TOWARDS A COMPETENCE THEORY OF THE FIRM

Edited by Nicolai J. Foss and Christian Knudsen

London and New York

First Published 1996
by Routledge
11 New Fetter Lane, London EC4P 4EE

Simultaneously published in the USA and Canada
by Routledge
29 West 35th Street, New York, NY 10001

© 1996 Nicolai J. Foss and Christian Knudsen

Typeset in Garamond by
Keystroke, Jacaranda Lodge, Wolverhampton

Printed and bound in Great Britain by
TJ Press (Padstow) Ltd, Padstow, Cornwall

British Library Cataloguing in Publication Data

A catalogue record for this book is available from the British Library

Library of Congress Cataloging in Publication Data

Towards a competence theory of the firm/edited by Nicolai J. Foss
and Christian Knudsen.
p. cm. — (Routledge studies in business organization and
networks ; 2)
Includes bibliographical references and index.
1. Industrial organization (Economic theory) 2. Competition.
I. Foss, Nicolai J., 1964– . II. Knudsen, Christian, 1951– .
III. Series.
HD2326.T69 1996
338.5—dc20 96–11896
CIP

ISBN 0-415-14472-8

CONTENTS

CONTENTS

ILLUSTRATIONS

FIGURES

TABLES

CONTRIBUTORS

Raphael Amit holds a PhD from Northwestern University, Evanston, Ill. He is the Peter Wall Distinguished Professor of Entrepreneurship and the Director of the Entrepreneurship and Venture Capital Research Centre at University of British Columbia, Faculty of Commerce and Business Administration. His research interests include entrepreneurship and venture capital research, strategic management and strategic planning methods.

Jens Frøslev Christensen is Associate Professor, Department of Industrial Economics and Strategy, Copenhagen Business School. A specialist in the management of innovation, he is the author of *Produktinnovation* (Copenhagen: Copenhagen Business School Press, 1992). His work has appeared in journals such as *Research Policy.*

Bo Eriksen holds an MSc from Copenhagen Business School. He is currently enrolled as a PhD student at Odense University. His current research interests include business and corporate strategy, strategic planning methods and organization design. His doctoral dissertation centres on the relations between competitive advantage and organization structure.

Kirsten Foss, PhD, is Assistant Professor, Department of Industrial Economics and Strategy, Copenhagen Business School. She has written mainly on the economics of the food sector, and has been associated with the Danish research programme on Market-Based Product and Process Innovations (MAPP). Her work has been published in *Research Policy.*

Nicolai J. Foss, PhD, is Assistant Professor, Department of Industrial Economics and Strategy, Copenhagen Business School. A recipient of the Tietgen and Zeuthen Prizes, Nicolai J. Foss has published in several journals (e.g. *Journal of Evolutionary Economics, Review of Political Economy, Scandinavian Journal of Management, Journal of Management Studies*) and has written *The Austrian School and Modern Economics* (Copenhagen: Copenhagen Business School Press, 1994). Together with Brian Loasby, Nicolai Foss is editor of *Capabilities and Coordination: Essays in Honor of G. B. Richardson* (forthcoming).

Hanne Harmsen, PhD, is Assistant Professor, Department of Marketing, Aarhus School of Business. Her research has mainly been on product innovation. She is associated with the MAPP research project, where she is a project coordinator.

Christian Knudsen, PhD, is Associate Professor, Department of Industrial Economics and Strategy, Copenhagen Business School. A specialist in the methodology of economics, Christian Knudsen's work has appeared in several Danish volumes. He edited (together with Uskali Mäki and Bo Gustafsson) *Rationality, Institutions and Economic Methodology* (Routledge, 1993), and has recently written *Economic Methodology* (two volumes, Routledge 1994).

Brian Loasby is Professor of Management Economics, University of Stirling. The author of numerous articles, Brian Loasby has written *Choice, Complexity and Ignorance* (Cambridge University Press, 1976), *The Mind and Methods of Economists* (Edward Elgar, 1989) and *Equilibrium and Evolution* (Manchester University Press, 1991). His research centres on the theory of the firm, doctrinal history and methodology.

Jesper Mikkelsen is an MSc in Business Administration and Business Law. He is an associate of A. T. Kearney.

Torben Pedersen, PhD, is Assistant Professor, Department of International Economics and Management, Copenhagen Business School. A recipient of the Tietgen Prize, Torben Pedersen has written *Danske virksomheders etableringer i udlandet* (with Poul Schultz and Harald Vestergaard, Copenhagen: Copenhagen Business School Press, 1992) and *Udenlandsk ejet industri i Danmark* (with Finn Valentin, Copenhagen: Ministry of Industry, 1994).

Paul Robertson is Senior Lecturer in the Department of Economics and Management at University College, University of New South Wales. He has previously taught at Boston University, the Johns Hopkins University and the University of Melbourne. In addition to many articles, he is co-author with Richard Langlois of *Firms, Markets and Economic Change: A Dynamic Theory of Business Institutions* (Routledge, 1995) and co-author with Sidney Pollard of *The British Shipbuilding Industry, 1870–1914* (Cambridge, Mass.: Harvard University Press, 1979).

Finn Valentin is Associate Professor, Department of Industrial Economics and Strategy, Copenhagen Business School. He specializes in the economics and sociology of technological change, and has directed research projects on industrial R&D and technology strategy and policy. In recent years, his focus has been on interorganizational issues relating to collaborative R&D and to the R&D function within multinational enterprises.

1

INTRODUCTION
The emerging competence perspective
Nicolai J. Foss

THE EMERGENCE OF A NEW PERSPECTIVE IN STRATEGY RESEARCH

This book contributes to the *competence perspective* on firms and firm strategies that has been emerging within the strategic management field over the last decade. Arguably, the competence perspective is – in its various guises – the dominant perspective on firm strategy today. Thus, strategic management scholars are very much agreed on ascribing primary importance to the resource and competence side of firms when accounting for the sources of long-lived competitive advantage, which is perhaps the central theme of strategic management research. This dominance can also be found in the thinking of managers and strategists; for example, the necessity of a 'return to the core business' is now almost universally emphasized by practitioners.

In this version, the competence perspective may perhaps be seen as a rediscovery of the proposition advanced by Adam Smith more than two hundred years ago, that specialization yields productivity advantages. But whereas Smith can be read as emphasizing specialization in terms of products, the modern competence perspective rather emphasizes specialization in terms of competence.

By 'competence', we understand a typically idiosyncratic knowledge capital that allows its holder to perform activities – in particular, to solve problems – in certain ways, and typically do this more efficiently than others. Because of its skill-like character, competence has a large tacit component, and is asymmetrically distributed. It may reside in individuals, but is in the context of the theory of the firm and strategic management perhaps best seen as a property of organizations rather than of individuals (it is therefore hard to imitate and transfer). At least, that is how the concept is used in this book.

By 'a competence perspective on firms and firm strategies', then, is meant, first, a consistent conceptualization of firms in terms of competence: firms are seen *essentially* as repositories of competence. And, second, it is firms' ability to accumulate, protect and eventually to deploy competences to product markets that is seen as determinative of their long-run competitive advantages. Moreover, firms' competence endowments co-determine their boundaries, notably their degree of diversification.

This view of the firm is not only to be found within the strategic management field; it is also emerging within economics, particularly in the evolutionary theory of the firm, as propounded by Richard Nelson and Sidney Winter in their 1982 book, *An Evolutionary Theory of Economic Change*. Here, too, firms are seen as essentially heterogeneous entities, characterized by their unique and path-dependent knowledge-bases (rather than simply by scale).

The same year, 1982, that saw the publication of Nelson and Winter's book also witnessed the publication of a seminal article by Stephen Lippman and Richard Rumelt, 'Uncertain Imitability: An Analysis of Interfirm Differences in Efficiency under Competition'. They demonstrated that, if one assumed that firms had difficulties imitating the firm-specific sources of superior performance, an equilibrium with firm of diverging efficiencies could be sustained. This opened the door for a rigorous economic approach to the analysis of firm strategies as a matter of the accumulation and protection of resources that yield Ricardian rents because of their superior inherent efficiencies.

Two years later, Birger Wernerfelt, building on Edith Penrose's *The Theory of the Growth of the Firm* (1959) and on Lippman and Rumelt's article, published his 'A Resource-based View of the Firm', probably the most influential academic article on firm resources. Since then, the more academic and largely US-based part of the competence perspective has normally been referred to as 'the resource-based view'. Important contributors to this strand within the competence perspective include, in addition to Wernerfelt and Rumelt, Jay Barney, Cynthia Montgomery, Ingemar Dierickx and Karel Cool.

Closely related to the resource-based view, but with a somewhat more practical orientation, is a string of contributions beginning with C. K. Prahalad and Gary Hamel's enormously successful 1990 article in the *Harvard Business Review*, 'The Core Competence of the Corporation'. Work that is closely related to the resource-based or core competence work is 'the capabilities approach' (Langlois 1992), 'the competence perspective' (Foss 1993), and 'the dynamic capabilities approach' (Teece, Pisano and Shuen 1990). Recent European-based work on 'competence-based competition' (Hamel and Heene 1994) also falls within this group.[1]

In this book, we use the term '*the competence-based perspective*' or, even simpler, 'the competence perspective' as the common denominator for these different, though closely related, influences. This is because all the above theories are agreed on ascribing primary strategic importance to those firm-specific assets that are knowledge-related and intangible, often tacit, hard to trade and shared among the agents of the firm. The assets that conform to these characteristics are what we understand as 'competences'.

Although it may seem so, the interest in conceptualizing the firm in terms of its competences is no new phenomenon *per se*. As Christian Knudsen argues in chapter 2 and Brian Loasby in chapter 3, it is in a sense a *renewed* interest, since

2

a knowledge-based conceptualization of the firm was present in the important British economist, Alfred Marshall's (1925) work, and blossomed in the classic work of Edith Penrose (1959) on *The Theory of the Growth of the Firm*. Penrose's work in particular has provided much inspiration for resource-based scholars (Wernerfelt 1984), and also for evolutionary theorists such as Richard Nelson and Sidney Winter (1982). In fact, it may with much justice be said that what Ronald Coase is to the contractual approach, Penrose is to the competence perspective.

However, in spite of its many precursors, the competence perspective did not really blossom until the end of the 1980s. Since that time, however, it has virtually dominated strategy content research; the percentage of articles written from a competence perspective in such journals as *Strategic Management Journal, Journal of Management*, and also more popular journals such as *California Management Review* or *Harvard Business Review*, is now quite high. Even the weekly, *The Economist*, well known for its harsh comments on management thinking, now routinely employ concepts such as 'core competences' in its business section. Given this quite widespread acceptance, why did it take so long before the competence perspective became influential?

There are several causal factors behind the emergence of the competence perspective, some of which are external and some of which are internal to the strategy field. They include:

- The death of the conglomerate: the need for a return to core business becomes conventional wisdom.
- The empirical importance of internal factors for understanding competitive advantage, exemplified by the superior efficiencies ascribed to Japanese production methods.
- Advances in economic theory, particularly with respect to the treatment of contracts, incentives, information and strategic interdependence.
- An increasing interest in firm heterogeneity within economics.
- A related and also increasing interest in emphasizing the knowledge dimensions of the firm within economics and strategic management.

The first two reasons on this list are clearly external, empirically based reasons. They both refer to the changes in organizational forms and in dimensions of competition that have accompanied the increasing internationalization and the more fervent technological change that have characterized many industries.

Let us consider the case of ITT (*The Economist* 1995). On 13 June 1995 Rand Araskog, president of the American conglomerate, ITT, announced that ITT was soon to be broken up into three free-standing firms, concentrating on insurance, hotels and manufacturing, respectively. The news made ITT rise on the New York Stock Exchange. In fact, stocks had been rising for some time in the expectation that ITT's divestment plans were soon to be announced. This suggests that investors are no longer particularly fond of conglomerate organization.

Perhaps more than any other firm, ITT was instrumental in defining the conglomerate as a viable organizational form in the 1960s. Under the remarkable Harold Geneen, ITT expanded strongly, primarily by merging with other firms, and consisted by 1970 of more than 400 businesses, operating in more than 70 countries all over the world. Under Rand Araskog, ITT has divested itself of more than 200 businesses, but still covers areas ranging from casinos to phone directories. In fact, Araskog has had difficulties determining precisely where ITT's core business lies.

Dozens of similar stories can be found. They all serve to illustrate the increasing emphasis in managerial practice on concentrating on core strengths. These are seen as the more permanent features of the firm, while products and strategic business units are seen as much more transitory. This is a view of the corporation that harmonizes with an increasingly internationalized world with shortening product life-cycles. In such a world, competitive success cannot rest on anything as fleeting as products or strategic business units; rather, it must be founded on something deeper – namely the knowledge capital in the form of competences that allow a firm to spawn new unanticipated products. The cultivation and management of synergistic learning processes in the firm therefore become key in this process. Strategy is about stretching knowledge assets and applying these to new areas.

According to some writers, notably Prahalad and Hamel, the above competence view on the corporation and on strategy has been near-standard fare in Japanese and other East Asian management practice for years and to a large extent accounts for the competitive successes of Asian firms in many industries. However, it has only recently been reflected in strategic thinking, and it has yet to make a substantial impact on Western management and strategy practice.

In addition to these external, more empirical reasons for the recent change in strategy thinking, there are some more internal developments. These may be summarized as having to do with a more intimate liaison between economics and strategy, a liaison that has become stimulated by a more realistic treatment of the firm within economics.

ECONOMICS AND MANAGEMENT STUDIES

It has gradually become an increasingly prevalent recognition that economic theory may be important to management studies, and perhaps particularly to the strategy discipline.[2] This has not always been so. Consider the verdict issued by the prominent British economist, Arthur Pigou:

> it is not the business of economists to teach woollen manufacturers to make and sell wool, or brewers how to make and sell beer, or any other business men how to do their job. If that was what we were out for, we should, I imagine, immediately quit our desks and get somebody –

doubtless at a heavy premium, for we should be thoroughly inefficient
– to take us into his woollen mill or his brewery.

(Pigou 1922: 463)

Now, business firms still employ relatively few microeconomists, and the
influence of economics on management may arguably primarily manifest itself
through the curricula of business schools. Through this route, however,
economics is bound to have an influence on the practical execution of firms'
strategies. As some prominent proponents of the economic turn in strategy
thinking have recently emphasized, this is not the same as saying, in an
'imperialist' manner, that strategy thinking should be *only* applied to microeconomics (Rumelt, Schendel and Teece 1994: 547–9). Instead, economics is
thought of as being able to *further* 'conversation' within the strategy discipline
and management studies in general, rather than to block it.

This is because economics provides a relatively clear and unambiguous
'language' in which many – if not all – strategy issues may be precisely represented. Furthermore, many would agree that the basic insights of economics[3]
have a high degree of validity – which means that economics may supply a
body of well-corroborated knowledge that may serve as a foundational element
for strategy research. For example, economics helps better understanding and
answering questions such as the following. What are the sources of competitive
advantage? How can competitive advantage be sustained? How sensitive is
competitive advantage to environmental changes?

Such questions are quite simply hard to understand and answer without
understanding the nature of basic competitive forces. Sociology and psychology
do not tell us much directly about what is perhaps the key question of strategy
research: which factors may make a competitive advantage sustainable? In order
to pose and answer this question meaningfully, knowledge of the mechanisms
that may off-set the equalization of returns over firms is necessary. For example,
economics may supply the answer that a competitive advantage can be made
sustainable to the extent that the relevant rent-yielding competences can be made
costly to imitate.

What makes it more plausible that economic modes of thought may help us
address and understand such questions is also the fact that economics has become,
in many ways, much more 'realistic'. There is now a much more sophisticated
treatment of information, incentives, coordination and strategic interaction than
was the case, say, two decades ago. It is not that all of these developments are
equally obviously helpful; but some of them clearly are helpful. This is perhaps
particularly obvious in the domain of the theory of the firm.

Early importers of economics to the strategy discipline were for a long time
inspired by a kind of economics that did not leave much room for resources and
competences, and, in effect, had little to say about the firm. To strategy scholars
such as Richard Caves and Michael Porter, economics meant the Bain–Mason
structuralist approach in industrial organization (IO) economics. To them, basic

5

IO concepts such as entry barriers and collusion behind such barriers offered an explanation of, for example, the observed persistence of above-normal profit.

However, would-be importers of IO to the strategy field confronted a number of translation problems. For example, the unit of analysis in IO was the industry, whereas the strategy scholars took the firm as the unit of analysis. Although the most prominent importer of IO to the strategy field, Michael Porter, was well aware of the problems these differences raised (Porter 1981), many of the unfortunate characteristics of IO did in fact carry over to his own industry analysis approach (Porter 1980). An example is the black-box conceptualization of the firm that is characteristic of older IO. It is present in *Competitive Strategy* (Porter 1980), as demonstrated by the complete *absence* of any comprehensive discussion in that book of the internal aspects of firms.

It is by no means illegitimate to black-box the firm – *if* one's primary interest is in short-run business strategy. But strategy is about much more than this. Almost any strategy textbook will conceptualize strategy as a matter of achieving fit between the strengths of the firm and the opportunities of the environment, while simultaneously safeguarding the weaknesses of the firm from threats of the same environment.

Notice that this basic SWOT conceptualization inherently involves the resource and competence side of firms by referring to strengths and weaknesses.[4] More specifically, strategy is also about the direction of firms' diversification activities (Montgomery and Wernerfelt 1988), the firm-specific (imitation) barriers that block the equalization of rents over firms (Rumelt 1984, Wernerfelt 1984), and the growth strategies of firms (Penrose 1959). What is important about these issues in the present context is that they necessitate theorizing the resource and competence side of firms at some level of detail. Recent developments in the theory of the firm have at least begun to take more seriously the internal aspects of firms.

THE CONTEMPORARY THEORY OF THE FIRM

During the last two decades, the theory of the firm, broadly conceived, has made considerable progress, as marked, for example, by the conferment of the Nobel Prize in economics to Ronald Coase in 1991. However, recent developments have been far from homogeneous, have not been constructed from a common set of assumptions, have been based on different research traditions, and have addressed widely different phenomena. Thus, we have theories – different theories – for understanding such aspects of the firm as its contractual character, its boundaries relative to the market (other firms), and its role as a repository for productive knowledge and a learning device. In other words, the current theoretical situation may be described as one of creative turmoil.

One way to put all this in perspective is to say that contemporary developments break in almost all relevant dimensions with the theory of the firm of neoclassical price theory (what is often referred to as 'the production function approach'). They break up the 'black box' and address the inner workings of the business firm; raise the question of the existence of firms and other types of economic organization; reject the uniformity postulate and try to describe firms as essentially heterogeneous entities; break with the given knowledge assumption and attempt to account for the firm as a learning entity; and so on.

This should of course not be taken to mean that it is analytically wrong to represent the firm as merely a production function: it depends on what analytical purpose this conceptualization is applied to (Machlup 1967). For simple price-theoretic analysis, it may not be wrong; if all we are interested in is addressing questions such as how much industry supply changes given a certain increase in sales taxes, we can make do with a very stylized picture of the firm, since what we are after is not really firm behaviour, but industry behaviour. However, for other purposes – such as those that interest us in this book – the conventional neo-classical conceptualization of the firm represents a serious affront to realism. It does not help us understand internal organization, the whole issue of firms' boundaries and contractual relations in general, it is a poor guide to understanding firm strategy, and it will not assist understanding how firm performance and national economic performance are connected.

To some extent it is because these 'other purposes' have become more pressing to the economics profession that we have during the last two decades seen a flurry of work on the theory of the firm. Reinforcing this tendency have been the more refined tools that are now available to economists, and a cumulative and relevant theoretical development within such areas as the economics of information and uncertainty, law and economics and industrial organization. Many branches of the modern theory of the firm have drawn extensively on these areas. For example, Armen Alchian and Harold Demsetz's (1972) classic work on the theory of the firm was a rather natural outgrowth of their own previous work within property rights economics, and of Ronald Coase's (1960) work on property rights, transaction costs and externalities. And Sanford Grossman and Oliver Hart (1986) draw extensively on game theory in developing their incomplete contract approach to the firm.

Building on foundations laid by Ronald Coase (1937, 1960), these writers and others, such as the extremely influential Oliver Williamson, have detailed the economic organization of the firm, and of many other types of economic organization. In fact, research in this area has been so broad and intensive that it may well be the most rapidly expanding research area in modern economics. Its impact on management research has been quite impressive, too; for example, Milgrom and Roberts's (1992) textbook on contractual economics is entitled *Economics, Organization, and Management*,[5] and Paul Rubin (1990) undertook a project to make transaction cost theory accessible to managers. In the present book, the fruitfulness of a rather orthodox contractual approach in the context of the competence perspective is demonstrated by Raphael Amit and Bo Eriksen's chapter (6) on business process engineering.

Briefly, within the contractual approach the firm is seen as an efficient contractual entity, in the sense of aligning the incentives of the various input-owners that enter into contractual relations with the legal entity known as 'the firm'. Although the contractual approaches are far from homogeneous, they are all agreed on giving the exchange aspects of the firm primary emphasis, to the relative neglect of the production side. That is to say, what they view as interesting about firms is not their role as repositories of productive knowledge *per se*, but rather their role as contractual entities, in other words, their particular way of structuring deals between input-owners. There is thus a separation between 'production' and 'governance', with maximum attention being paid to governance rather than production.

Again, it is important to emphasize that this may be a completely defensible procedure, depending on the purpose at hand. However, it has clear limits.[6] Among the more serious is that by suppressing interest in the production side of firms, the make-or-buy decision (and other aspects of economic organization) is not allowed to turn on differences in production costs: only transaction costs matter (see Demsetz 1993, Foss 1993). In fact, Paul Robertson, building on Richard Langlois's and his (1995) joint work, in chapter 5 makes a number of related points and argues that a distinct perspective on economic organization can be distilled from the competence perspective.

Furthermore, because of their lack of interest in the production side, contractual theories have difficulties addressing a number of important real-world phenomena. One example may be found in the much-debated outsourcing question. In terms of contractual economics, this may simply be seen as a matter of choosing the optimal boundaries of the firm: which activities should be left to the market (be outsourced) and which should be undertaken internally?

However, as Bettis, Bradley and Hamel (1992) argue, outsourcing may influence the firm's accumulation of productive knowledge and therefore its future competitive position. For example, careless use of outsourcing may imply the transfer of valuable knowledge to suppliers who later emerge as strong competitors, or it may imply that it becomes harder for the firm to produce new valuable knowledge, for example, if its development efforts require direct access to functions that have been outsourced.

Such dynamic aspects of the outsourcing decision cannot be accounted for in terms of contractual theories of the firm. In order to address, for example, the outsourcing problem in its complex entirety, something more is needed: specifically, a notion of firms as repositories of productive knowledge. This notion is supplied by the competence perspective. It is much less adequately treated by neoclassical theories of the firm, although here too, some advances have been made with respect to treating firms as knowledge-bearing entities (e.g. Prescott and Wisscher 1980). The deep problem is that the rationality assumptions of orthodox economics seem to hinder an adequate treatment of competence, understood as idiosyncratic problem-solving knowledge capital: whereas orthodox theory in principle assumes that competence is unbounded, the competence perspective breaks with this assumption.

8

COMMON THEMES

In spite of what has been said, the competence perspective is far from homogeneous, as argued by Christian Knudsen in chapter 2 and myself in the final chapter of this book. It is certainly not possible to speak of a 'research tradition' yet, and even less of a 'research programme'. This is so because, although there seems to be substantial agreement on which problems the competence perspective should address, there is little agreement on which means should be used to accomplish this problem-solving.

In spite of the relatively large bulk of recent work on the competence perspective, it is probably fair to say that it is considerably less homogeneous and more fragmented and implies much more conceptual ambiguity than, say, the contractual perspective on the firm. In short, when contractual theorists talk about 'contracts', 'incentives', 'team-production', 'residual rights', and so on, they know what they are talking about, and know that other scholars within their field to a large extent agree with their interpretation of such concepts. There is much shared knowledge within this field of research.

In contrast, it is unlikely that two competence-based scholars will be in agreement on the precise details of, most significantly, the meaning of the word 'competence', not to speak of 'core competence'.[7] As a reflection of the much more 'mature' state of contractual research, recent work within this area is stark, highly abstract and very formalized, whereas work within the competence perspective is loose, purely verbal and often quite ambiguous.

A number of circumstances are responsible for this state of affairs. For example, most research within the contractual perspective draws on relatively standard economics, whereas the competence perspective draws on a multitude of theoretical traditions. Exemplifying this is that the contractual perspective is overwhelmingly in debt to the work of a single man, namely Ronald Coase. In contrast, there is no Coase of the competence perspective (although Edith Penrose and perhaps Harold Demsetz are strong candidates here). Furthermore, the competence perspective has entertained a strong practice-orientation, much in contrast to the contractual perspective, which has implied the use of a looser terminology, more willingness to bend concepts, employing new ones where necessary, and so on.

Thus, while competence insights clearly appeal to managers, while there is some empirical support for the approach, and while the approach does not reduce management research to a minor branch of economics, the approach certainly still lacks both a *strong* empirical base and extensive theoretical elaboration (cf. Doz 1994). Moreover, the domains of application of the perspective needs to be clarified.

This book is an attempt to reduce conceptual confusion. For example, we have rather consistently used the 'competence' terminology. And it is also an attempt to clarify the domains of application of the perspective. For example, innovative discussions apply the competence perspective to technology strategy (chapters 7 and 8) and to the international setting (chapter 9). Moreover, the various contributions to this book begin from a set of related themes: more specifically, from central propositions characterizing the competence perspective and constituting a sort of 'minimum programme'.

My proposal for a list of common themes includes the following points:

- *Proposition 1*: The competence perspective is a strategic perspective, in the sense that it tries to uncover the sources of competitive advantages and account for the boundaries of firms in terms of the properties of competences.
- *Proposition 2*: Competencies are the key assets of firms; they are tacit and social knowledge-capital that tells its holders how to go on with problem-solving.
- *Proposition 3*: Firms are the basic units of analysis; they should be conceptualized in terms of the endowments of essentially heterogeneous but productive stocks of knowledge capital – competences – that are associated with differential levels of efficiency.
- *Proposition 4*: Efficiency differences yield rents. A primary research task is to account for the mechanisms producing long-lived rents, that is to say, long-lived competitive advantage. This will include going into the cognitive dimensions of competence and also investigating processes of emergence of competence.
- *Proposition 5*: The boundaries of the firm – that is to say, the firm's degree of vertical and horizontal diversification – should be explained using competences as part of the explanatory apparatus. For example, the nature of a firm's competences put restrictions on the sort of activities it can undertake and internalize.
- *Proposition 6*: The competence ultimately is a dynamic theory; that is to say, it is concerned with the creation, maintenance and creative destruction of competitive advantages in terms that refer to the creation, the protection and the obsolescence of competence. Learning processes must ultimately loom large in the competence perspective.

All of the chapters in this book represent first stabs at advancing the competence perspective based on the acceptance of the above points as unifying common themes.

NOTES

1 In the final chapter of this book, I undertake an analysis of the differences between the various perspectives within the overall competence-based approach.
2 There is currently a rather heated debate on how much economics should be allowed to influence management studies. See Camerer (1985) and Hirsch, Friedman and Koza (1990) for the extreme positions. Foss (1996) is an attempt to construct a middle position.
3 Such as the propositions that agents react predictably to changing incentives, that firms change input demands as relative prices change, that demand curves slope downwards, and so on.

4 As early contributors to the stategy field were well aware of; for example, Kenneth
   Andrews's classic *The Concept of Corporate Strategy* repeatedly makes the point.
5 See, however, the critical review by Brian Loasby (1995) that makes the point that
   while the book has much to say about economics and organization, it actually has
   very little to say about management proper.
6 Milgrom and Roberts (1992: 33–4) highlight some of the theoretical and conceptual
   problems involved in trying to separate production and governance, and the corresponding costs of these activities.
7 Those who doubt this can try to find out how many different definitions of 'core
   competence' they can distil from Prahalad and Hamel's 'The Core Competence
   of the Corporation'. Judging from my own experiments with students, ten different
   definitions seems to be the median response.

REFERENCES

Alchian, A. A. and Demsetz, H. (1972) 'Production, Information Costs, and Economic
   Organization', in A. A. Alchian (1977) *Economic Forces at Work*, Indianapolis: Liberty
   Press.
Andrews, K. (1993) *The Concept of Corporate Strategy*, 3rd edn, Homewood, Ill.: Dow
   Jones-Irwin.
Bettis, R. A., Bradley, S. P. and Hamel, G. (1992) 'Outsourcing and Industrial Decline',
   Academy of Management Executive 6: 7–22.
Camerer, C. (1985) 'Redirecting Research in Business Policy and Strategy', *Strategic
   Management Journal* 6: 1–15.
Coase, R. H. (1937) 'The Nature of the Firm', *Economica* 4: 386–405.
Coase, R. H. (1960) 'The Problem of Social Cost', *Journal of Law and Economics*
   3: 1–44.
Demsetz, H. (1993) 'The Nature of the Firm Revisited', in O. E. Williamson and
   S. G. Winter, *The Nature of the Firm*, Oxford: Oxford University Press.
Doz, Y. (1994) 'Managing Core Competence for Corporate Renewal: Towards a
   Managerial Theory of Core Competencies', *INSEAD Working Paper*, Corporate
   Renewal Initiative, Paris.
The Economist (1995) 'ITT: The Death of the Geneen Machine', 17 June, pp. 74–6.
Foss, N. J. (1993) 'The Theory of the Firm: Contractual and Competence Perspectives',
   Journal of Evolutionary Economics 3: 127–44.
Foss, N. J. (1996) 'Research in Strategy, Economics, and Michael Porter', forthcoming
   in *Journal of Management Studies*.
Grossman, S. and Hart, O. (1986) 'The Costs and Benefits of Ownership: A Theory of
   Lateral and Vertical Integration', *Journal of Political Economy* 94: 691–719.
Hamel, G. and Heene, A. (eds) (1994) *Competence-based Competition*, New York: John
   Wiley.
Hirsch, P. M., Friedman, R. and Koza, M. P. (1990) 'Collaboration or Paradigm Shift?
   Caveat Emptor and the Risk of Romance with Economic Models for Strategy and
   Policy Research', *Organization Science* 1: 87–97.
Langlois, R. N. (1992) 'Transaction Cost Economics in Real Time', *Industrial and
   Corporate Change*, 1: 99–127.
Langlois, R. N. and Robertson, P. (1995) *Firms, Markets and Economic Change*, London:
   Routledge.
Lippman, S. and Rumelt, R. P. (1982) 'Uncertain Imitability: An Analysis of Inter-
   firm Differences in Efficiency under Competition', *Bell Journal of Economics* 13:
   418–38.
Loasby, B. J. (1995) 'Running a Business: An Appraisal of Economics, Organization and

Management by Paul Milgrom and John Roberts', *Industrial and Corporate Change* 4: 471–89.

Machlup, F. (1967) 'Theories of the Firm: Marginalist, Behavioural, Managerial', in F. Machlup (ed.) (1978) *Methodology of Economics and Other Social Sciences*, New York: Wiley.

Marshall, A. (1925) *Principles of Economics*, London: Macmillan.

Milgrom, P. and Roberts, J. (1992) *Economics, Organization, and Management*, London: Prentice-Hall.

Montgomery, C. A. and Wernerfelt, B. (1988) 'Diversification, Ricardian Rents, and Tobin's q', *RAND Journal of Economics* 19: 623–32.

Nelson, R. R. and Winter, S. G. (1982) *An Evolutionary Theory of Economic Change*, Cambridge, Mass.: Belknap Press.

Penrose, E. T. (1959) *The Theory of the Growth of the Firm*, Oxford: Oxford University Press.

Pigou, A. C. (1922) 'Empty Economic Boxes: A Reply', *Economic Journal* 32: 458–65.

Porter, M. E. (1980) *Competitive Strategy*, New York: Free Press.

Porter, M. E. (1981) 'The Contributions of Industrial Organization to Strategic Management', *Academy of Management Review* 6: 609–20.

Prahalad, C. K. and Hamel, G. (1990) 'The Core Competence of the Corporation', *Harvard Business Review* 66 (May/June): 79–91.

Prescott, E. C. and Wisscher, M. (1980) 'Organization Capital', *Journal of Political Economy* 80: 446–61.

Rubin, P. (1990) *Managing Business Transactions*, New York: Free Press.

Rumelt, R. P. (1984) 'Towards a Strategic Theory of the Firm', in R. B. Lamb (ed.) *Competitive Strategic Management*, Englewood Cliffs, NJ: Prentice-Hall.

Rumelt, R. P., Schendel, D. E. and Teece, D. J. (1994) 'Fundamental Issues in Strategy: A Research Agenda for the 1990s', in R. P. Rumelt, D. E. Schendel and D. J. Teece (eds) *Fundamental Issues in Strategy*, Cambridge, Mass.: Harvard Business School Press.

Teece, D. J., Pisano, G. and Shuen, A. (1990) 'Firm Capabilities, Resources and the Concept of Strategy', mimeo, University of California, at Berkeley.

Wernerfelt, B. (1984) 'A Resource-based View of the Firm', *Strategic Management Journal* 5: 171–80.

2

THE COMPETENCE PERSPECTIVE

A historical view

Christian Knudsen

INTRODUCTION

In the present book, the term 'competence perspective' is used as the common denominator of a series of theories and research traditions within contemporary theories of the firm and strategic management. The concept includes *resource-based theory* (Wernerfelt 1984), *dynamic capabilities theory* (Teece, Pisano and Shuen 1990; Langlois 1992) and *knowledge-based theory* of the firm (Demsetz 1988). Common to these theories is the decisive importance given to the firm's internal, rather than to its external conditions for understanding its competitive market position. Internal competences, capabilities and accumulated knowledge are crucial concepts used to explain a firm's above-normal return and sustainable competitive advantages. Thus, the competence perspective is not only an alternative to orthodox theories of the firm and industry within the 'structure–conduct–performance' (SCP) tradition, but also an alternative to Porter's (1980) use of this tradition within strategic management. Porter identifies competitive advantages almost exclusively in terms of the firm's market power, which is assumed to be identical with its ability to position itself in a market, erecting entry and mobility barriers.

Although the competence perspective may appear as relatively homogeneous compared to orthodox neoclassical theory, a closer analysis and comparison of individual contributions within this perspective nevertheless seem to indicate considerable heterogeneity. Therefore, it is probably not reasonable at this point to describe the competence perspective as a coherent research programme, or paradigm, characterized by a common hard core and positive heuristic (cf. Imre Lakatos 1970). On the contrary, the competence perspective should rather be characterized as a series of theories of a certain familiarity, being derived from a number of shared underlying themes. In the following, I will discuss three themes that seem to be central to the distinct identity of the competence perspective.

First, the competence perspective views the firm (and the market) from an endogenous growth perspective. The firm is seen as a knowledge-accumulating entity, acquiring new knowledge through cumulative processes. New knowledge is gradually 'built into' the organization's formal and informal structure, and becomes a significant determinant for the direction of future accumulation of knowledge. The firm's developmental process can thus be characterized as path-dependent and constructive, creating still more complex structures from structures already in place to handle new and more demanding functions.

Second, scholars have used the competence perspective to explain how some firms within an industry are capable of maintaining above-normal return even in the long term. Contrary to the theme of endogenous growth, which focuses on how the individual firm creates competitive advantages, scholars have also used the competence perspective on the industry level to explain how existing advantages can be sustained, and perhaps even made permanent. This perspective is used to explain why 'successful' firms can maintain their competitive advantages despite the fact that competition, according to orthodox theory, should eliminate these advantages.

The *third* theme underlying the competence perspective, I shall argue, consists of a fairly homogeneous understanding of strategy. Prahalad and Hamel's (1990) discussion of 'core competences', Teece *et al.*'s (1994) discussion of the importance of assuring 'coherence' between the firm's different activities, and Montgomery and Wernerfelt's (1988) 'focus'-strategy and emphasis on related rather than unrelated diversification strategies seem to be derived from the same basic understanding. The problem is, however, whether it is possible, behind these fairly identical perceptions of strategy, to identify a common theoretical framework that can be used to categorize the various propositions. In this context, returning to classical scholars within strategic management, such as Kenneth Andrews (1971) and Philip Selznick (1957), may prove rewarding.

In the following, I will discuss the historical contributions within economic theory and strategic management underlying the three themes mentioned above. In the following section, I demonstrate, at both the firm and industry levels, that the theme of endogenous growth, developed by Alfred Marshall, and further expanded by post-Marshallians, such as Edith Penrose and G. B. Richardson, can be traced back to Adam Smith and his discussion of the relation between division of labour and economic growth. In recent years, the theme of endogenous growth has been studied from a resource-based perspective to determine if the most appropriate strategy for growth is a related diversification rather than one which is unrelated (Montgomery and Wernerfelt 1988; Teece 1980, 1982, 1984).

Under the heading 'On the Intellectual Background to the Theme of "Sustainable Competitive Advantage"', we argue that the theme of 'sustainable competitive advantages' can be traced back both to Schumpeter's dynamic view of competition and to the Chicago School's contributions to industrial organization (including the associated UCLA School). Important contributions made within the competence perspective for understanding the concept of sustainable competitive advantages come from Lippman and Rumelt (1982), Barney (1986a, 1991), Kathleen Conner (1991) and Dierickx and Cool (1989). Consequently, we discusses whether it is possible to identify and theoretically to reconstruct one common conception of strategy underlying the competence perspective. This is undertaken in the final section, 'On the Concept of Strategy and the Return to the Classical Theory of Strategy'.

ON THE ORIGIN OF THE ENDOGENOUS GROWTH PERSPECTIVE IN THE COMPETENCE PERSPECTIVE

How do competitive advantages emerge, and how are they sustained? This seems to be the core issue of the literature that I have designated *the competence perspective*. However, these issues will be discussed separately, because attempts to resolve them lead to two rather different types of literature, and hence to two different themes within the competence perspective. The question of how sustainable competitive advantages arise will be discussed primarily within the framework of a theory of endogenous growth (of the firm), whereas the question of how to secure sustainable competitive advantages must be resolved within an economic theory of competition at industry level. Even though the two issues are evidently interrelated, their intellectual history seems different and will be discussed in subsequent sections.

The classical heritage: Adam Smith and Charles Babbage

The theme of endogenous growth can be traced back to Adam Smith's *The Wealth of Nations* in 1776. In the first part of his book, Smith tries to analyse how the division of labour affects labour productivity and hence economic growth. In Smith's terminology, division of labour refers to how tasks in the productive process are divided among various individuals each doing their part. As an example, he mentions the pin factory, where the production process at that time was divided into no less than twenty-two distinct operations, each performed by individual workers.

Smith advances three arguments in favour of division of labour leading to higher productivity. First, repeating a task most likely leads to improved performance, and as simpler tasks can be repeated more often than complex tasks, there is more to gain from dividing production into simple tasks. Second, due to fewer costs of switching from one job to another, division of labour will lead to a reduction in costs. Third, a worker focusing on a simple set of tasks may see some way of developing machines to handle these.

But what are, according to Adam Smith, the factors limiting the division of labour, increasing return to scale and economic growth? In answering this question, Smith advanced his famous thesis 'that the division of labour is limited by the extent of the market'. Some 150 years later, Allan Young (1928) describes this thesis as 'one of the most illuminating and fruitful generalizations which can be found anywhere in the whole literature of economics'. The division of a complex task into finer and finer sub-operations would be possible as long as the market could be expanded.

In his 'classical production theory', Charles Babbage (1833) also argues that division of labour makes it possible for firms to differentiate between and specialize in those functions that, due to mechanization and standardization, lead to increased productivity and growth. Babbage formulates this 'principle of economy of scale' as 'That the master manufacturer, by dividing the work to be executed into different processes, each requiring different degrees of skill or of force, can purchase exactly that precise quantity of both which is necessary for each process; whereas, if the whole work were executed by one workman, that person must possess sufficient strength to execute the most laborious of the operations into which the art is divided' (1833: 175–6). Therefore, division of labour may imply savings, because a 'partial worker' does not need as high a wage as a 'general worker'. The qualifications of workers can be fitted to match the complexity of tasks. That division of labour would result in a higher productivity was, according to Babbage, a result of workers being gradually replaced by machines.

Classical theorists, such as Smith and Babbage, did not take division of labour and specialist roles for granted. On the contrary, they attempted to explain these concepts from a processual perspective, that is, they assumed economic agents to be basically more or less homogeneous, but gradually becoming differentiated in consequence of a decision to specialize. Conversely, other classical economists, headed by David Ricardo (1953), assumed the economic agents' capabilities and competences in producing to be exogenously given and thus requiring no explanation. The main example is Ricardo's theory of foreign trade, where England's trade with Portugal is explained in terms of the two countries' specialization patterns or competences in producing. In his example, Portugal was better at producing wine, and England at producing linen. This difference led to trade that was advantageous to both parties, because each had specialized in producing what they knew most about.

Leijonhufvud (1986) characterizes classical production theory of Smith and Babbage as distinctly different from the modern neoclassical theory of production in that it views the firm's productive opportunities from an evolutionary and endogenous growth perspective. According to Leijonhufvud, dividing the production process into increasingly simpler elements is a continuous 'discovery process', yielding new knowledge about production possibilities endogenously (rather than being a choice between a series of given alternatives, as assumed by neoclassical production theory).

Alfred Marshall: intra-firm differentiation and inter-firm specialization

Although the classical growth perspective, along with the emergence of the 'marginalist revolution', by and large disappeared from economic theory Alfred

Marshall, nevertheless, insisted on this perspective as a necessary correction of, and supplement to, the neoclassicists' static theory of production and competition. He referred to the logical inconsistency problem between increasing returns of scale and perfect competition, characterizing marginalist theory:

> we are here verging on the high theme of economic progress; and here therefore it is especially needful to remember that economic problems are imperfectly presented when they are treated as problems of static equilibrium, and not of organic growth . . . The static theory of equilibrium is only an introduction to economic studies; and it is barely even an introduction to the study of the progress and development of industries which show a tendency towards increasing return. Its limitations are so constantly overlooked, especially by those who approach it from an abstract point of view, that there is a danger in throwing it into definite form at all.
>
> (Marshall 1920: 461)

Marshall based his endogenous growth perspective primarily on Herbert Spencer's theory of 'differentiation', the permanent division of work functions into new sub-functions, which led to the development of a series of new specialized capabilities and knowledge. However, the increase in specialization caused new coordination problems which required the integration of newly developed specialist functions. Marshall argued that these processes of differentiation and knowledge accumulation took place not only within the framework of the individual firm, but also at the level of industry and society. Therefore, Marshall suggested there be a distinction between 'internal' economies, originating in the firm, and 'external' economies, originating in the interplay between firms. These two types of economy became central to the two post-Marshallian theories, developed during the 1950s and 1960s by Edith Penrose and G. B. Richardson, respectively.

Through the development of the theories of monopolistic and imperfect competition during the 1930s, Marshall's 'evolutionary perspective' by and large vanished from economic theory and did not play any role until 1950, when Alchian's classic article, 'Uncertainty, Evolution and Economic Theory', reintroduced the evolutionary perspective. Alchian even argued that his analysis should be considered a return to Marshall's method of analysis: 'we shall be reverting to a Marshallian type of analysis combined with the essentials of Darwinian evolutionary selection' (1950: 19).

Against this background, it may seem unreasonable that post-Marshallians, such as Penrose (1952, 1953) and Richardson (1960), were among the harshest critics of Alchian. In the so-called 'debate on biological analogies', they rejected Alchian's main thesis that economists could do without the hypothesis of profit maximization (and about individual rationality and adaptation), because the market would guarantee survival of more profitable firms at the expense of the less profitable. It is important to Penrose's and Richardson's criticisms of this argument that Alchian, in his attempt to develop a market theory along the lines of Darwin's theory, was not true to Marshall's specific evolutionary perspective (1920).

Based on Spencer's 'differentiation–integration' perspective, Marshall (1920: ix) had built his evolutionary understanding of economic phenomena on an analogy to the development of organisms, and only secondarily on Darwin's theory of the mechanisms of transmission, selection and variation. Thus, Marshall's foundation was what biologists call an *ontogenetic* perspective, rather than Alchian's *phylogenetic*. These perspectives are not independent of one another, but the theme of endogenous growth in the competence perspective clearly induces an ontogenetic theory. On the other hand, the theme of 'sustainable competitive advantages' can be analysed more adequately by applying a phylogenetic theory. I will pursue this argument in the section 'On the Intellectual Background . . . ' (p.24).

Edith Penrose

Compared to Marshall, Edith Penrose (1959) focused almost exclusively on the growth process of the individual firm, viewing the process from what she called 'an unfolding perspective' (Penrose 1955). That is, the firm was analysed from an endogenous growth perspective, particularly focusing on the inherent tendency to accumulate knowledge, which gradually expanded its set of production opportunities. Therefore, Penrose's theory can also be seen as an attempt to specify exactly which economies were actually at work within a single firm.

What did Penrose contribute toward furthering the development of Marshall's 'endogenous growth' perspective on the firm? In short, Penrose explained, more adequately than Marshall, the mechanism which enabled the individual firm to accumulate knowledge, and thus gradually to expand its production set. Like Marshall, Penrose assumed the firm to be subject to a consistent differentiation process that increased the need for coordination and integration. However, in line with Adam Smith, Marshall assumed that the increasing division of labour propelled this process. Penrose, on the other hand, postulated that releasing new 'surplus' was decisive for the firm's growth process.

According to Penrose, ever new managerial tasks and decision-making problems take up the manager's time and attention. However, having familiarized him- or herself with these problems, the manager becomes capable of handling them fairly routinely, and gradually replaces explicit and articulated problem formulations with an understanding which is almost exclusively based on tacit knowledge. The advantage of applying the solution to various tasks in certain routines, capabilities and heuristics is that the single decision-maker can economize on his or her scarce decision resources. Consequently, resources are made available that allow the decision-maker to direct attention towards tasks that have not yet been routinized. The condition for releasing new managerial resources is the gradual routinization of tasks, which leads to increased possibilities for management to expand its repertoire of actions, as well as expanding the activities of the organization.

Penrose primarily centres on the mechanism facilitating new knowledge and its subsequent accumulation in the firm. It is also characteristic of Penrose's theory that it focuses on how the firm accumulates knowledge of 'standard operating procedures' and 'routines' (Cyert and March 1963, Nelson and Winter 1982).

But what is the main difference between Penrose's and Marshall's theories of the accumulation of new knowledge? I suggest that we use the framework of Nonaka and Takeuchi (1995) and Hedlund (1994) in order to make one possible interpretation of this difference. They distinguish between *internalization* and *articulation* processes. In the former, formal knowledge is transformed into informal and tacit knowledge. In the latter, new knowledge is acquired by transforming tacit and unarticulated knowledge into formal and articulated knowledge.

Penrose's theory is primarily based on an internalization process. New knowledge is accumulated by transforming articulated and formalized knowledge about the best way to solve a certain problem into routines containing a strong element of tacit knowledge. To Penrose, the accumulation of knowledge is primarily the result of internalization, which implies economizing on scarce decision competences. In turn, new managerial resources are released that can be used to solve new problems and hence facilitate new growth.

Contrary to Penrose, Marshall's endogenous growth theory assumes that new knowledge is accumulated through an articulation process in which tacit knowledge is transformed into explicit and formal knowledge. In line with Adam Smith, Marshall sees division of labour as the cause for certain work functions being reduced to simple and standardized procedures that gradually become codified and mechanical. Thus, previous fairly complex work functions, containing a substantial element of tacit knowledge, are transformed into a series of specific sub-functions characterized by much more explicit and codified knowledge.

Even though Penrose focused on the impact of managerial and individually oriented resources on the growth of firms, she did not neglect the existence of similar mechanisms for accumulating knowledge at the social and organizational level:

> When men have become used to working in a particular group of other men, they become individually and as a group more valuable to the firm in that the services they can render are enhanced by their knowledge of their fellow workers, of the methods of the firm, and of the best way of doing things in the particular set of circumstances in which they are working.
>
> (1959: 52)

Initially, a team is confronted with a new coordination problem that can be solved in several equally appropriate, but unpredictable ways. However, since the team has not yet established any convention specifying which of these equivalent solutions has priority in the organization, each team-member must devote considerable attention, and decision-making resources, to the coordination of mutual performance. However, at some point, solutions to the coordination problem will crystallize, and a social rule of action will be established that, viewed from the single team-member's perspective, stabilizes his or her expectations of how the remaining team-members will act. Consequently, resources are released that can be invested in other tasks. In this case, too, knowledge is accumulated through internalization processes. We move from a situation in which the team-members have to spend much time and attention on coordinating their actions to another in which coordination happens almost automatically, requiring little attention and few decision-making resources. In the terminology of the American sociologist, James Coleman (1988, 1990), such conventions are the *social capital* of the organization.

George Richardson: inter-firm specialization

Penrose's primary aim was to further the development of Marshall's theory of 'internal economies', while Richardson focused on Marshall's theory of 'external economies'. In a series of contributions made from the 1960s to the mid-1970s, Richardson developed a knowledge perspective on how to organize economic activities in an attempt to overcome some of the major weaknesses of orthodox price theory. In his book *Information and Investment* from 1960, Richardson argues that orthodox price theory has not furnished us with a satisfactory solution to the coordination problem in an economy of decentralized decision-makers. Richardson was preoccupied with the dilemma of how producers could acquire sufficient information about each other's investment plans to secure 'convergence of expectations' (Malmgren 1961), and hence a solution to the problem of coordination (for a review of Richardson's contributions, see Foss 1994).

Richardson claimed that orthodox price theory had offered no adequate solutions for determining how producers could 'appropriately' anticipate each other's plans. The model of perfect competition attempted to solve this problem by introducing an auctioneer as a pure *ad hoc* construction. In Richardson's opinion, this construction had contributed to the postponement of an 'empirically based' solution to the problem. Therefore, Richardson suggested abandoning the auctioneer-construction in favour of studying models that contained both coordination success and failure. Nothing seemed to prevent a perfect-competition economy from getting into 'counterfinal situations' in which the producers acted on the basis of non-generalizable expectations of each other's plans, and therefore realized results that nobody actually wanted.

Richardson was aware that in many cases, interaction between producers in a real competitive economy did not lead to counterfinal results, but rather to reasonably well-coordinated results. According to Richardson, coordination in a decentral economy was not achieved through the price mechanism, as postulated by orthodox microeconomics. Instead, producers found organizational and/or institutional solutions to situations of great behavioural uncertainty. For example, by forming a strategic alliance, two parties may significantly reduce behavioural uncertainty about each other's investment plans. Interorganizational collaboration may help stabilize the parties' predictability of one another's future actions, and hence add to the predictability of their environment.

In both *Information and Investment* from 1960 and his article 'The Organization of Industry' from 1972, Richardson presents an institutional solution to the problem of coordination. He argues that classical microeconomics abstracts 'totally from the roles of organization, knowledge, experience, and skills, and thereby makes it the more difficult to bring these into theoretical foreground in the way needed to construct a theory of industrial organization' (1972: 888). In keeping with Penrose's resource-based theory of the firm, which distinguishes between resources and services, Richardson differentiates between a firm's *capabilities*, which reflect the knowledge, experience and skills accumulated by the firm, and its concrete *activities* (production, marketing, research and development) which are based on these capabilities.

In order to establish a typology about ways of organizing economic activities, Richardson distinguishes between 'similar' and 'complementary' activities. Activities are similar when they draw on the same capabilities, whereas activities that, in terms of scale and specifications, are meant to match one another, are referred to as 'complementary'. On this basis, Richardson advances a theory defining when we can expect the producers in a decentralized economy to use the following three organizational forms or institutional arrangements: the firm, the market and interorganizational collaboration. It is to be expected that similar activities are organized internally within the framework of the firm, because 'organizations will tend to specialize in activities for which their capabilities offer some comparative advantage' (1972: 888). However, when faced with activities that are neither similar nor complementary, the preferred mode of organizing will be the market, as there is no need for coordinating investment activities.

Finally, Richardson claims that between the two fundamental institutional forms, the firm and the market, there is a third, and hitherto neglected, way of organizing economic activities, namely *interorganizational collaboration*. To Richardson, the rationale of these institutional arrangements is to solve some of the coordination problems that he discussed in his book in 1960 (cf. Foss 1994). That is, viewed from the individual producer's perspective, the purpose of interorganizational arrangements was to reduce uncertainty about other producers' investment plans in order to coordinate different, but complementary activities. Richardson argued that

> this co-ordination cannot be left entirely to direction within firms because the activities are dissimilar, and cannot be left to market forces in that it requires not the balancing of the aggregate supply of something with the aggregate demand for it, but rather the matching, both qualitative and quantitative, of individual enterprise plans.

(1972: 892)

Orthodox price theory viewed interorganizational arrangements as monopolistic restraints on free competition, while Richardson argued that restraints were absolutely necessary for the functioning of the price mechanism and free competition.

Richardson's (1972) 'knowledge-based' theory of organizing economic activities may, on certain dimensions, be viewed as complementary to Coase's transaction cost theory. This is most conspicuous in terms of the market and hierarchy dichotomy, which Coase (1937) had taken an exclusive interest in as providing alternative coordination mechanisms. Richardson, on the other hand, perceived market and hierarchy as the extreme points of a continuum in which interorganizational arrangements constituted the intervening organizational forms. Indirectly, Richardson's emphasis on the 'knowledge' dimensions of economic activities also represents a more fundamental explanatory variable than do transaction costs. Or, as Richardson indicates: 'The explanation that I have provided is not inconsistent with his [Coase's] but might be taken as giving content to the notion of his relative cost [transaction costs] by specifying the factors that effect it' (1972: 896).

However, Richardson's 1972 formulation of an alternative knowledge-based theory of organizing economic activities does not transgress the 'comparative institutional' and 'efficiency-oriented' explanations of transaction cost theory by, for example, viewing economic phenomena from a genuine 'endogenous growth' perspective. However, Richardson's concept of capability could be claimed to presuppose an endogenous growth perspective. He introduced his capability theory in an attempt to account for the process that ensured the emergence of a coordination equilibrium and must consequently be built on an endogenous growth perspective. Specific capabilities can therefore only be understood as having emerged gradually through a cumulative learning process. Transaction costs, on the other hand, are just assumed to be exogenously given.

Nothing seems to prevent making Richardson's 1972 analysis more 'dynamic' or 'process-oriented' (Richardson 1975). Although Richardson's 1975 article was an attempt to reconstruct Adam Smith's theory of 'the division of labour' and 'increasing return to scale', it can also be interpreted as an attempt to place his own capability theory in a more explicit 'endogenous growth' perspective. A growing market for the firm's output may lead not only to purely quantitative and uniform growth in the individual firm, but also to qualitative changes. Richardson argues that market growth will cause the individual firm to specialize in more uniform activities, while at the same time becoming even more dependent on market and interorganizational relations.

More recent contributions

During the last decade, the endogenous growth perspective, as used by Marshall, Penrose and Richardson, has gained considerable ground, particularly within the strategy field, but also among certain theorists of the firm, and industrial economists. Currently, the competence perspective seems to be characterized by two relatively distinct, but complementary schools, which have both contributed to the further development of the endogenous growth theme. One of the schools is resource-based theory (Wernerfelt 1984), which has based its theory of strategic management explicitly on Penrose's theory of the firm's limits to growth. The central thesis of this school of strategic management is the necessity for firms to establish strong *resource* positions, rather than strong *market* positions. The other school is dynamic capability theory (Teece, Pisano and Shuen 1990). Like resource-based theory, dynamic capability theory develops Penrose's works from the 1950s. However, this theory focuses on developing Richardson's works on interorganizational collaboration and what Teece (1986) calls 'co-specialized activities' and 'complementary assets'.

Based on an endogenous growth perspective, both of these theories have attempted to formulate an explanation of the multi-product firm's choices between related and unrelated diversification. The main thesis is that the firm's growth is, or should be, related to the process from which new knowledge and capabilities emerge, making it possible to expand the fields of production. As Penrose stressed, an endogenous growth perspective of a firm tends to encourage a related, as opposed to an unrelated, diversification strategy:

> A firm may go into many fields, but to maintain itself against competitive pressures it must be prepared to continue putting new funds into each field. This need for continuous new investment will restrict the number of fields a firm can support at any given time. The further from its existing areas of specialization it goes, the greater the effort required of the firm to attain the necessary competence not only in dealing with present production and market conditions, but also in making the adaptations and innovations necessary to keep up with competition.
>
> (Penrose 1959: 134)

In a classic study from 1974, Rumelt tested the validity of this rule by examining whether multi-product firms, that had pursued a related diversification strategy, did better than firms pursuing a non-related diversification strategy. In keeping with Penrose, Rumelt argued that 'successful' diversification was based on a number of 'core skills' in the firm that could be employed in related markets. Similar studies conducted by Montgomery and Wernerfelt (1988) and Chatterjee and Wernerfelt (1991) have confirmed this thesis. Montgomery and Wernerfelt (1988), for instance, demonstrate that more narrowly focused firms in general score higher on 'Tobin's q' (measurement for the value produced by a firm) than non-related, conglomerate-type firms.

Contrary to these mainly empirical contributions, Teece (1980, 1982, 1986) and Teece *et al.* (1994) have strived to formulate a new dynamic theory of the multi-product firm, which focuses on the accumulation of resources, capabilities, and the forces that set limits to this growth. While orthodox theory tried to understand the multi-product firm from the perspective of a static model of production, using the concept of 'economies of scope' (Panzar and Willig 1981), the competence perspective has introduced the concept of 'coherence' as a dynamic counterpart to this. The essence of this concept is that the firm's growth process must be balanced, allowing for coherence between existing and new activities. The concept of coherence thus involves having the 'strategy perception' that underlies the competence perspective. The next section discusses this theme in detail.

ON THE INTELLECTUAL BACKGROUND TO THE THEME OF 'SUSTAINABLE COMPETITIVE ADVANTAGE'

The theme of 'endogenous growth' has primarily focused on the process through which new knowledge and capabilities are accumulated within the framework of the individual firm. So far, literature on this theme has primarily discussed it from a processual, or firm-oriented perspective. On the other hand, the theme of sustainable competitive advantage has been discussed within the framework of equilibrium and industrial economics. The latter theme deals with whether knowledge and capabilities acquired endogenously may produce above-normal profits in the long run, or whether these advantages are eliminated as a result of competition between firms. That is, the focal point is the nature of competitive relations between firms (cf. Barney 1986a, Conner 1991). Despite the distinct differences within the competence perspective between the themes of 'endogenous growth' and 'sustainable competitive advantages', both perspectives seem to draw on evolutionary theories. As to the theme of sustainable competitive advantage it again seems natural to use Marshall and his understanding of competition.

The Marshallian starting point

In contrast to modern theories of competition, such as the neoclassical and SCP traditions, Marshall operated with an 'evolutionary'-based industry perspective. Marshall viewed an industry as consisting of a series of heterogeneous firms that were different in terms of costs, market conditions, and so on. Theoretically, he considered each industry to be comprised of a series of heterogeneous firms that differed as to size, age, knowledge, organization, and so on. Moreover, the industry's structure was not exogenously given, but rather an entity existing in historical time and undergoing a gradual transformation process: 'Thus the rise and fall of individual firms may be frequent, while a great industry is going through one long oscillation, or even moving steadily forwards; as the leaves of a tree grown to maturity, reach equilibrium, and decay many times, while the tree is steadily growing upwards year by year' (Marshall 1920: 457). In order for industries to represent both *heterogeneous* firms and historical entities, Marshall introduced the concept of a 'representative agent'. Contrary to the modern usage of this concept, Marshall used it to define the *average* of firms within an industry as to age, size, and so on. Viewed from this perspective, an equilibrium position would thus represent a balance 'between the forces of progress, and of decay' (Marshall 1920: 460), not a position of rest as in orthodox theory.

The suppression of evolutionary perspectives

During the 1930s, with the emergence of theories of imperfect and monopolistic competition, this evolutionary and population-based perspective on industries was abandoned from mainstream economic theory. Not only did a new set of theories come to dominate economics, but industries and competition were to be analysed from a fundamentally different perspective. A more 'mechanical' perspective gained ground that only allowed for situations of equilibrium at the industry level when all firms were in equilibrium. This is consistent with how an industry was now being conceptualized as consisting of a series of fundamentally homogeneous firms. Economic theory could no longer embrace 'variations' and 'heterogeneity'. 'Representative agents' were no longer identical with an 'average' of firms, but with an 'ideal type' towards which existing firms in an industry converged.

The difference between these two industry perspectives can also be described in terms of Mayr's (1976) important distinction between a *population* and a *typological* perspective: 'The ultimate conclusions of the population thinker and of the typologist are precisely the opposite. For the typologist, the type is real and variation an illusion, while for the populationist, the type (average) is an abstraction and only the variation is real. No two ways of looking at nature could be more different' (Mayr 1976: 28). During the 1930s, typological thinking came to dominate economics at the expense of Marshall's populational understanding. A major consequence of this was that, since firms were now viewed as fundamentally homogeneous, there was no reason to continue studying them from an intraorganizational perspective. Consequently, scholars were expected to explain the existence of above-normal profits by referring to the market rather than internal firm factors. Various 'market imperfections', such as entry barriers, were used to explain why certain firms, capable of establishing an appropriate market positioning, made above-normal returns, and thus gained sustainable competitive advantages.

Despite the fact that the populational perspective was gradually being superseded in economics during the 1930s, important contributions to this perspective were nonetheless published during this decade, such as Schumpeter's *The Theory of Economic Development* in 1934. Several decades passed before economists scrutinized his understanding of competition. During the 1930s, economists were building a static theory of competition based on a typological perspective which assumed market structures to be given. Schumpeter's ambition was to construct a theory of dynamic competition based on an evolutionary perspective. Orthodox theory had viewed the market institution as a solution to the coordination problem of the decentralized economy where prices provided the agents with correct signals and incentives. However, to Schumpeter, the primary purpose of the market system was to produce, and subsequently test, new ways of doing things. This could be anything from developing new products and production processes, to investigating new outlets and markets. Being an evolutionary theorist, Schumpeter focused on endogenously generated novelties that entrepreneurs tested in the market, via new ways of combining known elements, in order to see whether these would yield above-normal profits, or rents. In some cases, new combinations of known elements destroyed previous routines. That is, through a process of 'creative destruction', new routines replaced old ones.

The return to evolutionary modes of thought

During the 1930s, mainstream economics was primarily engaged in adding theories of imperfect and monopolistic competition to the orthodox programme, which meant that Schumpeter's dynamic theory of competition had little impact. Not until the 1950s and 1960s did evolutionary and population theories become important for the understanding of competition in economics. The Chicago School and Demsetz and Alchian at UCLA criticized both the SCP paradigm and the theory of monopolistic competition from the perspectives of evolutionary and population theory. During the 1980s, this criticism, and its alternative view of the sources of above-normal profits, has been used by some resource-based theorists to understand the nature of competitive advantages and how they can be sustained over a certain period.

In his article from 1950, 'Uncertainty, Evolution and Economic Theory', Alchian formulated the foundation of the Chicago School's population-theoretical understanding of the market. Alchian's main idea was that:

All individual rationality, motivation, and foresight will be temporarily abandoned in order to concentrate upon the ability of the environment to adopt 'appropriate' survivors even in the absence of any adaptive behavior.
(1950: 21)

Thus, firms were no longer viewed as 'perfect rational decision-makers', as in orthodox theory. On the contrary, they were viewed as 'adaptive institutional arrangements', 'shaped' by the market forces. In consequence, the market was seen as a selection mechanism that, through a differential survival process (profitable firms expand and non-profitable firms contract), ensures that only the more efficient firms survive.

Alchian (1950) emphasized that the selection mechanism only ensured 'survival-of-the-fitter', and not necessarily 'survival-of-the-fittest', but his reservations were soon forgotten. In 1953, Friedman used Alchian's selection argument in his 'Methodology of Positive Economics' for an *ad hoc* defence of why economic theory maintained the hypothesis of maximization of return and prioritized studying situations of equilibrium over processes. Friedman's argument was that situations of equilibrium and profit-maximizing behaviour were merely the 'end result' of a selection process. Therefore, there was no need for studying this selection process which produced certain rules of action, or certain institutional arrangements. We could only assume the result to be the most efficient rules and institutions. That is, 'maximization-cum-equilibrium' explanations could be interpreted as compatible with 'adaptive' or 'functionalist' explanations. On the other hand, these were not compatible with the 'endogenous growth' explanation mentioned earlier.

The adaptive and functional explanatory model also underlies Alchian and Demsetz's (1972) explanation of why firms exist. According to Alchian and Demsetz, the capitalist firm has emerged – through non-specified learning and selection processes – as the institutional solution to the 'metering' problem related to team-production. This way of organizing production makes it impossible to measure the individual's performance and pay him/her accordingly. Therefore, the individual is faced with a 'contribution' dilemma, which incites shirking at the expense of the collectivity.

Confronted with this problem, a series of more or less appropriate institutional solutions are bound to materialize. Alchian and Demsetz (1972) do not presume that a perfect rational solution to the metering problems will be designed *ex ante*. On the contrary, they surmise that, over time, numerous different solutions will occur that are tested and compared, making it possible to point to the most appropriate solution. In other words, a solution that ensures individual compensation according to his/her true, but non-observable, marginal productivity. According to Alchian and Demsetz (1972), the best solution to the 'metering' problem is the capitalist firm in which one of the team-members has residual rights to the team-production while simultaneously monitoring the others' performance.

However, what is to be concluded about the competitive relations between firms characterized by team-production? Demsetz concludes that above-normal returns will not necessarily be eliminated in the short run simply as a result of competition. The reason is that it will be difficult for less profitable firms to imitate more profitable firms that have adopted team-production, since it is impossible to identify the types of input that give a firm certain competitive advantages. Demsetz (1973) describes this deficient ability to identify the correct causes of a firm's success in the following way:

> It may be very difficult for . . . firms to understand the reasons for . . . difference in performance, or to know to which inputs to attribute the performance of the successful firm. It is not easy to ascertain just why GM and IBM perform better than their competitors. The complexity of these organizations defied easy analysis, so that the inputs responsible for success may be undervalued by the market for some time.
>
> (1973: 2)

Situations in which the firm and/or its competitors find it difficult to ascertain the causes of success are referred to as 'causal ambiguity' (Lippman and Rumelt 1982). In general, Demsetz argues that the existence of information costs in an economy makes it difficult or impossible to duplicate or imitate another firm's competitive advantages, such as superior technology, market knowledge, organizing, and so on. In keeping with Alchian's 1950 model, Demsetz assumes the individual firm to be confronted with genuine uncertainty, and that market selection rather than rational calculus decides which firms are profitable, and which die out. Compared to the orthodox theory and the SCP paradigm, which are based on a typological schema, above-normal returns will 'not arise because the firm creates "artificial scarcity" through a reduction in its output. Nor does it arise because of collusion.' Rather, from a population model perspective, 'superior performance can be attributed to the combination of great uncertainty plus luck or atypical insights by the management of a firm' (1973: 3). The consequence is that the concept of 'sustainable competitive advantages' is not, as in the SCP paradigm, in accordance with a theory of monopoly, but rather with the rent analysis of classical political economy.

Modern resource-based theorists

Inspired by both the Chicago School's industrial organization analysis and Schumpeter's vision about the dynamic competition in a capitalist economy, strategy scholars such as Barney (1986a), Lippman and Rumelt (1982) and Rumelt (1984), tried during the 1980s to clarify the conditions for the existence of *sustainable* competitive advantages. Like other evolutionist theorists, they based their settlement on the typological conception:

> The traditional model of industry in industrial organization is taken from oligopoly theory and remains that of identical firms or firms that are homogeneous but for scale. The effect of this modelling assumption has been to reduce the study of industrial competition to the study of relative scale, all other differences being ignored.
>
> (Rumelt 1984)

In line with Demsetz, Rumelt argued that sustainable competitive advantages had to be explained by the existence of a fundamental uncertainty as to which particular resource in a firm caused success. This 'causal ambiguity' implied that a situation of equilibrium might exist, making it possible for firms within the industry to cash in on greater profits than outside firms, without the latter necessarily attempting to penetrate the industry and hence cause profits to erode. Here, Rumelt (1984) introduced the term *isolating mechanism* to explain those phenomena that *ex post* restrict the equalization of rent differentials between firms. Examples of this are: experience-based managerial resources (Penrose 1959); organizational culture that is valuable, rare and imperfectly imitable (Barney 1986b); invisible assets such as product reputations that are difficult to imitate (Itami 1987); and heuristics that a successful firm uses to solve new problems (Schoemaker 1990).

28

A common denominator of these examples is that resources have been accumulated over a long period of time, through an uncertain, unpredictable accumulation process that is almost impossible for other firms to replicate (and which, in some cases, may even be impossible for the firm itself to duplicate). To the imitating firm, the problem is that the given resources are 'a result of human action, but not of human design'. That is, they cannot be designed *ex ante*, but only produced as a by-product through a spontaneous and highly uncertain accumulation process, in which the chances of failure are greater than those of success.

It is a weakness of the competence perspective that no attempts have been systematically made to integrate the theme of sustainable competitive advantages with the theme of the endogenous growth perspective. The resource-based literature on sustainable competitive advantages has been based primarily on a model of equilibrium, and has focused on how different isolating mechanisms determine non-classical situations of equilibrium. The existence of isolating mechanisms is justified within the model, because the processes of accumulating resources, which are the background of these isolating mechanisms, are not incorporated into the model itself. Attempts to anchor the resource-based theory in an evolutionary research programme, such as Nelson and Winter's (1982) theory of economic change, or Hannan and Freeman's (1989) organization ecology, could contribute to solving this problem (cf. Montgomery 1995). As early as 1982, Nelson and Winter argued that the background for introducing an evolutionary paradigm in economic theory was a wish to be able to handle change processes in a non-*ad hoc* way, contrary to orthodox price theory. Also, Winter (1987) has introduced a series of dimensions that can be used to characterize a firm's knowledge and technology base, and hence to understand the backdrop to the isolating mechanisms in competition between the firms.

ON THE CONCEPT OF STRATEGY AND THE RETURN TO THE CLASSICAL THEORY OF STRATEGY

The classical concept of strategy

The competence perspective emphasizes understanding the firm's competitive situation primarily in regard to its resources, rather than its market position. This implies that scholars within strategy have returned to a perception widely shared by classic strategy theorists, such as Barnard (1938), Selznick (1957), Chandler (1962, 1990, 1992) and Andrews (1971). As Rumelt formulates it:

> In essence, the [strategy] concept is that a firm's competitive position is defined by a bundle of unique resources and relationships, and that the task of general management is to adjust and renew these resources and relationships as time, competition, and change erode their value. This way of looking at the firm . . . is . . . useful in describing and summarizing

the empirical studies of firm behavior that form the core of the business policy literature.

(1984: 57–8)

However, I will go a step further than Rumelt, arguing that employing the classical strategy literature more actively may contribute to solving some of the problems for which modern literature on the competence perspective apparently has no solution. At the general level, this includes how to merge the theme of 'endogenous growth' with the theme of 'sustainable competitive advantage'.

Endogenous growth and sustainable competitive advantage

The reason why it seems difficult to merge the theme of 'sustainable competitive advantage' with the theme of 'endogenous growth' is perhaps because the two themes build on two apparently different perceptions of the firm and firm behaviour. Like the Chicago School, the theme of 'sustainable competitive advantage' views the firm and its behaviour from an equilibrium perspective, and explains ad hoc those processes that must be assumed to have produced the firm's heterogeneous resource positions. Under the theme of endogenous growth, the firm is analysed as a historical entity, which implies giving a 'cumulative process' perspective priority over an 'equilibrium' perspective. Thus, two fairly dissimilar behavioural foundations are maintained within the two streams of literature, both of which can be traced back to the classical debate on biological analogies within economics in the early 1950s.

At that time, Alchian (1950) advocated interpreting firm behaviour as being determined by the environment via a fairly unspecified selection process. In opposition to this, Penrose argued that Alchian's perception of economic agents was too 'passive', 'the growth approach has so far been expounded in any systematic form only by the "biological economists" – by those who view firms as organisms and conclude that they grow like organisms. That variant of the growth approach leaves no room for human motivation and conscious human decision and I think should be rejected on that ground' (1952). The danger of focusing too much on an evolutionary perspective was that it excluded a more active 'perception of actors' in economics. Viewed from the strategy perspective, it is obviously inconvenient not to leave room for pro-active actions of a strategic nature. Sidney Winter, for example, argues that:

In the theoretical world [of evolutionary economics], strategic analysis, in the sense defined here, has no place, although of course there is abundant scope for *ex post facto* discussion of which habits and impulses proved successful. As a response to a need for guidance in the real world, this fatalistic perspective has obvious and severe limitations.

(1987: 161–2)

One explanation for this is that, to Alchian (1950) and Nelson and Winter (1982), the dominant analytical level was the industry rather than the firm.

Viewed from this level, it is quite natural to explain 'success' in terms of 'blind luck', rather than as a consequence of superior knowledge, resources or capabilities. After having published *An Evolutionary Theory of Economic Change* in 1982, Nelson and Winter partially changed analytical levels from industry to firm, which then improved the importance and relevance of the evolutionary paradigm within strategy. An evident example of this is Teece *et al.*'s (1994) introduction of the concept of coherence.

Against this background one could ask, what is the behavioural foundation of the competence perspective? And what are the implications of this foundation for the perception of strategy? In order to answer these questions, we should look for inspiration among some of the classic theorists of strategy. A very inspiring piece of work is Philip Selznick's *Leadership in Administration: A Sociological Interpretation* from 1957 (cf. Knudsen 1995a, b).

Selznick's work

Even though Selznick's theory of 'distinctive competence' was primarily a contribution to sociological and organizational theories, there are several reasons for perceiving it as an important precursor to the current competence perspective. In keeping with Penrose's resource-based theory, Selznick argued that an adequate study of organizations would entail a 'genetic and developmental approach, an emphasis on historical origin and growth stages. There is a need to see the enterprise as a whole and to see how it is transformed as new ways of dealing with a changing environment emerge.' Selznick clearly dissociated himself from earlier attempts to see organizations either as perfectly rational agents or as adaptive institutions that, via selection, fitted into their environment. Viewing organizations from the former perspective would imply seeing them as purely 'technical instruments', exploited by the management to achieve its goals.

On the other hand, viewing organizations as institutions that adapt to the environment via selection processes may raise two types of criticism. First, this perspective on firms, or organizations, leaves no room for 'pro-active' actions and hence strategic management. Second, operating with an 'opportunistic' understanding of organizations, focusing on short-term adaptation, leaves no room for 'active' and 'long-term' learning. As an alternative to these two perceptions of organizations, and their implicit understanding of strategy, Selznick suggests:

> accepting the obligation of giving direction instead of merely ministering to organizational equilibrium; in adapting aspiration to the character of organization, bearing in mind that what the organization has been will affect what it can be and do; transcending bare organizational survival by seeing that specialized decisions do not weaken or confuse the distinctive identity of the enterprise.

(1957: 149)

31

Selznick's view of the firm in many ways tallies with that of Penrose. However, the behavioural foundation of Selznick's theory is far more explicit. In the light of modern economics, Selznick's theory is an example of what decision-making theory terms 'the problem of time inconsistency' (cf. Strotz 1956). That is, faced with an intertemporal decision-making problem, a firm will not follow its original long-term plan. It will choose the solution that is most optimal in the specific period. Consequently, the firm will be confronted with what Schelling (1984) calls a problem of 'self-command', and Elster (1985) terms 'weakness of the will'. That is, the individual's long-term interests ('the planner') attempt to dominate, or control, the short-term interests ('the doers'). According to Elster, this problem of 'self-control' can be modelled as an *intrapersonal* prisoner's dilemma game between the individual's long- and short-term interests, leading to a suboptimal outcome if nothing is done by the 'controller' to constrain the 'doers'.

Reconstructing Selznick's analysis

It is possible to reconstruct Selznick's theory of distinct competences and identities of organizations on the basis of a 'multiple-self' model. That is, the purpose of strategy and leadership is to impede 'the pursuit of immediate short-run advantages in a way inadequately controlled by considerations of principle and ultimate consequences'. To Selznick, this 'case-by-case' adaptation represents an 'irresponsible form of leadership', as it does not make the organization autonomous in relation to the environment, which signals weakness of the will. To solve the problems of 'self-command', Selznick argues for *institutional* leadership to 'look . . . [at] . . . the long-run effect of present advantage . . . and . . . [to study] . . . how changes affect personal or institutional identity' (1957: 143).

To solve such problems of self-command, an organization employs a series of various *pre-commitment* strategies to shape its character or identity. This involves analysing how an organization limits its own future freedom of choice by making 'character-defining commitments' in order to create, or develop, its own identity. Paradoxically, by limiting their own freedom of action through commitment to certain future behavioural patterns, individuals, as well as organizations, develop their own unique identity. It is through an institutionalization process that formal organizations are infused with value, and thus acquire a certain character or role. It is in this sense that organizations are not seen as passive 'role adaptors', but rather as very active in creating their own future role.

This is a model of what one could call the 'self-constituted' or 'self-constructed' agent which is the basic foundation of Selznick's theory of 'distinct competences' and thus his perception of the concept of strategy. This model of the 'cumulative creation of character' is different from the more conventional pre-commitment models within economics in that the individual is not modelled as invariant over time. Not only does the model assume former 'selves'

32

to limit future possibilities of action by imposing restrictions on the individual's future strategies, but they also prompt the individual to change the quality of his/her set of action and hence his/her identity or nature. In focusing on how the individual can coordinate his/her actions in a cumulative process over time, Selznick is said to be operating with a far more organic and coherent perception of identity than that characterizing conventional pre-commitment models. In keeping with this, the concept of strategy is therefore closely tied to the idea of the best possible way of handling intertemporal coordination and hence guaranteeing a sustainable growth process.

Endogenous growth processes and the concept of strategy in a competence perspective

The multiple, and often diverging, perceptions of how to define or interpret the concept of strategy often seem to stem from the very different perceptions of what constitutes the basic nature of organizations or firms (Knudsen 1995a, b). Being based on an endogenous growth perspective on the firm, competence theorists operate with a concept of strategy very different from that characterizing theories based on either an 'equilibrium-orientation' or a 'functionalist' perception of the firm or the organization. Competence theorists, thus, refute 'equilibrium-oriented' theorists' attempts to identify the concept of strategy with both the formulation of 'rational plans' and attempts to position oneself in markets where one can exploit entrance barriers. Likewise, adherents of the competence perspective reject the functionalist theorists' desire to identify the concept of strategy with attempts to guarantee static, efficient structures through matching environments and structures.

A major explanation of why competence theorists not only are critical of these two perceptions, but also seem to converge towards an almost identical perception of strategy, is that they view the firm from the same endogenous growth perspective. And viewed in this perspective it is reasonable to link strategy to the question of which means to apply to guarantee a sustainable growth process.

Teece *et al.* (1994) discussing the concept of coherence, Prahalad and Hamel (1990) discussing 'core competences', Levinthal and March (1993) discussing the necessity of balancing 'exploitation' and 'exploration' and avoiding development traps, and Montgomery and Wernerfelt's (1988) criticism of an unrelated diversification strategy and prioritizing a 'focused' strategy, all seem to be preoccupied by the most adequate way of handling the growth process in a firm in order to guarantee sustainable growth. One can argue that these seemingly very different perceptions of the concept of strategy are merely variations of the same theme, which could be described in the terminology of Schumpeter's discussion of how one during a growth process should strive to strike a balance between static and dynamic efficiency. Or as formulated by Wernerfelt: 'the optimal growth of the firm involves a balance between exploitation of existing resources and the development of new ones' (1984: 178).

core

Thus, if focusing too one-sidedly on achieving static efficiency, the organization or the firm may undermine its long-term growth process. Likewise, staking too much on dynamic efficiency, in terms of the organization's incessant striving to renew its competences, may result in competences adequate to demonstrate any form of 'distinct competences' never developing. Hence, the strategic task becomes one of striking a balance between static and dynamic efficiency, making it possible to initiate new activities, if they can function as *stepping stones* for further expansion (Wernerfelt 1984).

Viewed in this light, management's major task becomes to guarantee the firm's strategic flexibility, that is, over time to reduce costs by adapting to new and unanticipated events. Striking the balance between static and dynamic efficiency implies that the firm develops a set of routines and capabilities, guaranteeing that it always holds new options in readiness when facing unexpected events to avoid being caught up in a 'competence trap' (Levinthal and March 1993).

CONCLUSION

Contrary to Mahoney and Pandian (1992) and Teece, Pisano and Shuen (1990), who have argued that the competence perspective constitutes a 'unifying paradigm for strategy research', I have argued that the competence perspective still harbours too much tension and heterogeneity to be considered an integrating paradigm or research programme. However, if using classics – such as Selznick (1957) and Andrews (1971) – makes it possible to bridge various schools of behavioural theory, and to specify the behavioural foundation of the competence perspective and its understanding of strategy, then the most important barriers to developing a unifying research programme in strategy will be eliminated.

REFERENCES

Alchian, A. A. (1950) 'Uncertainty, Evolution and Economic Theory', *Journal of Political Economy* 58: 211–21.

Alchian, A. A. and Demsetz, H. (1972) 'Production, Information Costs, and Economic Organization', in A. A. Alchian (1977) *Economic Forces at Work*, Indianapolis: Liberty Press.

Andrews, K. R. (1971) *The Concept of Corporate Strategy*, Homewood, Ill.: Richard D. Irwin.

Babbage, C. (1833) *On the Economy of Machinery and Manufactures*, 3rd edn, London: Charles Knight.

Barnard, C. (1938) *The Functions of the Executive*, Cambridge, Mass.: Harvard University Press.

Barney, J. B. (1986a) 'Strategic Factor Markets: Expectations, Luck, and Business Strategy', *Management Science* 32: 1231–41.

Barney, J. B. (1986b) 'Organizational Culture: Can it Be a Source of Sustained Competitive Advantage?', *Academy of Management Review* 11: 656–65.

Barney, J. B. (1991) 'Firm Resources and Sustainable Competitive Advantage', *Journal of Management* 17: 99–120.

Chandler, A. D. (1962) *Strategy and Structure*, Cambridge, Mass.: MIT Press.

Chandler, A. D. (1990) *Scale and Scope. The Dynamics of Industrial Capitalism*, Cambridge, Mass.: The Belknap Press of Harvard University Press.

Chandler, A. D. (1992) 'Organizational Capabilities and the Economic History of the Industrial Enterprise', *Journal of Economic Perspectives* 6 (3): 79–100.

Chatterjee, S. and Wernerfelt, B. (1991) 'The Link between Resources and Type of Diversification', *Strategic Management Journal* 12: 33–48.

Coase, R. H. (1937) 'The Nature of the Firm', *Economica* 4: 386–405.

Coleman, J. S. (1988) 'Social Capital in the Creation of Human Capital', *American Journal of Sociology*, suppl. 94: 95–120.

Coleman, J. S. (1990) *Foundation of Social Theory*, Cambridge, Mass.: Harvard University Press.

Conner, K. R. (1991) 'A Historical Comparison of Resource-based Theory and Five Schools of Thought within Industrial Organization Economics: Do we Have a New Theory of the Firm?', *Journal of Management* 17: 121–54.

Cyert, R. M. and March, J. G. (1963) *A Behavioral Theory of the Firm*, Englewood Cliffs, NJ: Prentice-Hall.

Demsetz, H. (1973) 'Industry Structure, Market Rivalry, and Public Policy', *Journal of Law and Economics* 16: 1–9.

Demsetz, H. (1988) 'The Theory of the Firm Revisited', *Journal of Law, Economics and Organization* 4: 141–62.

Dierickx, I. and Cool, K. (1989) 'Asset Stock Accumulation and Sustainability of Competitive Advantage', *Management Science* 35: 1504–11.

Elster, J. (1985) 'Weakness of the Will and the Free-rider Problem', *Economics and Philosophy* 1: 231–65.

Foss, N. J. (1994) 'Cooperation is Competition: George Richardson on Coordination and Interfirm Relations', *British Review of Economic Issues* 40: 25–50.

Friedman, M. (1953) 'The Methodology of Positive Economics', in M. Friedman, *Essays in Positive Economics*, Chicago: University of Chicago Press.

Hannan, M. T. and Freeman, J. (1989) *Organizational Ecology*, Cambridge, Mass.: Harvard University Press.

Hedlund, G. (1994) 'A Model of Knowledge Management and the N-form Corporation', *Strategic Management Journal* 15: 73–90.

Itami, H. (1987) *Mobilizing Invisible Assets*, Cambridge, Mass.: Harvard University Press.

Knudsen, C. (1995a) 'The Competence View of the Firm: What Can Modern Economists Learn from Philip Selznick's Sociological Theory of Leadership', in W. R. Scott and S. Christensen (eds) *Institutional Construction of Organizations: International and Longitudinal Studies*, London: Sage.

Knudsen, C. (1995b) 'Theories of the Firm, Strategic Management and Leadership', in C. Montgomery (ed.) *Towards a Synthesis of Evolutionary and Resource-based Approaches to Strategy*, Boston: Kluwer.

Lakatos, I. (1970) 'Falsification and the Methodology of Scientific Research Programmes', in I. Lakatos and J. Musgrave (eds) *Criticism and the Growth of Knowledge*, Cambridge: Cambridge University Press.

Langlois, R. N. (1992) 'Transaction Cost Economics in Real Time', *Industrial and Corporate Change* 1: 99–127.

Leijonhufvud, A. (1986) 'Capitalism and the Factory System', in R. N. Langlois (ed.) *Economics as a Process. Essays in the New Institutional Economics*, Cambridge: Cambridge University Press.

Lippman, S. and Rumelt, R. P. (1982) 'Uncertain Imitability: An Analysis of Interfirm Differences in Efficiency under Competition', *Bell Journal of Economics* 13: 418–38.

Mahoney, J. T. and Pandian, J. R. (1992) 'The Resource-based View within the Conversation of Strategic Management', *Strategic Management Journal* 13: 363–80.

Malmgren, H. B. (1961) 'Information, Expectations and the Theory of the Firm', *Quarterly Journal of Economics* 75: 399–421.

Marshall, A. (1920) *Principles of Economics. An Introductory Volume*, 8th edn, London: Macmillan.

Mayr, E. (1976) *Evolution and the Diversity of Life*, Cambridge, Mass.: Harvard University Press.

Montgomery, C. A. (1995) *Resource-based and Evolutionary Theories of the Firm. Towards a Synthesis*, Boston: Kluwer Academic Publishers.

Montgomery, C. A. and Wernerfelt, B. (1988) 'Tobin's q and the Importance of Focus in Firm Performance', *American Economic Review* 78: 246–50.

Nelson, R. and Winter, S. (1982) *An Evolutionary Theory of Economic Change*, Cambridge, Mass.: Belknap Press of Harvard University Press.

Nonaka, I. and Takeuchi, H. (1995) *The Knowledge-creating Company. How Japanese Companies Create the Dynamics of Innovation*, Oxford: Oxford University Press.

Panzar, J. C. and Willig, R. D. (1981) 'Economies of Scope', *American Economic Review* 71: 268–72.

Penrose, E. T. (1952): 'Biological Analogies in the Theory of the Firm', *American Economic Review* 52: 804–19.

Penrose, E. T. (1953) 'Rejoinder', *American Economic Review* 43: 603–9.

Penrose, E. T. (1955) 'Limits to the Growth and Size of Firms', *American Economic Review, Papers and Proceedings*: 531–43.

Penrose, E. T. (1959) *The Theory of the Growth of the Firm*, Oxford: Oxford University Press.

Porter, M. E. (1980) *Competitive Strategy: Techniques for Analyzing Industries and Competitors*, New York: The Free Press.

Prahalad C. K. and Hamel, G. (1990) 'The Core Competences of the Firm', *Harvard Business Review* 66: 79–91.

Ricardo, D. (1953) *The Principles of Political Economy and Taxation*, London: Dent.

Richardson, G. B. (1960/1990) *Information and Investment*, Oxford: Oxford University Press.

Richardson, G. B. (1972) 'The Organisation of Industry', *Economic Journal* 82: 883–96.

Richardson, G. B. (1975) 'Adam Smith on Competition and Increasing Returns', in A. S. Skinner and T. Wilson (eds) *Essays on Adam Smith*, Oxford: Oxford University Press.

Rumelt, R. P. (1974) *Strategy, Structure and Economic Performance*, Boston: Division of Research, Harvard Business School.

Rumelt, R. P. (1984) 'Towards a Strategic Theory of the Firm', in R. B. Lamb (ed.) *Competitive Strategic Management*, Englewood Cliffs, NJ: Prentice-Hall.

Schelling, T. (1984) *Choice and Consequence. Perspectives of an Errant Economist*, Cambridge, Mass.: Harvard University Press.

Schoemaker, P. J. (1990) 'Strategy, Complexity, and Economic Rent', *Management Science* 36: 1178–92.

Schumpeter, J. (1934) *The Theory of Economic Development*, Cambridge, Mass.: Harvard University Press.

Selznick, P. (1957) *Leadership in Administration. A Sociological Interpretation*, Berkeley: Harper & Row.

Strotz, R. H. (1956) 'Myopia and Inconsistencies in Dynamic Utility Maximization', *Review of Economic Studies* 23: 165–80.

Teece, D. J. (1980) 'Economics of Scope and the Scope of the Enterprise', *Journal of Economic Behavior and Organization* 1: 223–47.

Teece, D. J. (1982) 'Towards an Economic Theory of the Multiproduct Firm', *Journal of Economic Behavior and Organization* 3: 39–64.

36

Teece, D. J. (1984) 'Economic Analysis and Strategic Management', *California Management Review* 26: 87–110.

Teece, D. J. (1986) 'Profiting from Technological Innovation: Implications for Integration, Collaboration, Licensing, and Public Policy', *Research Policy* 15: 285–305.

Teece, D. J., Pisano, G. and Shuen, A. (1990) 'Firm Capabilities, Resources, and the Concept of Strategy', CCP Working Paper 90–8.

Teece, D. J., Dosi, G., Winter, S. G. and Rumelt, R. P. (1994) 'Understanding Corporate Coherence: Theory and Evidence', *Journal of Economic Behavior and Organization* 23: 1–30.

Wernerfelt, B. (1984) 'A Resource-based View of the Firm', *Strategic Management Journal* 5: 171–80.

Winter, S. G. (1987) 'Knowledge and Competence as Strategic Assets', in D. J. Teece (ed.) *The Competitive Challenge: Strategies for Industrial Innovation and Renewal*, Cambridge, Mass.: Ballinger.

Young, A. (1928) 'Increasing Returns and Economic Progress', *Economic Journal* 38: 527–42.

3

THE ORGANIZATION OF INDUSTRY

Brian Loasby

INTRODUCTION

This chapter is founded on two of Hayek's principles: first, that 'economic problems arise always and only in consequence of change' (Hayek 1945: 523), and second, that the question is not 'whether planning is to be done or not, but *who* is to do the planning' (Hayek 1945: 520). My intention is to examine the organization of industry as a system of dispersed planning to cope with, and also to generate, various kinds of change. I shall therefore consider the advantages and limitations of firms and markets, and of various ways of organizing firms and markets, interactions between firms, and the ways in which these advantages and limitations may evolve over time. What follows is no more than a sketch, but it is intended to be a sketch from a distinct perspective: the analysis will be conducted on the assumption of incomplete knowledge. The theme and the perspective are those of G. B. Richardson (1960, 1972, 1990), as is the title of this chapter.

I would like to begin by explaining why Hayek's principles provide an appropriate basis. The first precondition of economics is scarcity; hence the most fundamental economic idea is that of opportunity cost. But, as Adam Smith realized, it is because scarcity can be alleviated by a very extensive system of specialization, with its consequent pervasive interdependences, that economics becomes an essential part of the study of society. Yet the study even of a highly interdependent system has only limited scope if the pattern of interactions, once established, does not change.

Let us consider a world in which there is no change, in Hayek's (1937: 35) sense of 'any divergence of the actual from the expected development'. There may be cycles and trends, even discontinuities, provided that everyone knows about them in advance, and that they always happen when they are expected. There seems no reason why this definition of 'no change relative to expectations' should not include an agreed list of possible states of the world: the absence of change implies that such a list is never falsified. Now we have a model of a world without change in this sense: it is the Arrow–Debreu model of general equilibrium, which has been considered the supreme achievement of economic

38

theory. It is normally presented as a world of perfectly competitive markets, though we are occasionally reminded that it has an alter ego as a world of perfect central planning. In fact, however, it is a world in which neither markets nor planning is needed: every contingency is already covered by contracts or instructions. All that is necessary is that each person continues to perform an appropriate set of routines, whether this set has been chosen, or imposed, or even genetically determined. Apart from complexity, there is no identifiable difference between behaviour in such an economy and behaviour in a colony of social insects. It is not at all obvious that economists have any comparative advantage in studying such a system.

Yet it is in this direction that economists' obsession with rationality has taken them. The paradox is well displayed by Schumpeter (1934: 80), although – surprisingly for one who often took delight in disturbing conventional wisdom – he does not draw attention to it. 'The assumption that conduct is prompt and rational is in all cases a fiction. But it proves to be sufficiently near to reality, if things have time to hammer logic into men . . . Outside of these limits our fiction loses its closeness to reality . . . the choice of new methods is not simply an element in the concept of rational economic action . . . but a distinct process which stands in need of special explanation.' In Schumpeter's system, rational choice theory provides a predictive model of the routines of the circular flow, but does not explain how they arise; economic development depends on entrepreneurial plans which are based on 'figments of our imagination' (Schumpeter 1934: 85). Furthermore, when these entrepreneurial plans invalidate the pattern of rational routines, people have no algorithms of rational choice for devising a new pattern; that is why Schumpeterian innovation leads to recession.

Economists should note that there can indeed be no algorithm of rational choice, as they define it, for devising patterns: patterns – indeed closed systems – are not a product but a precondition of rationality, as that has come to be interpreted in mainstream economics. We appear therefore to have a problem. Rational choice theory is efficiently and exclusively tailored to equilibrium, in which there are no decisions to be made, and there is no need for markets; markets are needed only out of equilibrium. In an Arrow–Debreu world, as its expositors have insisted, markets open once only, and close before agents begin to execute their equilibrium plans. A rational choice theory of markets seems therefore strictly applicable only to an empty set of phenomena. That it may nevertheless sometimes be quite useful I would be prepared to argue on another occasion; but in this chapter I shall be looking elsewhere.

That does not mean that I shall be abandoning the idea of reasoned behaviour. But I turn to Marshall (1920: 5) for an account of

the fundamental characteristics of modern industrial life . . . They are . . . a certain independence and habit of choosing one's own course for oneself, a self-reliance; a deliberation and yet a promptness of choice and judgement, and a habit of forecasting the future and of shaping one's course with reference to distant aims. They may and often do cause people to compete with one another; but on the other hand they may tend, and just now are tending, in the direction of co-operation and combination of all kinds, good and evil.

He adds 'It is deliberateness, and not selfishness, that is the characteristic of the modern age' (Marshall 1920: 6). This care in working out a plan of action is contrasted by Marshall with the habit and custom which, as Schumpeter observed, provides the closest practical approximation to the constructions of rational choice theory. Planning, as a process, is required because of change, in Hayek's sense of divergence from what was predicted; instead of following routines, people need to work out what they should do. Planning also has the effect of introducing change, both intended and unintended. So Hayek's two propositions are closely linked: it is change that gives rise to economic problems which have to be tackled by some kind of planning, and the actions which result are major sources of change.

These propositions have twin corollaries: the problems arise because the economy is not in equilibrium – at least, not an equilibrium of prices and quantities, on which so much effort has been focused; and they cannot be resolved by the rigorous application of rational choice theory, in which action is a formal consequence of the data. This does not mean the abandonment of logic, or of the routine which is its twin; what it does mean is investigating systems of planning, and methods of organization, which do not depend on the availability of a complete specification of the possibilities, but which may be regarded as equilibrium configurations of theory and policy (Loasby 1991). It perhaps should not be necessary to add that the process of planning is more important than the plan which results from it.

KNOWLEDGE AND COMPETENCE

To find an alternative organizing principle to that of rational choice equilibrium we turn to the problem of knowledge. Both economic agents and those seeking to analyse their behaviour require a knowledge base on which to work; and if they are to behave sensibly they must recognize the incompleteness of knowledge, which is the fundamental reason for 'divergence of the actual from the expected development'. We now know that it is logically impossible to exclude such divergences, because it is impossible to prove the truth of any general empirical proposition. Knowledge is fallible, and so therefore must be expectation; but both are capable of improvement. We may invent novel conjectures to challenge or supplement the conjectures which presently pass for knowledge, and these conjectures may be criticized and tested within a selection process in which better conjectures, we believe, are likely to have a better chance of surviving.

If our economic system is to be a vehicle for the improvement of knowledge, and for the use of that improved knowledge in relaxing the constraints of scarcity, then what needs to be coordinated is the generation and testing of novel conjectures. What makes coordination inherently problematic is the impossibility of determining what new knowledge is to be found, and how it may be found: distributing probabilities over supposedly complete lists is a pretence of knowledge. The chief practical difficulty is the conflict between the need for agreement, possibly tacit, on a framework within which conjectures will be criticized and tested, and the desirability of variety among these conjectures, which may require some diversity of frameworks. One possible solution is a pattern in which several types of product or technologies, or analytical systems, are simultaneously developed, each by a number of close rivals. What is clearly not appropriate is the homogeneity of product and process that is usually associated with Pareto efficiency.

We are here envisaging, in Hayek's (1937: 49) phrase, a division of knowledge to set beside the division of labour, offering similar prospects of economic betterment, but generating similar needs for coordination. Indeed, the finer the division of labour and of knowledge, the greater the expertise that results, but also the greater is likely to be the experts' ignorance of those matters in which they are not expert; and sometimes the greater the ignorance of the extent of that ignorance. But this is a special case – an important special case, as we can observe – of the general problem of living in a world where we cannot foresee the future. Something can be done about that too: as Menger (1871) pointed out, we can make provision through the accumulation of various kinds of reserves, such as fire extinguishers, medicine chests and money. In contemplating the organization of industry, we may like to replace the term 'reserves' with the currently fashionable label of 'competences'.

We may think of competences in two ways, which are not entirely unrelated. The first is the degree of specificity. What is the range of uses to which a particular kind of knowledge or skill can be put? What threats or opportunities will it prepare us for? It should be noted that this assessment is necessarily comparative: what matters is our standing in relation to actual or potential rivals. The second perspective is the degree of control: to what extent is the use of any particular competence dependent on other people, either directly or because of their control over complementary competences? It is important to distinguish between nominal and effective control; the latter may depend not only on appropriate incentives but also on knowledge. Many people and organizations have discovered that the skills which they believed they could command were quite inadequate for their purposes.

What should be remembered, but is often forgotten, is that every competence, like every other form of knowledge, is always a conjecture: whatever the past record it is impossible to guarantee that our skills or knowledge will be up to the next task that we believe them capable of performing. Nevertheless, it is reasonable to include the development of competences in any plan of action which is formulated. (This is a notable, if underdeveloped, feature of Ansoff's (1965) foundational analysis of corporate strategy.) In an economic context, this is what

41

we do when we seek to increase our knowledge; thus our consideration of competences leads to a wider definition of the organization of industry as a system for the coordination of the growth of knowledge.

However, as Hayek argued, the attempt to coordinate through centralization inevitably frustrates many of the potential benefits of the division of knowledge. Specialization increases the total of knowledge; but it reduces the fraction of that total which can be understood by any individual or group of decision-makers. However, control of competences is unnecessary if we can have ready access to them; and they may sometimes be much more effective competences if we do not try to control them, but leave decisions to those who know better, as is recommended by those who advocate empowering subordinates. The use of cash, or other liquid assets, as reserves reveals a preference for access over control, and is particularly attractive when we are very uncertain what competences will prove valuable in the future; for we can access much more than we can control. But a preference for liquidity is a rejection by potential purchasers of the possibility of contingent contracts; and this makes sense only if matched by a rejection of contingent contracts by potential suppliers. For if, when purchasers wish to take advantage of their liquidity, suppliers are already fully committed to other customers, the availability of ready cash is not enough to ensure access to those suppliers, and to the competences which they control. If the absence of contingent contracts causes suppliers to neglect their own skills, matters are even worse. Liquidity requires continuing markets, and continuing participation on both sides of these markets. But these markets are not adequately represented by the bloodless fictions of demand and supply functions. They are structures – sometimes physical structures, always structures of relationships and routines – which facilitate access to distinctive skills, and allow those who possess such skills to make effective use of them.

MARKETS

Let us examine markets from this perspective. A society that is governed by routines can work very well without markets; but when people wish to modify or replace routines then markets may provide a very convenient form of organization in which to coordinate their evolving individual plans into a coherent pattern. It is surely no coincidence that the rise of medieval markets coincided with a general tendency to move from status to contract as a coordinating principle; and it is certainly not accidental that Walras turned to markets as a device for organizing the process of equilibration. What is worth noting is the kind of market that he used as his model. This was the Paris Bourse: a highly organized market, with clear rules, in which one could be reasonably confident of finding everyone who was interested in trading in the particular commodities of that market – and, indeed, of finding many of the same people on each successive visit. It is hardly the anonymous market of perfect competition; nor did Walras intend it to be.

It is helpful to compare Walras's model with Marshall's (1920: 332–4) example of a market in which temporary equilibrium is established. The corn-market in a country town is also highly organized, the recognized focus for trade in its district, with clear rules, regular participants and a long history. Both Walras and Marshall invoke markets which are effective institutions for the establishment of an equilibrium set of trades upon a particular occasion. Their function may therefore seem obvious. But economists should never think of value without enquiring about cost; and here we should take note of one of the most remarkable, yet unremarked, coincidences in economic theory.

Hayek's (1937) famous article on 'Economics and Knowledge' was followed in *Economica* by another famous article by Coase (1937) on 'The Nature of the Firm'; and the connections between the two have not received the attention that they deserve. A major reason for this is that Coase, in recognizing the need for some explanation of firms within a theoretical structure which attributed coordination entirely to markets, failed to see that the explanation which he gave implicitly called into question the reason for markets. For in order to develop his argument that a firm sometimes offered a more economical way of arranging transactions than was possible through the use of a market, Coase drew attention to the costs of using a market. That itself is enough to demonstrate that there is no place for markets in an Arrow–Debreu equilibrium, in which no one wishes to make any new contracts, and in which these costs therefore have no purpose; but it also raises the question of how markets come into existence. Who bears the cost of organizing markets, and why? Now a much-neglected theme in transaction cost economics is the possibility of reducing the direct cost of individual transactions through investments in transaction technology. (As we shall shortly observe, Casson (1982) is the outstanding exception.) It is not neglected in the study of marketing, nor in Chandler's (1977, 1990) explanation of the rise of large firms; but the analytical implications have not been developed.

Since there are at least two parties to any transaction, investments in transaction technology are likely to reduce the direct cost of transacting for the party who does not invest. If the objective of the investment is to facilitate a continuing stream of transactions, then substantial externalities are unavoidable – indeed they may be implicit in such an objective. A market is a public good; and who can be expected to invest in the provision of a public good? One obvious motivation for such investment is the desire to levy tolls or taxes; and that gives some clues about the kinds of commodities for which markets may be highly organized.

However, markets do not usually begin by being highly organized; and many remain rather poorly organized, because no one can see sufficient prospect of recovering the investment that is necessary to create a highly organized structure. But every market requires investment by someone; and where no one sees a prospect of recovering that investment by charging market participants (as happens, for example, in the great Exchanges, and also in the major auction markets created by Sothebys and Christies, as well as in the classified advertisement columns of newspapers) then the investment must be made by some of the participants themselves, in the hope of recovering it through the additional gains from trade which the market will make possible.

Which participants will these be? The obvious requirement is that they must expect to engage in a large volume of transactions, which directs us to manufacturers and retailers, especially those who operate on a large scale, as in Chandler's story. But there is another requirement, that the sum of production and transaction costs must be expected to be less than the revenue received. Thus, something more is needed than the most efficient transaction mode for organizing a given technology. Instead of the usual comparison of market and hierarchy, it is worth returning to Adam Smith's comparison of specialization and self-sufficiency, which is the charter for all subsequent economics. Transaction costs can be avoided altogether if we all produce everything for ourselves. Thus the benefits of specialization must outweigh the costs of coordination by the most effective method, whether this be direction or exchange; but the greater these benefits, the higher the transaction costs it is worth incurring to achieve them. We are occasionally reminded that in explaining industrial structure, it is the total of production and transaction costs that matters; but it is standard practice to assume that production costs are uniform across transaction modes. This is historically false: over the last two hundred years both transaction and governance costs have greatly increased, because changes in the organization of industry which entailed such increases have permitted even greater reductions in production costs, through the effects of the division of labour and the division of knowledge. This is precisely what Chandler has explained to us.

It is a little-noticed feature of Marshall's analysis that such investments in both governance and markets are seen as necessary costs of building any business; firms must create not only an internal but also an external organization. This is no trivial matter; it necessarily takes time (Marshall 1920: 500), because it includes elements of learning by doing and of reputation-building, and it may in certain cases require as much capital as is embodied in fixed plant (Marshall 1919: 270). It is in this context that we must interpret Marshall's (1920: 458) reference to the 'very steep' demand curve faced by a firm which is seeking to build a market for a new product – a reference which is linked to the observation that the required return on investment in developing its external organization is 'a large part' of a firm's supplementary costs. What is at issue, as in all Marshall's discussion of individual firms, is a process of change – even when he is attempting to construct a model of long-term equilibrium for an industry, which requires, not the equilibrium, but the transience of individual firms.

Two other features of Marshall's analysis of external organization should be noted. First, this investment is a major potential source of external economies: parallel investments in market-building by firms within a single industry improve the overall organization of the market and thus offer benefits to all participants. Firms seeking to develop a new market often welcome rivals for this reason. Marshall's principal examples of these benefits are provided in his discussion of industrial districts, where they are most easily observed. This form of industrial organization, which was conspicuous in Britain during most of Marshall's lifetime, is less obvious, though not absent, there today; but its importance in contemporary Italy has attracted increasing attention in recent years, and has been interpreted along Marshallian lines (Becattini 1990).

The other aspect of Marshall's analysis which requires attention is that investment in market development does not simply create capabilities which improve the firm's response to external change. 'Deliberation and forethought' were welcomed by Marshall not only because they might be expected to lead to better use of what was available, but because they would generate a continual stream of improvements. Not the least of Marshall's reasons for approving an industrial structure of many firms was his belief in the scope that this division of knowledge afforded for many people to introduce their own ideas for better products and better methods; indeed, the ability to do this was included in his specification of the abilities required of the ordinary manufacturer (Marshall 1920: 297). To do this effectively requires an appropriate basis of knowledge and a system for trying out ideas; and these too are provided by the firm's external organization. Markets are one of the forms of organization which aid knowledge: not only the knowledge required to negotiate an efficient set of contracts, but the knowledge required to improve the choice set on which contracts can be based. With this extension, it becomes possible to compare market forms not only in respect of the relative costs of transacting, but also in respect of their relative capacity to generate value through improvements.

To conclude this section on market organization, it may be helpful to mention two other economists who have recognized the importance of developing markets. The first is Edward Chamberlin (1933). His *Theory of Monopolistic Competition* is based on the assumption of diverse preferences, which entail product diversity in an effectively coordinated economy. Though his analysis is formally presented in terms of equilibrium, it has been persuasively argued that the underlying problem in such an economy is that of developing diverse products and finding the customers for whom they are appropriate: Chamberlin's theory is therefore to be interpreted as a theory in which producers have to organize their own markets, and bear the costs of doing so (Robinson 1971: 33–4). On this interpretation, the explicit introduction of selling costs, though an important analytical innovation, is not at all conceptually clear; for, as Marshall (1919: 181) had observed, 'Production and marketing are parts of the single process of adjustment of supply to demand', and the allocation of costs between these activities must be in part arbitrary. The obvious difference between Marshall and Chamberlin is that the falling demand curve for the individual firm, which had been introduced by Marshall to indicate that markets take time to develop, is transformed by Chamberlin into a feature of equilibrium. As Andrews (1964) pointed out, this transformation rests on a confusion between the long-run demand for the differentiated commodity and the long-run demand facing the present producer of that commodity in the presence of other potential producers; if these other producers have access to similar skills, Chamberlin's assumptions imply what we would now call a contestable market. The need for investment by new entrants gives the incumbent some protection, but in the form of time rather than any permanent advantage. That was Marshall's view: it was later developed by Richardson (1960).

The other economist who should be mentioned is Mark Casson (1982). Casson begins by developing a formal model of entrepreneurship, derived from Kirzner (1973), as arbitrage in markets where transactions are costless, which is the traditional neoclassical assumption; he then discards this assumption and discusses the obstacles to trade. If the entrepreneur is simply profiting from disparities between the prices of a uniform commodity in different places or at different dates, then it may be possible to free-ride, or nearly so, on the institutions which have already been created to facilitate trade; but if the entrepreneur is seeking to profit from a new idea, then, as Casson points out, there may be substantial obstacles to be overcome, and it will be up to the entrepreneur to overcome them. Casson's (1982: 164) list of market-making activities comprises contact-making, specification of the proposed trade, negotiation, transport and administration, monitoring and enforcement. From his examination of what is required, Casson (1982: 179) concludes that 'the set-up costs of a market organization is likely to be quite high compared with its recurrent costs'; therefore new markets will normally be organized by firms who see a good prospect of recovering these set-up costs over a reasonable time-scale. As we have seen, this emphasis on the capital element in transaction costs, which Casson shares with Marshall, is surprisingly rare in transaction cost analysis. That is perhaps a consequence of accepting the proposition that 'in the beginning there were markets', with its apparent corollaries that only the current costs of these markets are relevant, and that the markets themselves are already well defined. But if market structures are created by investment, we should also recognize that the decision to invest must be based on a conjecture about the appropriate definition of this particular market and that, like all conjectures, any such definition may be falsified. Inappropriate market definition is indeed a common reason for the failure of innovations.

ORGANIZATIONAL COMPETENCES

We have seen that markets require investment, and in most cases investment in developing relationships which not only reduce the cost of making individual contracts but also encourage the growth of knowledge. Though we should not understate the value of prices in assisting the organization of economic activity, we should recognize that prices alone are rarely sufficient statistics. In the first place, the information conveyed by equilibrium prices is much more useful than that conveyed by prices which are not in equilibrium, and which therefore do not provide a secure basis for future commitments; and the price itself does not reveal the category to which it belongs. In conventional theory everyone is supposed to know, but we are not told how they can find out. Second, as Richardson (1960) pointed out, the optimal response to a price signal depends on the responses of others, even in what is called a perfectly competitive market. Future prices depend on present decisions by many people, based on their current expectations; how convenient, then, is the assumption that these expectations are rational. But though rational expectations may be a condition of equilibrium, they are not sufficient to explain how equilibrium is achieved.

Third, how best to respond to a price signal typically requires an understanding of more than the commodity to which that price refers; it usually requires a good deal of knowledge of other commodities with which it might be combined, either as inputs into production or in use by customers, and of the technology of such combinations. There is an implicit assumption in much market theory that the economy is completely decomposable – that the knowledge which is needed to make the best use of one commodity, if not already possessed by the decision-maker, is effectively packaged in the goods or services which are bought in order to make that best use. The decision-maker has detailed specialist knowledge; everything outside that range can be handled as a set of black boxes, the performance characteristics of which are public knowledge. Now there are many goods which are designed to be used as black boxes – especially, but not only, consumer products; but there are many which are not.

Access to some of this complementary knowledge is gained through a firm's external organization, in which voice is generally preferred to exit; but where there is substantial tacit knowledge, or close complementarity between knowledge clusters, then the most effective way of organizing such knowledge may lie within the firm itself. The choice may be explained by transaction costs, if one chooses – the costs need not include opportunism, bounded rationality will suffice – but it may be more informative to focus on the additional value that can be created within an administrative framework which facilitates interaction, and thereby creates opportunities. The possible benefits of such internalization, and some of the conditions of success, can be illustrated from the history of Du Pont (Hounshell and Smith 1988).

Du Pont's explosives business was politically sensitive, and a desire to hedge the risks led to the company's first diversifications into artificial leather and celluloid. The outbreak of war in Europe in 1914 quickly raised profits to twice the prewar level of sales; it also magnified the political risk, for while Americans were being denied access to German dyes, Du Pont was multiplying its profits by making explosives from a chemical intermediate which was also a major input into dyestuffs manufacture. So Du Pont became a dye-maker in order to protect its core business (Hounshell and Smith 1988: 78–81). It quickly discovered that its knowledge base was inadequate, and lost money on a large scale until 1923; even then profitability depended on the recruitment of German dye chemists and tariff protection.

Taken over its life-cycle to its abandonment in 1980, it is not at all clear that dyestuffs, as a business, justified the resources that Du Pont devoted to it; but it created two centres of knowledge which were at least close to being indispensable for the company's outstanding success in synthetic fibres. The first was knowledge about the formulation and application of dyes: nylon and some later fibres would not take up the dyes which were available at the time that they were discovered, and must have been restricted to minor markets if that problem had not been solved; and without good reasons for believing that the company was competent to solve it, development would not have started. The second contribution of the dyestuffs business was that it brought Du Pont for the first time into a market populated by many customers with varying needs; this required not only a new kind of marketing organization with a new focus, but also a new relationship between marketing and production; in Marshall's terminology, it required new forms of internal and external organization. People in Du Pont understood these things by the time that nylon was being developed.

The story of nylon exemplifies the value of deliberately organizing the growth of knowledge. Nylon was not the result of targeted research, as that is usually understood; it was a planned accident. The Research Director, Charles Stine, who conceived the plan, stated beforehand:

> I do not believe that it would be possible for a central Chemical Department to produce the desired results if the department were . . . set off to one side and, in a manner of speaking, directed to 'invent some good, big, profitable things'. The intimate touch with the various industrial lines of the Company is, to my mind, absolutely indispensable.
>
> (Hounshell and Smith 1988: 135)

Stine had taken care to develop that intimate touch, and based his plan upon it. By the mid-1920s Du Pont's strength lay in the development of businesses that it had acquired, through the continuous application and improvement of technical and marketing skills. What Stine recognized was, first, that there were a few core technologies which underlay this range of businesses, and, second, that the fundamental principles of these technologies were not well understood, neither by Du Pont, nor by anyone else. So the process of improvement depended on craft skills of an advanced kind.

A better understanding of underlying principles, Stine argued, was almost certain to improve Du Pont's competence in product and process development somewhere within its current range of activities; and since future circumstances were not predictable, the development of such competence was the best available research strategy (Hounshell and Smith 1988: 233). There were other reasonably certain benefits, in scientific prestige, morale, recruitment and information exchange; and there was the possibility that something substantially new would emerge. If it did, then Stine's programme would go as near as possible to ensuring that what emerged would be precisely the kind of new idea that Du Pont would be best placed to develop. Nylon was just that; and so too was neoprene, also an outcome of this research programme, and the second most profitable product in Du Pont's history.

The importance of organizing knowledge appropriately can be demonstrated by comparing this triumphant episode with Du Pont's disastrous search for 'new nylons' after 1945, when the corporate research department was encouraged – in Du Pont's devolved system, none of the 'barons' could be directed, even by the company's President – to do precisely what Stine had warned against: to invent one or more major new products which could gradually replace nylon as the main profit generator, and to do so outside the range of the company's current business.

In fostering this strategy, it appears that the President at that time, Howard Greenewalt, the first chemical engineer to occupy the position, was much more influenced by his own wartime experience than by the history of the original nylon, if indeed he understood that history. The US Government had given Du Pont the task of designing, constructing and operating the Hanford plutonium plant as part of the atomic bomb programme, and Greenewalt, who had been put in charge, had demonstrated that his team understood the problems of developing the plutonium process much better than the physicists who had invented it: indeed, if the physicists' advice has been followed, the plant would not have worked (Hounshell and Smith 1988: 338–41).

It is perhaps not surprising, therefore, that Greenewalt should come to believe that Du Pont's skills in product and process development now gave it access to very extensive economies of scope. Whether the relevant skills existed within the company is not clear; what did become clear was that its management system could not mobilize them. Organizational design is based on a conjecture, as Egidi (1992) has pointed out, and the conjecture which had served Du Pont so well for twenty-five years was not appropriate to Greenewalt's strategy. Stine's appraisal was corroborated. In pursuit of its search for major diversification, corporate research became increasingly detached from the operating divisions, which had quite enough to do in serving and expanding their established markets with the help of their own research staff. The chief result of this costly effort was a significant enhancement of Du Pont's reputation for basic science (Hounshell and Smith 1988: 376); and that is not surprising, because corporate researchers need a reference point, and if they were turning away from the operating divisions, academic science was the most natural alternative.

Penrose (1995: 149) defined a firm as 'a pool of resources the utilization of which is organized in an administrative framework'; and the history of Du Pont demonstrates the importance of both halves of that definition. Organization shapes and constrains both the development and the use of knowledge. But before we conclude that the failure of Du Pont's search for 'new nylons' was the result of an inappropriate administrative framework, which was capable of being remedied, we should remember why a framework is necessary. It is required to promote compatibility within a group, or a set of interlocking groups, by encouraging or imposing connecting principles which will guide, not merely choices, but the concepts to be used in framing problems. Its purpose is to integrate a cluster of activities, and, since human rationality is bounded, it does so by differentiating this cluster from others. The division of knowledge is necessary for the growth of knowledge. Limits to rationality imply limits to the competence of any formal organization; the skills that Greenewalt assumed to be available were probably incompatible with the formidable range of competence which Du Pont actually possessed. Within any administrative framework it is likely to be difficult to cope with activities which are not similar, as similarity is defined by that framework.

INTERORGANIZATIONAL COMPETENCE

Now among the relatively neglected issues in the economic analysis of industrial organization are those that arise when activities which are dissimilar are nevertheless closely complementary: they rest on different knowledge bases, which are best kept distinct, and yet they need to be carefully fitted together in order to produce the required results. The coordination of these activities cannot be achieved by price-mediated arm's-length exchanges, for what is at issue is the precise definition of the goods or services which are to be provided. Yet integration, which is the standard conclusion from transaction cost theory when there are major obstacles to efficient market transactions, threatens to impede the efficiency with which each activity is managed; indeed, this has now become a fashionable criticism of previously fashionable strategies of diversified corporate growth. The preferred solution in many instances, as was pointed out by Richardson (1972) in the first substantial treatment of this issue in modern economics, is the management of coordination across organizational boundaries. Since that article was written, there has been greater appreciation, at least among businessmen, of the value of suppliers and customers as sources of knowledge which may be more effectively used through personal contact and even through joint activity than by attempting to incorporate them within a single administrative framework. When knowledge bases are incompatible, access, if effectively organized, is better than control.

From the perspective of the present chapter, in which markets are seen as institutions which assist change by aiding the organization of knowledge, there is no difference of principle between investing in an external organization in order to acquire knowledge and to build reputation, which Marshall so clearly recognized but failed to impress on his successors, and investing in specific relationships in order to create knowledge through the combination of closely complementary but dissimilar connecting principles. Any external organization is a network of specific relationships, or, in the language of Austrian economics, a structure of complementary capitals. Much of the knowledge needed by any firm, or by any individual, in order to plan effectively, lies outside that firm or individual.

The creation of markets helps to make some of that necessary knowledge accessible through the use of products or services in which it is embodied, and also by identifying the potential partners who are capable of providing them.

'The function of competition', as Hayek (1946: 97) observed, 'is here precisely to teach us *who* will serve us well: which grocer or travel agency, which department store or hotel, which doctor or solicitor, we can expect to provide the most satisfactory solution for whatever particular personal problem we may have to face.' Hayek's formulation correctly identifies the customer's problem as that of identifying distinctive competence, and the role of markets as that of providing options for future contracts, rather than contracts for future options – a perspective that can be found in Menger (1871). It is, however, unfortunate that Hayek's illustrations all relate to final consumption; for the organization of production gives rise to problems which are similar, but of much greater scale and complexity. Indeed, it is surprising that Austrian economists, who have given commendable emphasis to the importance of complementary capital structures, and to the issues of coordination that they entail, have not paid more attention to the kinds of inter-firm relationships which may arise in the attempts to achieve effective coordination. Competition often provides a similar function here; but sometimes it does not supply the knowledge which is necessary for planning, and then the appropriate setting for planning requires the participants to disregard conventional organizational boundaries.

THE EVOLUTION OF ORGANIZATION

Since economic problems arise only because of change, we might reasonably expect that the organizational arrangements most suitable for any section of the economy will vary from time to time. What knowledge is relevant depends on the situation, and different kinds of knowledge are to be found in different locations, and need to be accessed in different ways. But we should remember that forms of organization not only provide frameworks within which knowledge is mobilized; they also provide the structures within which knowledge develops. Therefore the forms of organization that are best fitted for one environment at one point in time may generate knowledge which is less appropriate to a changed environment. Transaction costs and the need for frameworks both entail path-dependency, and the division of knowledge ensures that the creation of capabilities exacts an opportunity cost.

Such indeed appears to be a major cause of the recent troubles of IBM. IBM, it should be remembered, was not among the early favourites for the title of leading computer company; it achieved that position because it had the best-organized knowledge of those business practices to which the new technology could be applied, and succeeded in combining this knowledge with the best understanding of how these applications should be made. This combination, rather than the hardware, was what its customers were willing to pay for, although it was the hardware for which they were billed. But now not only are there many organizations which are proficient in the technology, especially with smaller machines; many of the large customers have developed their own skills in applying the technology, and have relatively little need of IBM's expertise.

They are therefore naturally unwilling to pay for it in the price of IBM equipment; and what they do need can be obtained elsewhere. Knowledge has changed, and been diffused; different forms of organization are therefore appropriate. IBM has now begun to disentangle the marketing of equipment from the marketing of business expertise.

The theme of changing organizational arrangements as the kind and location of knowledge changes has been explored by Langlois (1992a, b). It may be regarded as an extension of Popperian ideas of knowledge, to which Hayek was sympathetic; ways of organizing knowledge, like scientific hypotheses, are fallible conjectures, which no amount of apparently confirmatory evidence can prove to be correct. Therefore, just as particular organizational forms, such as individual firms and markets, may be justified as ways of preserving particular sets of options, so may a variety of forms be justified as a way of preserving the option within an economy of moving to a different form as conditions change, without having to make the necessary investment from scratch. At both levels, the attempt to secure maximum efficiency at a point in time – which must be on the basis of an imposed specification – is likely to impede efficiency over time (Schumpeter 1943: 83).

Maximum efficiency at a point of time requires the full commitment of resources to provide for the contingencies that are currently envisaged – as is best exemplified by an Arrow–Debreu equilibrium; holding back reserves against the possibility that contingencies not envisaged may occur is wasteful in terms of that specification, which assumes that they cannot occur. But, as Menger (1871) realized, reserves are an appropriate response to uncertainty: they offer the hope of countering a threat or seizing an opportunity. Among such reserves, the categories which should be of most interest to economists are money, firms and markets. Money has been omitted from this discussion, though, as many firms have discovered, there are times when it is the most important resource of all. It has been omitted because money is not enough; organized networks of skills are required for a successful economy, and they are the product of continued investment. Were this proposition not being so convincingly demonstrated in the former European planned economies, it might be clearly observed in Britain. If these networks of skills are to provide a satisfactory range of options, this investment should come from a variety of sources, and reflect a variety of opinions about the range of future threats and prospects. This conclusion is a restatement of one of Hayek's objections to central planning, which may be extended to notions of 'national champions', and any versions of belief in 'the one best way', whether propounded by politicians, management consultants or economists.

REFERENCES

Andrews, P. W. A. (1964) *On Competition in Economic Theory*, London: Macmillan.
Ansoff, H. I. (1965) *Corporate Strategy*, New York: McGraw-Hill.

Becattini, G. (1990) 'The Marshallian Industrial District as a Socio-Economic Notion', in F. Pyke, W. Sengenberger and G. Becattini, *Industrial Districts and Inter-Firm Co-operation*, Geneva: ILO.

Casson, M. (1982) *The Entrepreneur: An Economic Theory*, Oxford: Martin Robertson.

Chamberlin, E. H. (1933) *The Theory of Monopolistic Competition*, Cambridge, Mass.: Harvard University Press.

Chandler, A. D. (1977) *The Visible Hand*, Cambridge, Mass.: Harvard University Press.

Chandler, A. D. (1990) *Scale and Scope*, Cambridge, Mass.: Harvard University Press.

Coase, R. H. (1937) 'The Nature of the Firm', *Economica* 4: 386–405.

Egidi, M. (1992) 'Organizational Learning, Problem Solving and the Division of Labor', in H. Simon, with M. Egidi, R. Marris and R. Viale, *Economics, Bounded Rationality and the Cognitive Revolution*, Aldershot: Edward Elgar.

Hayek, F. A. von (1937) 'Economics and Knowledge', *Economica* 4: 33–54.

Hayek, F. A. von (1945) 'The Use of Knowledge in Society', *American Economic Review* 35: 519–30.

Hayek, F. A. von (1946) 'The Meaning of Competition', Stafford Little lecture, Princeton University; reprinted in F. A. Hayek (1948) *Individualism and Economic Order*, Chicago: University of Chicago Press, pp. 92–106.

Hounshell, D. A. and Smith, J. K. Jr (1988) *Science and Corporate Strategy*, Cambridge: Cambridge University Press.

Kirzner, I. M. (1973) *Competition and Entrepreneurship*, Chicago: University of Chicago Press.

Langlois, R. N. (1992a) 'Transaction Cost Economics in Real Time', *Industrial and Corporate Change* 1 (1): 99–127.

Langlois, R. N. (1992b) 'External Economies and Economic Progress: The Case of the Microcomputer Industry', *Business History Review* 66: 1–50.

Loasby, B. J. (1991) *Equilibrium and Evolution*, Manchester: Manchester University Press.

Marshall, A. (1919) *Industry and Trade*, London: Macmillan.

Marshall, A. (1920) *Principles of Economics*, 8th edn, London: Macmillan.

Menger, C. (1871) *Principles of Economics*, translated by Dingwall, J. and Hoselitz, B. F., Glencoe, Ill.: Free Press, 1950.

Penrose, E. T. (1995) *The Theory of the Growth of the Firm* (originally published 1959), Oxford: Oxford University Press.

Richardson, G. B. (1960, 1990) *Information and Investment*, 1st and 2nd edns, Oxford: Oxford University Press.

Richardson, G. B. (1972) 'The Organization of Industry', *Economic Journal* 82: 883–96; reprinted in Richardson (1990), pp. 224–42.

Robinson, R. (1971) *Edward H Chamberlin*, New York and London: Columbia University Press.

Schumpeter, J. A. (1934) *The Theory of Economic Development*, Cambridge, Mass.: Harvard University Press.

Schumpeter, J. A. (1943) *Capitalism, Socialism, and Democracy*, London: Allen and Unwin.

4

COMPETITIVE ADVANTAGE AND THE CONCEPT OF CORE COMPETENCE

Bo Eriksen and Jesper Mikkelsen

INTRODUCTION

The concepts of competences, capabilities and resources have received much attention lately in strategic management theory. It has become important to compete on capabilities (Stalk, Evans and Schulman 1992a) and leverage the firm's core competence (Prahalad and Hamel 1990) as opposed to the emphasis on positioning within an industry during the early and mid-1980s. Some writers are even announcing the arrival of a new paradigm: the so-called 'resource-based perspective' within strategic management (e.g. Peteraf 1993; Teece, Pisano and Shuen 1990). While there is good reason to caution against uncritically adopting concepts such as resource base, core competences, competing on capabilities, and the other slogans that academics and consultants use to promote their ideas, we argue that the general idea holds some promise for research as well as the practice of strategic management. However, it is our contention that much of the reasoning behind the 'new' competence literature does not rest on a particularly coherent theoretical ground. The concept of core competences should be regarded as *a concept in need of clarification*. We argue that anchoring core competence in economic theory may indeed provide this clarification.

Thus, it is the main purpose of this chapter to provide a clarification of the concept of core competence. On the basis of these clarifying discussions it should be possible to contribute to new insights into the phenomenon of sustained competitive advantage. One aim is to circumvent the charge of circularity raised by, among others, Porter (1991: 108). We wish to address two issues in this chapter. First, does the concept of core competence make theoretical sense, and second, what should managers look for when they attempt to identify and develop core competences? We start by tracing the antecedents of the concept of core competence, giving the background for its present state of development. That review will set the stage for our attempt to define more precisely the concept of core competence. Subsequently we shall discuss the concept of core competence in lieu of sustained competitive advantage and attempt to provide some guidelines for operationalizing the concept.

TRACING THE CONCEPT OF COMPETENCE

The concept of competence, or distinctive competence to be more precise, has its origin in Philip Selznick's (1957) sociological analysis of leadership in administration. By this concept Selznick referred to what an organization does especially well in comparison to other organizations. Although Selznick's insights on strategic management were advanced at that time, it was not until other authors, such as Ansoff (1965) and Andrews (1971), popularized the concept that distinctive competence came to have an impact on conventional writing and business practice.

In spite of the apparent success of the design (Andrews and others) and planning (Ansoff) schools in strategic management, analytical rigour and theoretical consistency did not characterize the strategy field until the early 1980s (Mintzberg 1990). In the early 1980s a more analytical approach to strategy became popular, spurred by Porter's (1980) industrial organization (IO) approach to strategy.

Porter's approach has accepted most of the premises underlying the traditional business policy approach which focused almost exclusively on strategy formation. With Porter's competitive forces model, built on the SCP (structure–conduct–performance) paradigm, as the underlying theoretical foundation, research in the strategic management field turned its main research efforts towards analysis of market structures as determinants of inter- as well as intra-industrial performance differences. This effort has led to the definition of generic strategies which firms are prescribed to follow depending on their position in the industry.

In spite of its analytical appeal and theoretical rigour, the competitive strategy approach has been the target of much criticism from economists, other strategy researchers and, perhaps especially, organization theorists. In this chapter we will mainly focus on the critique originating from a recent revival of a resource-based approach to strategic management. Within this approach, the concept of distinctive competence is of central importance.

Revival of a competence approach to strategy

Three, more or less interrelated, developments within both economics and strategy research may be seen as antecedents to the present status of the concept of competence.

First, there has been an increasing dissatisfaction with the industry analysis approach to strategy as embodied in Porter (1980). The disagreement may be traced back to early methodological debates in the field of industrial organization economics, particularly Chicago School IO (Demsetz) vs Harvard University SCP (Bain–Mason).

Second, a somewhat related debate has been going on concerning the theory of the firm. Dissatisfaction with the neoclassical perception of the firm as a production function has led to alternative approaches. One early alternative approach was Penrose's (1959) theory of firm growth. Penrose departed from the neoclassical paradigm in important ways. One departure was to conceive of the firm as a collection of heterogeneous resources that each have several potential services to render. The range of services available from existing resources is determined by the present knowledge of the firm. A second departure was the change in theoretical emphasis from a comparative-static to a change-oriented, or dynamic explanation. This was echoed by Nelson and Winter (1982) in their evolutionary theory of economic change. Based on evolutionary insights, Winter (1987, 1988) argued that differences in the competences with which firms are endowed are important in understanding the competitive differences between firms.

Third, empirical evidence from the early 1980s raised doubt about the value of the positioning school. In particular, Rumelt's (1974, 1982) analyses revealed that 'the dispersion of long-term profit rates within industries is very much larger than the dispersion of industry profit rates across industries' (Rumelt 1987: 141). In fact the intra-industry variance was three to five times larger than the inter-industry variance, and Rumelt (1987: 141) concludes: 'Clearly, the important sources of excess (or subnormal) profitability . . . were firm specific rather than the results of industry membership.' Although attempts have been made to develop and refine concepts such as mobility barriers and strategic groups in order to account for these findings, such developments are essentially ad hoc extensions of the theory.

Given this background it does not seem surprising that a stream of research, which turned the focus back to the firm, emerged successfully in the mid-1980s. After almost a decade of refining industry analysis models there seemed to be a very strong appeal to the idea that we have to look inside the firm in order to find the unique sources of competitive advantage. Following these tendencies there has been increasing interest in explaining systematic intra-industry performance differentials in the industrial organization literature and the strategy content literature (e.g. Schmalensee 1985, Wernerfelt and Montgomery 1988, Rumelt 1991). Several theoretical contributions have been made with the purpose of explaining competitive advantage or sustained competitive advantage with reference to unique and hard-to-imitate resources, competences and/or capabilities (e.g. Aaker 1989; Barney 1986a, b, 1991; Gabel 1984; Castanias and Helfat 1991; Hall 1992; Hitt and Ireland 1985; Prahalad and Hamel 1990; Stalk, Evans and Schulman 1992a; Wernerfelt 1989). Even in the so-called 'new IO economics', there has been a nascent interest in developing models that explain intra-industry heterogeneity (e.g. Dana 1991, Maksimovic and Zechner 1991, Hermalin 1994).

The resource-based view of the firm

The resource-based view of the firm views the firm as a bundle of resources, the services of which may have multiple uses (Penrose 1959). Resources may for analytical purposes be divided into three categories:[1] tangible resources, such as plant and capital; intangible resources, such as patents and trade marks; and knowledge about products and processes, which may be embedded in individuals or physical media of communication, such as paper and digital or analog storage.

At any point in time the firm will have a stock of resources which is the result of previous decisions on resource allocation, where the available resources have been assigned to a particular service. Major irreversible 'choices' about the time path of resource accumulation are usually made infrequently. Whenever such choices are made, the subsequent scope of the firm's *strategy space* is limited. Such choices function as meta-level decisions which lock the firm into a particular path from which deviation may become increasingly difficult to accomplish, should such change of direction become necessary (path-dependence). There are partly economic reasons (sunk costs, switching costs) and partly cognitive reasons (learning, attachment, etc.) for such inertia. Further, heterogeneity may result from indivisibilities of resources (Penrose 1959). For example, a firm can only choose between integer numbers of managers they wish to hire (see Hermalin 1994). Many choices are thus constrained by such non-convexities.

Although the process of resource development may tend to make the firm inflexible, the resource perspective views the uniqueness that this process may produce as a potential source of sustained competitive advantage and thus superior levels of return. The concept of rent has received much attention in the literature on the resource perspective. The reason for this is that it is substantially different from the profit concept used in the traditional IO approach, and that this has implications for the conception of strategy. Basically, the concept of rent implies resource scarcity and productivity differentials.[2] This conception of rent is different from the SCP notion of monopoly profit.[3] The main difference for our purposes lies in the strategy implications that may be derived from the underlying perspectives. The SCP theory assumes homogeneous technology within industries and therefore leads one to the only logical conclusion that collusion or effective positioning will lead to higher profits and that these positions may be protected by entry barriers. The resource perspective makes the assumption that resources are heterogeneous and immobile which leads to the conclusion that efficient resource allocation, development and protection (isolation) is the road to superior performance. In the words of Teece, Pisano and Shuen (1990: 13):

> The resource-based approach sees firms with superior capabilities and/or organizational structures being profitable not because they raise prices above long-run costs, but because they have markedly lower costs, or offer markedly higher quality or product performance.

THE CONCEPT OF COMPETENCE

In the preceding section we presented a basic version of the resource perspective. In that section we purposely refrained from using the concept of competence in order not to confuse the discussion of that concept. The purpose of the present section is to clarify what we think should be understood by competence and in particular to make a distinction between resources and competence.

Towards a definition of competence

Within strategic management the most popular definition of core competence seems to be the one proposed by Prahalad and Hamel (1990: 82) who define core competences as 'the collective learning in the organization, especially how to co-ordinate diverse production skills and integrate multiple streams of technologies'.

In spite of the very general definition, where emphasis is put on coordination, the examples provided by Prahalad and Hamel delineate competences in terms of the underlying production skills and technological know-how. As Stalk, Evans and Schulman (1992b: 170) state it: 'Hamel and Prahalad's examples, whatever their *ex post facto* definitions, focus on competences as pools of functionally specific technical skills (such as engine building) around which the corporation needs to identify and shape itself.'

In that sense there seems to be no difference between resources and competences; competences are just pools of resources capable of performing a specific function. For example, Hamel and Prahalad (1990) mention compact data storage and retrieval, as in the case of Philips's optical-media competence, or compactness and ease of use, as with Sony's micromotors and microprocessor controls. In the Honda case, also discussed by Prahalad and Hamel the engine-building competence that Honda had developed through its excellence in motorcycle production was seen as a 'stepping stone' for becoming one of the leading car manufacturers in the world.

If we settle for this quite general understanding of capabilities as resources we will have difficulties with understanding processes of competence development and the relationship between competences and sustained competitive advantage. But apart from the obvious, that the development of competences depends on prior deployment of resources, what characterizes competences? Briefly stated, we view competences as more than just a function of prior resource deployment. We argue that competences are closely related to organization structure, and that organization capital and social capital are useful in linking organization structure to competences. In the following we are going to take a closer look at the link between resources and competences in order to gain a deeper understanding of these concepts. We will do so by introducing two concepts which derive from economics and sociology respectively. The first is *organizational capital* and the second is *social capital*.

Organizational capital

According to Prescott and Visscher (1980: 447) information (or knowledge) is the basic source of organizational capital: 'Information is an asset to the firm, for it affects the production possibility set and is produced jointly with output. We call this asset of the firm its organization capital.' Essentially, organizational capital is viewed as an asset that allows improved coordination of the activities the organization undertakes. To be valuable, organizational capital must be asymmetrically distributed across firms, the efficient firms having larger endowments of organizational capital.

Prescott and Visscher (1980: 448–59) identify four types of organizational capital:

1 Information about employees (person–task matching), i.e. knowledge about the abilities of individuals and how they relate to the tasks that must be undertaken.
2 Information about teams of workers (personality matching), i.e. how to put together optimal work teams.
3 Human capital of employees (skills), i.e. knowledge about which skills are available in the organization, and which should be made available by investment or acquisition.
4 Task information (average productivity norm), i.e. information about the desired productivity of the tasks that are to be undertaken.

This information is valuable in the context of monitoring employees and providing them with proper work incentives, since it reduces the amount of private information that employees possess.

The concept of organizational capital embodies what the firm 'knows' about how to coordinate productive activities. Strictly speaking, *the firm* does not know anything, the information resides in some type of memory media. Nelson and Winter (1982) have suggested that this memory media consists of the firm's *routines*. The routines themselves, however, reside in some communication media in which they are stored and from which they may be retrieved whenever needed. As we suggested in the section on 'The resource-based view of the firm' (p. 57), the media may be the human brain or other physical media such as paper or digital or analog storage. In addition to these types of media it is possible to think of the organizational structure and the physical sequencing of the production process as a carrier of organizational capital. Organizational capital has a tacit dimension, and, although people leave the firm, most of the organizational capital may be left intact.

Although the tacit dimension of organizational capital may be problematic since it may refuse codification and thus the replication which may be necessary for purposes of growth, this may also be a strength because it isolates it from involuntary transfer to competitors. We will have more to say on that point later on.

The organizational capital concept provides a clue to a more sophisticated definition of the concept of competence, pointing to the types of knowledge necessary to allocate the resources of the firm in a manner which enables the firm to do things in a comparatively better (more efficient) way. The strength of the concept is in highlighting the importance of *efficient coordination* of activities. Also, the informational properties of organization capital are important for providing efficient incentives for employees. When the managers of the firm know more about individuals and teams and their abilities, there is less private information. This means that employees can extract less informational rent, and that salaries may get closer to full-information equilibrium salaries. A weakness of the concept of organizational capital is that it does not address motivation or values, which may be important factors in promoting efficiency. A further weakness of the concept is that it ignores the importance of social context, that is, the notion that the whole may be larger than the sum of its parts. This dimension is, however, captured in the notion of social capital (Coleman 1988).[4]

Social capital

Even casual empirical evidence attests to the fact that the social context, within which transactions are carried out, is important in shaping the decisions and actions that are carried out.[5] To Coleman (1988: 98), 'social capital is defined by its function. It is not a single entity but a variety of different entities, with two things in common: they all consist of some aspect of social structures, and they facilitate certain actions of actors – whether persons or corporate actors – within the structure.' Further, Coleman (1988: 101) asserts: 'The function identified by the concept of "social capital" is the value of these aspects of social structure to actors as resources that they can use to achieve their interests.' According to Coleman (1988: 100) social capital, 'comes about through changes in the relations among persons that facilitate action'. Although Coleman's (1988: 98) primary concern is with social capital as a resource for individuals, he underlines that even, 'relations among corporate actors can constitute social capital for them'.

Like other forms of capital, social capital is productive, making possible the achievement of certain ends that in its absence would not be possible. Like human and physical capital, social capital may be specific to certain activities. Unlike other forms of capital, social capital is inherent in the structure of relations between actors. It is not embedded in either the actors themselves or in physical artifacts of production.

Social capital is a relatively ill-defined concept, and some caution is called for in using social capital to define another concept. However, we find that some of the properties of social capital are of relevance in characterizing an organization in general, and competences in particular. Coleman (1988: 102–4) distinguishes between three groups of social capital:

1 obligations, expectations and trustworthiness of structures
2 norms and effective sanctions
3 information channels.

We view the norms and sanctions part of social capital as analogous to a corporate culture. As Barney (1986a) points out, some organization cultures may be efficiency-enhancing, whereas other cultures are not. The information channels part of social capital, in our view, refers to, for example, how individuals within an organization communicate with each other through informal channels, that is, through their social networks within the organization. When this clarification is made social capital in regard to firms emerges as a concept which covers *the willingness of individuals within a given firm, as well as of associated firms, to contribute unselfishly (loyally, non-opportunistically) to the attainment of joint objectives*. In order for the stock of social capital to remain stable, the social structure has to be characterized by closure, have unambiguous norms, and display credible commitments to enforcement. If these structural traits are absent the social-capital norm may be relatively vulnerable to problems of free-riding.

The value of the concept of social capital is that it assigns an economic meaning to the social context in which exchanges occur in the sense that social capital emerges as a result of individuals' cumulated actions. Furthermore, social capital complements the concept of organizational capital, which does not consider context at all. Both concepts will be linked in our ensuing interpretation of core competence. What is important to note is that social capital in some sense is a meta-routine. For example, corporate culture can be thought of as a meta-routine which constrains the actions of individuals in the firm.

Competence defined

To define the concept of competence let us return to the definition given by Prahalad and Hamel (1990: 82). According to this definition core competence is 'the collective learning in the organization, especially how to coordinate diverse production skills and integrate multiple streams of technologies'. Having presented the resource perspective and discussed the organizational capital and social capital concepts it is now possible to add some depth to this definition.

Competence is not just another resource which may be applied to the production of intermediate or end products. The important words in Prahalad and Hamel's definition are *learning, coordinate and integrate*. It is the accumulated organizational and social capital which makes coordination and integration possible. Organizational capital is necessary in order for people to be able to communicate and cooperate efficiently. Social capital will furthermore support the exchange of unselfish, loyal effort and support which may make the difference between being a mediocre and a world-class corporate player.

Core competence, then, is *both* organizational capital and social capital. Organizational capital reflects the 'technical' aspects of coordinating and integrating production, whereas social capital highlights the importance of social context. The former may, for example, be embodied in the organizational structure, whereas the latter, for example, reflects the corporate culture and, as such, emerges from particular structural conditions. Social capital and organizational capital are then to be considered complements. Both aspects of core competence have implications for the efficiency of the firm, since they both, under a limited set of 'states of the world', enhance the efficiency of the organization's operations.

The existence of a set of strong core competences defines the strategy space available to the firm, that is, it produces path-dependence. This is an advantage if the state of the world is one where such competences are valuable. Thus, an important point of core competences is that their value is exogenously determined. The managers' task, then, is to choose in which broad areas of competence development the firm should engage.

Core competences as foundations of competitive advantage

Analysing core competences as if they were similar to any other type of resource may yield some useful insights. We shall consider four aspects that each indicate whether core competences may be a source of sustained competitive advantage (Barney 1991). These aspects may be considered as the general logic of the resource-based view of the firm, tying competitive advantage to sustainability.

Core competences should be valuable

Obviously, core competences should improve the efficiency of the firm, that is, they should be helpful in delivering some combination of value and cost that is superior to that of their competitors. For example, one could attribute the superior growth record of McDonald's (compared to say Burger King) to its core competences (Irvin and Michaels 1989). The value created by McDonald's, such as cleanliness, family orientation, and so on, seems to be greater than what Burger King and other competitors are able to deliver, and can be traced back to the rather strict operating policies to which the franchisees must adhere.

Core competences should be heterogeneous

It is not a sufficient condition that value is created by core competences. The value should also be based on the deployment of different resources than those of the competition. An example is that of Merck, the American pharmaceutical giant. Merck was reportedly the first pharmaceutical company to adopt a more scientific/academic style of R&D, for example by forging closer ties to leading research universities. This distinguished the firm for a period, and has been interpreted as a key factor to its success. The strategy made Merck more innovative and thus able to create more value than its competitors. The manner in which it organized its R&D was clearly different from the traditional R&D laboratory in the pharmaceutical industry.

Core competences should be imperfectly imitable

As the example of Merck illustrates, competitive advantages seldom last for ever. Now practically all the world's pharmaceutical companies have emulated Merck's way of managing R&D, thus reducing the initial advantage that Merck may have had. To prevent imitation two types of isolating mechanism may be counterproductive to imitative efforts. One has to do with the very nature of the resource.[6] Secondly the innovative firm may employ various legal strategies to protect its valuable resources.[7]

Core competences should be difficult to substitute

Finally, even though core competences may be difficult to imitate, for example, because of their idiosyncratic nature, there is always the threat of substitution. Firms, such as Benetton from Italy and The Limited from the USA, have been successful in redefining the way design, manufacturing, distribution and marketing of fashion clothing is carried out. For example, Benetton has succeeded in obtaining variety and quality at low cost by using different principles of organization than was the tradition in the fashion garment industry (Baden-Fuller and Stopford 1992). Combining the two was previously unheard of in the garment industry, much like the (assumed) fundamental conflict between cost leadership and differentiation strategies in Porter (1980).

Core competences and sustainable competitive advantage

Core competences differ from most other types of resource in the mechanisms that sustain possible competitive advantage, as well as in the processes by which they are created. The latter also indicates something about the possible sustainability of competitive advantage that is based on core competences (Dierickx and Cool 1989). In this section we shall discuss some of the properties that are particular to core competences.

Difficulty of perceiving the value of competences

In a world where rational expectations are assumed and prices are fully flexible, the value of an asset will be fully reflected in its price. This is unless an actor has private information concerning the value of an asset. In this case it is possible to obtain above-normal profits for an extended period. Examples of such markets where the prices of assets fully reflect their value are financial markets. Extending this to the realm of competitive advantage, it is unlikely that an individual firm is in a position to enjoy sustained periods of cheap capital, since lenders (or shareholders) are likely to move their business to other borrowers who are willing to pay higher interest rates. However, as asserted earlier, markets for core competences do rarely exist. As a consequence, the information required to evaluate core competences is asymmetrically distributed across individuals, with the individuals employed in the firm, such as the management, being those with access to the best information. Therefore, the insiders of the firm are in a better position to know both which core competences the firm possesses and the value as well as possible applications of these, a point emphasized by Barney (1986b). Thus, the value of core competences is more difficult to evaluate than that of most other resources.

Ambiguity

The firm's core competences are quite complex compared to most of the firm's other resources. Even though it is possible to identify *what* the firm does better than its competitors, it may often be impossible to deduce *why* the firm is better and *how* such activities may be replicated by competitors. This has been referred to as 'causal ambiguity' by Lippman and Rumelt (1982), who also conclude that it may explain why firms may continue to earn above-normal returns.

Interconnectedness

The firm's core competences are complex, that is, they are created by interactions between many different entities/individuals. It is not always possible to replicate these interactions as they are unique to the firm's history, and perhaps to the mental models of the different individuals. Interconnectedness between individuals within a unique social structure should intuitively be more difficult to 'reverse-engineer' than a product. Therefore, valuable core competences are difficult to replicate by competing firms.

History-dependence

Not only are the firm's core competences ambiguous and interconnected, they are also the result of a unique historical process, termed 'administrative heritage' by Bartlett and Ghoshal (1992). The firm's 'administrative heritage' influences its future actions and strategic choices. For example, Collis (1991) proposes that the firm's administrative heritage may induce it to compete in structurally unattractive segments. Thus administrative heritage creates path-dependence.

Cumulative learning

Core competences are accumulated, rather than acquired in a corresponding factor market. What distinguishes core competences is the fact that the accumulation itself requires some learning. For example, a brand name, which is also accumulated, does not require that any substantial learning takes place within the firm, and its creation as well as its exploitation is fairly straightforward.

Irreversible investment

Due to the idiosyncrasy of core competences and their general untradability, the investments required to create core competences are totally irreversible. Such irreversible investments create a commitment to maintaining the firm's core competences, and create an incentive for corporate coherence.[8] Since choices of organizational form are generally made from non-convex sets (e.g. functional versus divisional), there are major switching costs between structures. This tends to reinforce path-dependence.

An important point about these determinants of sustainability is the fact that they are positive complements to each other. Increasing the level of, say, interconnectedness between competences may often increase the effect of cumulative learning on sustainability.

IDENTIFYING COMPETENCES

Recent strategy literature has begun to emphasize the importance of the heuristics managers employ in deciding upon the firm's strategy (e.g. Amit and Schoemaker 1993, 1994). In this approach to strategic management, due to path-dependence created by managers' choices about which resources to accumulate, the important point in strategy becomes to identify: (a) which rent-earning assets the firm should develop, and (b) the value of these assets under every imaginable future state of the world. The latter points to the value of scenario thinking and similar methods to reduce the cognitive biases in managerial decision-making (see e.g. Russo and Schoemaker 1992). It is the former task we shall focus upon in the ensuing: *given* expectations about the future state of the world, which competences are valuable?

Identifying core competences

Generally speaking, the reason we are interested in identifying the firm's core competences is that they are important in understanding the firm's ability to differentiate itself from competitors. The existence of some core competence is what allows the firm to become more efficient than its competitors under a limited subset of the firm's strategy space. In the following we shall discuss some central issues regarding the value of core competences.

Asset specificity

Not all competences are valuable, since some of them are in the public domain, where all firms have more or less equal access to them.[9] Such competences cannot endow the firm with sustainable competitive advantage since their value is likely to be fully reflected in their price. An example is that of skilled labour. If a particular kind of skilled labour is suddenly regarded as being important (i.e. valuable) in an industry, then it is likely that salaries will be bid up to the level where their value is fully reflected in their price. Further, competences may differ in their relative contributions to value creation. Some competences may be very valuable if they contribute much to enhance the firm's efficiency whereas other competences may contribute little to value creation. The first step is then to analyse which types of competence are likely to contribute to the firm's efficiency. The second step is to analyse whether they will endow the firm with sustainable advantage.

What characterizes those competences that are rare or unique is *asset specificity* (see e.g. Williamson 1985: 95–6 for a discussion of asset specificity): that is, assets that are in some way dedicated to a particular purpose, site, customer or organizational context. Further, the investments made in their creation will tend to be highly irreversible. The central feature in the context of strategy formation is that the firm has some degree of discretion over the use and development of such assets. It should be noted that Williamson's category of asset specificity does not include what we here define as core competences. Further, Williamsonian asset specificity is specificity in terms of *users*, whereas core competences are specific in terms of *uses*. Thus core competences do not necessarily limit the number of transaction partners (as in the case of Williamsonian asset specificity). Rather, the core competence limits the number of transaction *types* the firm can undertake.

Core competences may be seen as one of the firm's specific assets. Their specificity may be attributed to their cumulative nature, that is, administrative heritage (e.g. Bartlett and Ghoshal 1992). Core competences are highly dependent on the firm's human resources, as it is partly the firm's employees that are the bearers of its core competences. However, core competences do not reside in any single individual, but are tied to the organizational context, such as through a form of routinization (e.g. Nelson and Winter 1982).

Character of the knowledge embodied in core competence

In their recent writings Kogut and Zander (1992) and Winter (1987) offer some dimensions for evaluating the firm's knowledge. Their main argument, relating to the imitability of knowledge, is that knowledge that can be characterized as 'information' is relatively easy to imitate, and knowledge that can be characterized as 'know-how' is relatively difficult to imitate. The latter may be because it is tacit, unarticulated, unteachable, unobservable in use, complex and systemic (Winter 1987: 170), whereas 'information' has public-good characteristics. Core competences may be regarded as a form of knowledge about how to coordinate the services of the firm's resources. For example, the firm's culture may be interpreted as the firm's tacit knowledge about what it should do, and how it should do it. If the firm's competences may be characterized as having public-good nature, then they are unlikely to endow the firm with sustainable advantage, as they can be easily imitated.

When are core competences valuable?

The firm's core competences are valuable if they enable the firm to perform a set of activities more efficiently than competitors, and if they are difficult to imitate or substitute. A central issue is whether the firm will be able to expand the range of activities over which its core competences are valuable. This is dependent upon two conditions: (a) the productive capacity of the firm's competences, and (b) the flexibility of the firm's competences. The term 'productive capacity' denotes how many of the *same* activities the firm can handle efficiently, and whether it is possible to expand the number of similar activities if demand increases. The term 'flexibility' refers to the number of *different* activities the firm is able to pursue efficiently.

Lazonick (1992) provides an interesting account of the evolution of industrial organizational structures since the first industrial revolution. Before the first industrial revolution, British industry was the most dominant in the world, its competitive advantages relying upon shop-floor organizations with highly skilled craftsmen. However, with the technological advances that were made in production technology, Britain's initial competitive advantages were eroded as they failed to make the necessary organizational changes to take advantage of the new possibilities for mass production (see, e.g. Chandler 1990). In these organizations, characteristic of the United States, professional managerial hierarchies were built up, and operating tasks were standardized along with the introduction of scientific management. This type of organization professionalized the general management and functional management part of the organization, whereas it removed the necessity of skills on the operating level. Later, American industry lost leadership to Japanese industry, as it introduced yet new principles of organization, emphasizing organizational flexibility and skill creation in all levels of the organization.

The initial British way of organization had a limited productive capacity. Expansion was contingent upon the management abilities of the manager–owner, and upon the time it takes to train new skilled workers in apprenticeship positions. The American way of organizing mass production, on the other hand, was easier to replicate, although flexibility was low, due to the need to specialize jobs vertically and horizontally. But the system itself was easy to replicate, the most important constraint on expansion being the availability of professional specialists (managers). The Japanese way of organization seems to have improved the quality of the operating core, as well as retaining basic cost-competitiveness, their organizations typically being more flexible as well as having a high productive capacity.

The historical experiences of industrialization hold some implications for our understanding of core competences. First, different modes of organization differ in their flexibility and productive capacity. Second, different modes of organization have different core competences associated with them. The value of these core competences is dependent upon the state of prevailing expectations about

67

the future state of the world. This last point is important since it adds a certain (healthy) environmental determinism to our understanding of the nature of sustained competitive advantage.

The general point is that if the firm's core competences are flexible, that is, they are able to produce services that may be applied across a wide range of purposes, and they have a high productive capacity, that is, their productive capacity may be expanded as demand for their services increases, then these two dimensions are likely to be positively associated with the value of the firm. On the other hand, if the firm's core competences are rigid and cannot be expanded easily, then its basic strategy space is reduced, and the firm will be more *path-dependent.*[10]

Leveraging competences: efficient organization

Core competences may be created. However, it is not possible, *ex ante*, to determine whether the competences the firm wishes to create are going to endow the firm with sustainable competitive advantages, as this would be a formula for success that would quickly become part of the public domain, and the possible rents would then be competed away (Gabel 1984, Barney 1986b, Dierickx and Cool 1989). We *are* able to say something about how the firm may go about developing particular types of core competence. Organization design is one powerful medium for creating and maintaining core competences.

Prahalad and Hamel (1990) introduce the concept of strategic architecture as a way of integrating the notion of competitive advantage with choices about organization design. However, theirs is not a very explicit framework for designing organizations. Their main argument is that a firm should choose which competences it wishes to base its competitiveness on, and then ensure that these are diffused around the organization so they can be exploited, maintained and developed further. In this section, we will attempt to make more explicit where the central problems are in relating core competences to organization design.

Some types of knowledge can be easily transferred to other individuals or firms, requiring only a minimum level of user competence (Eliasson 1990). The use of language and a minimum level of training may be enough to transfer knowledge characterized as information. Knowledge characterized as know-how, on the other hand, is often difficult to transfer. In this dimension knowledge is tacit, and can only be transferred by long periods of interaction in a group. As we have discussed earlier, this distinction has important implications for long-term competitiveness, because core competences, if they are to be of any long-term economic importance, must be based on know-how rather than on information. Thus, the difficulty of imitating know-how is a vital factor in sustaining competitive advantage derived from the firm's organizational capital. One way of creating competences that are difficult to imitate or substitute is by some sort of routinization. Such routinization may be carried through in both the formal structure and the informal structure. It is likely to be the latter that offers the greater protection against imitative efforts, as the informal structure is more difficult to detect and interpret than the formal structure.

Further, competences may reside in many different parts of the organization, as proposed by Carlsson and Eliasson (1991). They distinguish between selective, organizational and technical/functional competence, as well as learning ability. Combining their notion of competences with Mintzberg's (1983) distinction between the five basic parts of the organization[11] may yield some useful insights. Selective capability should be expected to reside mainly in the strategic apex, as this is the place where major investment and market decisions are made (at least formally). Organizational ability should be expected to reside mainly in the middle line and technostructure with some upward reference to the top management. Technical ability should be expected to be most prominent in the operating core, as this is where the basic operating activities are carried out. And learning ability should be relevant throughout all levels of the organization, and may also be routinized in some manner. Further, following the idea of absorptive capacity, learning is most efficient in a known environment. In other words, diverging from the beaten-path behaviour is essentially inefficient, at least in the short run, whereas some degree of divergent behaviour is effective in the long run, such as when there is technological change (Cohen and Levinthal 1990).

Adopting the notion that there are different classes of competence and that these may reside in different places within the organization allows a more precise conception of the relations between competences and organization design. For example, if the firm's competence lies in its ability to organize production in an efficient manner, then some of the underlying resources for this may be the skill level of the workers and the way the work process is organized, such as by standardization of skills, output or work processes. Further, as this example indicates, some core competences may be contingent on the existence of other resources in the firm. Competences may often span beyond functional/departmental boundaries, and rather than speaking of specific departments as bearers of core competences, the firm as a whole is seen as the bearer of competences.

Developing core competences

Core competences are created by human action. However, unlike most types of resource, there is not necessarily a direct link between action and outcome in the creation of core competences, that is, the link is to some extent stochastic. For example, when it concerns investment in a brand name, tying a plausible link between the amount of effort, capital and creativity and the outcome is possible. This is considerably more difficult when it comes to core competences. In particular, the social capital component of core competence reduces the scope of designability of core competences. This problem is accentuated by the fact that not all members of the organization share the social capital; for example, not all goals are shared.

There may be further problems in developing core competences. First, defining the purpose of organizations; second, the role of organizational evolution in shaping the creation/emergence of core competences is unclear; and, finally, the decision-makers are boundedly rational and tend to use decision-making heuristics.

Intentionality

Typically, organizations are defined as purposeful organizations. Neoclassical economists define the firm's goal as one of profit maximizing, and many organization theorists assume a single utility function to be optimized when designing the organization. However, organizations may be viewed as coalitions of individuals that each derive some benefits and incur some costs from participating in the organization (Cyert and March 1963). One possible consequence of this view is that structures emerge and evolve through an ongoing process of negotiation (Grandori 1991). In this case, different efficient forms can be found, since there may be several points of Pareto optimality. Thus the unilateral visible hand of management may be questioned.

Organizational evolution

Further, questioning the logic of the visible hand, organizations may also be seen as evolving entities whose routines determine their development trajectories (Nelson and Winter 1982). Initially successful routines are retained in the organization and determine what kind of strategic alternatives the firm considers. As a corollary to Chandler's (1962) famous conclusion that organizational structure follows strategy, we may also conclude that strategy follows from organizational structure too. As core competences result from irreversible investments, structures may perhaps be considered partially sunk. Also, adopting the negotiation metaphor of organizations, changing utilities of the different groups and individuals may also influence the structural evolution of the corporation.

Social capital and organizational capital emerge as a result of cumulative learning and the development of norms. Top management learns about 'how to organize certain productive activities' – that is, 'organizational capital development', to use the terms developed earlier in this chapter. Social capital develops as the corporation develops certain norms about behaviour within the organization.

Bounded rationality

Finally, the bounded rationality of managers limits the scope of the visible hand somewhat. If some amount of intentionality is assumed, then it should be with reference to some form of bounded rationality. Bounded rationality may push the view of organizations more in the direction of emergent organization, since

70

the structuring of organizations to some extent may be assumed to be the result of experimental processes (Eliasson 1990). Successful experiments are adopted, and unsuccessful experiments are rejected. The key normative advice for managers to be derived from our previous discussion is that managers should devote time to consider *what they do not know*. Going through such a process may inform managers about the robustness of the firm's competitive advantages over a range of possible future states of the world. Scenario thinking may be a helpful tool in this respect.

CONCLUDING REMARKS: ARE WE GETTING ANY FURTHER?

Studying core competences with respect to both their economic and social implications is a relatively new phenomenon. Studying competences by themselves, however, is a relatively old phenomenon in the management and organizational sciences. However, as pointed out earlier, there has been a lack of consensus about what core competence actually is.

Our definition of core competence as *both* organizational capital and social capital has a number of advantages. First, it interprets the concept of competence as an asset of the firm, and, in some trivial ways, core competences behave like physical assets. For example, their value differs across various states of the world. Second, the definition highlights the *coordination* and *integration* part of the phenomenon, by introducing organizational capital to the concept. Third, our definition brings in the *social context* of competence, by introducing the concept of social capital. Fourth, including social context in the concept of competence raises some questions about the *designability* of core competences.

Much more research is needed. In particular, the behavioural side of strategy needs to be explored, for example, how the process of creating core competences takes place. It is exactly in the study of a phenomenon like core competences that insights from economics and behavioural science may supplement and enrich each other, and both areas should be included in a theory of core competences.

NOTES

1 Penrose (1959) divided resources into two categories, human and physical. But, as she pointed out, this division may be elaborated depending on the purpose at hand.
2 In some interpretations of the resource-based view of strategy, the rent concept implies a notion of entrepreneurial resource development contained in the Schumpeterian conception of entrepreneurial rents due to innovative activity (Rumelt 1987).
3 The rents due to resource scarcity can be considered as rents due to lower marginal costs of production than competitors'. In contrast, monopoly rent arises from the ability to set prices at the privately efficient level.
4 In this chapter we will not attempt to expand the model of man but limit ourselves to an expansion of the situational dimension: informational assumptions and social context.

5 See, for example, Granovetter (1985) for a critique reflecting the relative neglect of social context in economics.

6 Aspects like tacitness, social complexity, causal ambiguity and time-compression diseconomies are examples of this category of isolation mechanism.

7 Trade secrets, patents, trade marks and contractual safeguards are examples of this category of isolation mechanism.

8 This is parallel to the concept of exit barriers in industrial organization literature. A high level of irreversible commitment to a certain type of competences may also function as entry deterrent.

9 This assumption is similar to that of homogeneous technology in neoclassical price theory.

10 What should be noted, though, is that in general increased flexibility of resources is likely to be associated with less specificity.

11 These are the strategic apex, the technostructure, the middle line, the support staff and the operating core.

REFERENCES

Aaker, D. (1989) 'Managing Assets and Skills', *California Management Review* Winter: 91–106.

Amit, R. and Schoemaker, P. (1993) 'Strategic Assets and Organizational Rent', *Strategic Management Journal* 14 (1): 33–46.

Amit, R. and Schoemaker, P. (1994) 'Investment in Strategic Assets: Industry and Firm Level Perspectives', in P. Shrivastava, A. Huff and J. Dutton (eds) *Advances in Strategic Management 10*, Greenwich, Conn.: JAI Press, pp. 3–33.

Andrews, K. (1971) *The Concept of Corporate Strategy*, Homewood, Ill.: Irwin.

Ansoff, I. H. (1965) *Corporate Strategy*, New York: McGraw-Hill.

Baden-Fuller, C. and Stopford, J. M. (1992) *Rejuvenating the Mature Business*, London: Routledge.

Barney, J. B. (1986a) 'Organizational Culture: Can it Be a Source of Sustained Competitive Advantage?', *Academy of Management Review* 11 (3): 656–65.

Barney, J. B. (1986b) 'Strategic Factor Markets: Expectations, Luck, and Business Strategy', *Management Science* 32 (10): 1231–41.

Barney, J. B. (1991) 'Firm Resources and Sustained Competitive Advantage', *Journal of Management* 17 (1): 99–120.

Bartlett, C. and Ghoshal, S. (1992) *Transnational Management*, Homewood, Ill.: Irwin.

Carlsson, B. and Eliasson, G. (1991) 'The Nature and Importance of Economic Competence', IUI Working Paper no. 294, Industries Utretningsinstitut.

Castanias, R. P. and Helfat, C. E. (1991) 'Managerial Resources and Rents', *Journal of Management* 17 (1): 155–71.

Chandler, A. D. (1962) *Strategy and Structure: Chapters in the History of the Industrial Enterprise*, Cambridge, Mass.: MIT Press.

Chandler, A. D. (1990) *Scale and Scope*, New York: The Free Press.

Cohen, W. M. and Levinthal, D. (1990) 'Absorptive Capacity: A New Perspective on Learning and Innovation', *Administrative Science Quarterly* 35: 128–52.

Coleman, J. (1988) 'Social Capital in the Creation of Human Capital', *American Sociological Review* 94 (Supplement): 95–120.

Collis, D. (1991) 'A Resource-based Analysis of Global Competition: The Case of the Bearings Industry', *Strategic Management Journal* 12 (Special Issue): 49–68.

Cyert, R. M. and March, J. G. (1963) *A Behavioral Theory of the Firm*, Englewood Cliffs, NJ: Prentice-Hall.

Dana, J. (1991) 'Differentiation and Emulation in Games of Strategic Choice under Uncertainty', Mimeo, Department of Economics: Dartmouth College.

Dierickx, I. and Cool, K. (1989) 'Asset Stock Accumulation and Sustainability of Competitive Advantage', *Management Science* 35: 1504–11.

Eliasson, G. (1990) 'The Firm as a Competent Team', *Journal of Economic Behavior and Organization* 13: 275–98.

Gabel, H. L. (1984) 'The Microfoundations of Competitive Strategy', INSEAD Working Paper, Fontainebleau.

Grandori, A. (1991) 'Negotiating Efficient Organization Forms', *Journal of Economic Behavior and Organization* 16 (3): 319–40.

Granovetter, M. (1985) 'Economic Action and the Problem of Embeddedness', *American Journal of Sociology* 91 (3): 481–510.

Hall, R. (1992) 'The Strategic Analysis of Intangible Resources', *Strategic Management Journal* 13: 135–44.

Hermalin, B. (1994) 'Product-Market Competition and Heterogeneity in Organizational Form', Mimeo, University of California, Berkeley.

Hitt, M. and Ireland, D. (1985) 'Corporate Distinctive Competence: Strategy, Industry and Performance', *Strategic Management Journal* 6: 273–93.

Irvin, R. A. and Michaels, E. G. (1989) 'Core Skills: Doing the Right Things Right', *The McKinsey Quarterly* Summer: 4–19.

Kogut, B. and Zander, U. (1992) 'Knowledge of the Firm, Combinative Capabilities, and the Replication of Technology', *Organization Science* 3: 383–97.

Lazonick, W. (1992) 'Business Organization and Competitive Advantage: Capitalist Transformations in the Twentieth Century', in G. Dosi, R. Gianetti and P. A. Toninelli (eds) *Technology and Enterprise in a Historical Perspective*, Oxford: Clarendon Press.

Lippman, S. A. and Rumelt, R. P. (1982) 'Uncertain Imitability: An Analysis of Interfirm Differences in Efficiency under Competition', *Bell Journal of Economics* 13: 418–53.

Maksimovic, V. and Zechner, J. (1991) 'Debt, Agency Costs, and Industry Equilibrium', *The Journal of Finance* 46: 1619–44.

Mintzberg, H. (1983) *Structures in Fives – Designing Effective Organizations*, Englewood Cliffs, NJ: Prentice-Hall.

Mintzberg, H. (1990) 'Strategy Formation: Schools of Thought', in J. W. Frederickson (ed.) *Perspectives on Strategic Management*, New York: Harper & Row.

Nelson, R. R. and Winter, S. G. (1982) *An Evolutionary Theory of Economic Change*, Cambridge, Mass.: Harvard University Press.

Penrose, E. T. (1959) *The Theory of the Growth of the Firm*, Oxford: Basil Blackwell.

Peteraf, M. A. (1993) 'The Cornerstones of Competitive Advantage: A Resource-based View', *Strategic Management Journal* 14: 179–91.

Porter, M. E. (1980) *Competitive Strategy*, New York: The Free Press.

Porter, M. E. (1991) 'Towards a Dynamic Theory of Strategy', *Strategic Management Journal* 12 (Special Issue): 95–117.

Prahalad, C. K. and Hamel, G. (1990) 'The Core Competence of the Corporation', *Harvard Business Review* 66: 79–91.

Prescott, E. C. and Visscher, M. (1980) 'Organization Capital', *Journal of Political Economy* 88 (3): 446–61.

Reve, T. (1990) 'The Firm as a Nexus of Internal and External Contracts', in M. Aoki, B. Gustafsson and O. E. Williamson (eds) *The Firm as a Nexus of Treaties*, Beverly Hills, Calif.: Sage.

Rumelt, R. P. (1974) *Strategy, Structure, and Economic Performance*, Cambridge, Mass.: Harvard Business School Press.

Rumelt, R. P. (1982) 'Diversification Strategy and Profitability', *Strategic Management Journal* 3: 359–69.

Rumelt, R. P. (1987) 'Strategy, Economic Theory and Entrepreneurship', in D. J. Teece (ed.) *The Competitive Challenge*, Cambridge, Mass.: Ballinger Books.

Rumelt, R. P. (1991) 'How Much Does Industry Matter?', *Strategic Management Journal* 12 (3): 167–85.

Russo, E. J. and Schoemaker, P. J. H. (1992) 'Managing Overconfidence', *Sloan Management Review* 33 (2): 7–17.

Schmalensee, R. (1985) 'Do Markets Differ Much?' *American Economic Review* 75 (3): 341–51.

Selznick, P. (1957) *Leadership in Administration*, New York: Harper & Row.

Stalk, G., Evans, P. and Schulman, L. E. (1992a) 'Competing on Capabilities: The New Rules of Corporate Strategy', *Harvard Business Review* March–April: 57–69.

Stalk, G., Evans, P. and Schulman, L. E. (1992b) 'Comment', *Harvard Business Review* May–June.

Teece, D. J., Pisano, G. and Shuen, A. (1990) 'Firm Capabilities, Resources and the Concept of Strategy', CCC Working Paper no. 90–8, University of California at Berkeley.

Wernerfelt, B. (1989) 'From Critical Resources to Corporate Strategy', *Journal of General Management* 14 (3): 4–12.

Wernerfelt, B. and Montgomery, C. (1988) 'Tobin's q and the Importance of Focus in Firm Performance', *American Economic Review* 78 (1): 246–50.

Williamson, O. E. (1985) *The Economic Institutions of Capitalism*, New York: The Free Press.

Winter, S. G. (1987) 'Knowledge and Competence as Strategic Assets', in D. J. Teece (ed.) *The Competitive Challenge*, Cambridge, Mass.: Ballinger Books.

Winter, S. G. (1988) 'On Coase, Competence and the Corporation', *Journal of Law, Economics and Organization* 4 (1): 163–80.

5

COMPETENCES, TRANSACTION COSTS AND COMPETITIVE STRATEGY

Paul Robertson

INTRODUCTION

Over the last few years, a large literature has developed on the relationship between organizational resources and strategy.[1] The emphasis has generally been on attaining 'competitive advantage': that is, on positioning firms so that they can use superior inputs, or privileged access to inputs, to generate Ricardian rents or economic profits by implementing different strategies from those of their competitors. Prahalad and Hamel (1990), for example, contend that firms should determine what core competences are needed to achieve a particular strategy and then develop or acquire those competences that they do not already have. Kay (1993) is less optimistic about the ability of firms to gain important competences or capabilities, but he emphasizes that strategy should be built on existing competences.[2] Furthermore, in common with other writers, Prahalad and Hamel and Kay concentrate on the maintenance of competences-based advantages over a prolonged period. Thus Barney (1991: 102) defines competitive advantage as being 'sustained' only if 'it continues to exist after efforts to duplicate that advantage have ceased'. In order for this to occur, four conditions have been identified. In Peteraf's words (1993: 180), 'The first [condition] is *resource heterogeneity* from which come Ricardian or monopoly rents. *Ex post limits to competition* are necessary to sustain the rents. *Imperfect resource mobility* ensures that the rents are bound to the firm and shared by it. *Ex ante limits to competition* prevent costs from offsetting the rents.' (See also Barney 1991.)

The resource-based or competences approach has now developed to the point at which some authors contend that it is a full-bodied theory of industrial organization comparable to the neoclassical, structure–conduct–performance, Schumpeterian, Chicago School and transaction cost models in its range of applications (Conner 1991). However, there are still important aspects to be canvassed concerning the effects on firm strategy of possessing resources of various levels of quality. In this chapter, I look more deeply into three important emphases of the resource school in order to provide a more realistic guide to strategy formulation. In particular, I contend that an emphasis on the sustainability of unique or scarce

75

competences[3] is too narrow because uniqueness can be expected to decay as time passes. Dependence on current competences can therefore lull an organization into a feeling of complacency when it should instead be directing its efforts towards a search for new scarce competences. Secondly, firms generally need to combine a variety of resources in the course of generating outputs. It is therefore necessary to look at the whole bundle of necessary competences when choosing a strategy and to avoid placing excessive emphasis on so-called core competences. The possession of superior competences of production does not in itself guarantee that a firm can deliver outputs at a lower price than competitors can because transaction costs and questions of appropriability must also be considered. And finally, although staking out a position of competitive advantage may be desirable, it is too confined a perspective from which to approach strategy formulation. By definition, the collection of Ricardian rents or economic profits is not available to most firms in competitive markets. Firms must make the best use of their competences irrespective of whether this will lead to an absolute competitive advantage.

An evolutionary resource-based model of firm development that addresses these issues is presented in the first main section of this chapter, with a discussion of the implications of the model for strategy formulation in the following section.

AN EVOLUTIONARY MODEL OF COMPETENCES, TRANSACTION COSTS AND COMPETITIVE FIRM BEHAVIOUR[4]

Firms and markets are, in a sense, a continuum. Inputs that are not produced internally must be purchased and vice versa. The choice of which inputs to make and which to buy is one of the most important strategic decisions that confronts managers. Any useful analysis must therefore determine which activities, if any, must be contained within firms and which can be delegated to the market.

The 'why' of firms

In the modern debate over the economics of organization, one basic assumption that proponents of both the nexus-of-contracts view (Cheung 1983) and the property-rights view (Hart 1989, Moore 1992) have taken over from neoclassical economics is that firms are a second-best alternative that persist as a result of 'market failure'. Moreover, all of these schools of thought centre their theories on the premise that the primary behavioural goal of firms is to provide profits for their owners. In this view, the organizational form that a firm adopts is (consciously?) chosen because it will deliver a return on investment at least as great as any alternative form of organization. This assumption holds both for the relationship of the firm to its external environment – what the firm chooses to do itself and what it purchases and sells to others – and for the internal organization of the firm – how it goes about producing whatever goods or services it has decided belong within its proper sphere of activity.

From the perspective of real-world firm behaviour and the boundaries of the firm, these assumptions ignore some of the most important factors that determine firm organization and underpin the relationship between firms and markets. They essentially relegate to second place, or even assume away altogether, the activities that the people working for the firm are really engaged in. These include deciding what to produce and how to produce it and then actually producing it in the way that best rewards the firm's owners. Hence, success derives from the firm's provision of goods and services that meet the needs of potential customers in a way that generates the highest possible returns to its owners. In short, the behaviour of firms is determined with an eye on both blades of the Marshallian scissors (Langlois and Robertson 1992).[5]

If this is true, then we should conceive of firms as organizations that need to tackle a variety of goals. These goals are interdependent in the sense that, while all must be addressed in some form if the desired product is to eventuate, some may conflict with others if they are not coordinated or 'managed'. This holds even if we leave aside questions of opportunism and shirking. If a firm is to survive, let alone prosper, it must make sure that it produces something that customers desire, which means that it must acquire and accurately use information, or knowledge, about products and production processes. In fact, a firm must be organized to undertake one, several or all of the following activities associated with the profitable production of a good or service: conception, design and development, manufacturing, provision of inputs, marketing and distribution, and many others. A design that is outstanding in the sense that it meets the performance attributes (Lancaster 1971) potential purchasers desire, however, may for that very reason cost more to produce than those same purchasers are willing to pay; or it may be impossible to produce at all. Thus one reason for organizing such diverse activities is to provide coordination between aspects of production so that a plausible outcome results in the form of a good or service that (a) can be produced with non-cost attributes attractive to potential buyers; (b) can be produced at a price that is also acceptable to those buyers; and (c) allows for an acceptable return on the productive resources involved.

A variety of types of competences may be required, depending on the nature of the task at hand (Table 5.1). It is a separate question as to how the necessary competences are to be organized – whether the proper vehicle for generating such a plausible outcome is a vertically integrated firm, or several firms specializing in different links in the productive chain, or a group of independent and unattached workers. The answer depends in part, of course, on levels of transaction costs, but it also depends on the nature of the activities to be performed and on the types of competences that are needed, especially in the form of human skills or talents.

77

Table 5.1 Competences and the cost of selected strategies

| Competence | Acquisitions phase | | | Operations phase | |
	(1) Portfolio investment	(2) Unrelated diversification	(3) Related diversification	(4) Unrelated diversification	(5) Related diversification
1 Finance				Scope for internal capital market	Scope for internal capital market
2 Entrepreneurship	Cost of search relatively low	Cost of search relatively low	Cost of search relatively high		
3 Management				Higher internal management expense	Lower internal managerial expense
4 Production			(a) Possibly cheaper to integrate vertically than to buy or sell in market (b) Possible reductions in the expense of adding new lines because of shared facilities		Possible sharing in of supervision and assessment
5 Marketing			(a) Possibly cheaper to integrate vertically than to sell in market		

Table 5.1 Competences and the cost of selected strategies cont.

6 Research	(b) Possible reductions in expense of adding new lines because of shared facilities	(a) Possibly cheaper to integrate vertically than to sell in market (b) Possible reductions in expense of adding new lines because of shared facilities	Possible sharing in costs of supervision and assessment
7 Raw material procurement		(a) Possibly cheaper to integrate vertically than to sell in market (b) Possible reductions in expense of adding new lines because of shared facilities	Possible sharing in costs of supervision and assessment
8 Organizational	Lower probability of internal resistance		Higher probability of internal resistance

Williamson (1985) indicates that transactions can occur only across a 'technologically separable interface'. If it is technically impossible to perform two or more stages in a production process separately, then there can be no transactions as the product proceeds along these stages, and the activities must remain within a single organization. Otherwise, in Williamson's view, the movement from one stage to another does constitute a transaction that firms may either internalize or handle through market-based exchange. But technical considerations are not the only factors that determine the size of a firm's irreducible core. There are other types of interrelationship that provide organizational bonding, many of which are behavioural or cognitive in nature. When there is a low degree of interdependence among activities, the outcome of their operations is 'additive' in the sense that the total result is the sum of the outputs of the individual operations. However, when the performance of particular operations cannot proceed without the completion of other operations, the resulting high degree of interdependence may lead to 'superadditive' results. In this case, the outcome from the combined performance of the operations is greater than (and frequently different from) the outcome of the operations being undertaken separately (Cheung 1983).

Interdependence, therefore, leads by definition to certain types of operational inseparability or indivisibility. In itself, however, this does not mean that the possibility of transactions between components is ruled out. Although the coordinated efforts of several workers may be required to lift a slab, the workers can be hired and replaced individually. Similarly, in theory (and occasionally in practice) the machines in a factory may have varied ownership even though the production of a particular good depends on their coordinated use.

The real factor that can rule out transactions in the course of a productive process is not inseparability *per se* but a combination of interdependence of activities *and* the costliness of transferring knowledge about or imitating one or more of the components of a process. The extreme case here, of course, is when various components of a process are *inimitable*. Mahoney and Pandian (1992) capture this latter idea by distinguishing between 'contestable synergy' and 'idiosyncratic synergy'.[6] When there is contestability, as in the example of the lifting of the slab, there is 'a combination of resources that create value but are competitively available' (Mahoney and Pandian 1992: 368). Idiosyncratic synergy, on the other hand, occurs when the enhanced outcome is specific to the particular resources that are being combined and substitutes are not available.[7] In general, we should expect that the irreducible core of any organization would be the coordinated set of resources, or competences, that is idiosyncratically synergistic and vital to the goals of the organization.

What are examples of idiosyncratically synergistic competences? Although it is possible to conceive of a mineral that has only one use and a production process that cannot function without that mineral, one can usually purchase both minerals and processes. Similarly, although a group of people may have a higher total output when working together than when in other combinations, under most circumstances the people are legally free to move eventually even though they be under contract for the time being.

The idiosyncratically synergistic competences that bind organizations together are, in fact, most frequently forms of knowledge that are difficult both to acquire and to communicate to others. This knowledge is often expressed in the form of the individual and collective behaviour of members of the organization. As Prescott and Visscher put it, the 'firm is a structure within which agents have the incentive to acquire and reveal information in a manner that is less costly than in possible alternative institutions' (1980: 460). Through working together, people learn to behave in institutionally specific ways that are efficient but cannot be easily, cheaply or quickly taught to others. Therefore, these firms develop ways of acting that are competitively valuable but, because they have evolved within a particular context, are likely to vary from those of other firms. This variance increases as the industrial context of firms differs, but will be present to a degree even among firms in the same or similar industries. To the extent that this behaviour is efficient and hard to replicate, it provides an advantage to the firm that would be lost if the firm were split up or dispersed.

Intrinsic and ancillary competences

Thus idiosyncratically synergistic knowledge and ways of acting, or *intrinsic competences*, are at the heart of firms as organizations. In most cases, however, the production of a final product requires a range of resources or competences that extends well beyond the core of individual firms. To be successful, firms must choose ways of combining all of the necessary competences in a way that best meets all of the three conditions for satisfying customers and operating profitably.

The value of these competences will generally vary from a strategic standpoint. The intrinsic competences of a given firm may or may not be strategically advantageous. The fact that a firm possesses various characteristics that cannot be imitated and may be very hard to alter does not mean that these competences are optimal for producing any particular good or service. While firms are well advised in many cases to choose operations that make the best use of these characteristics, it may be that such operations are unattractive in a strategic sense. For example, they may be best suited to producing goods that sell in stagnant and highly competitive markets, or even to producing goods for which there is hardly any market at all.

Nevertheless, to survive, a firm in such a position must find ways of making the best of a bad thing by combining its inferior intrinsic competences with *ancillary*[8] competences in the most satisfactory way possible. This is not necessarily as dismal a prospect as may appear at first glance, because a firm with privileged access to vital ancillary competences may be highly competitive, at least over the short run, despite having poor intrinsic competences. For example, a firm that is the only one located in an area in which workers with rare skills are readily and cheaply available may, for a period, be able to compete very successfully in an industry in which these skills are essential even if the firm's intrinsic core endowment is not well suited to other aspects of producing that good. Eventually, of course, in the absence of barriers to entry or movement, we would expect competing firms to locate in the same area, driving up the price of labour and eliminating the advantage of the initial firm. If the intrinsic competences of the new firms were better suited to producing the good, the original firm would then find itself under pressure and perhaps fail, but for a period of time it would have had access to a better *overall* set of competences than its competitors had. When the vital ancillary competence is the ownership of an essential input such as a mineral, the initial firm's advantage may extend indefinitely, or at least until alternative sources are found, regardless of having to bear the burden of a poor intrinsic endowment of resources.

Internal and external competences

In general, this notion that competences have relative, rather than absolute, costs and values can be extended to all the internal and external resources available to a firm. The particular competences and the technology for combining them that a firm chooses to employ – its production function – will, as in the neoclassical model, vary with relative costs, as will the make/buy decision for inputs.

As is well known, the cost structure that a firm faces is composed of two elements, the direct costs of production and transaction costs. For current purposes, transaction costs, which may be characterized as the cost of *utilizing* competences, extend beyond the elements suggested by Williamson and others such as asset-specificity, opportunism and bounded rationality, and also beyond the governance costs which Alchian and Woodward (1988: 66) have called the costs of 'the administering, directing, negotiating, and monitoring of the joint productive teamwork in a firm'. Purchasing goods externally may also entail other factors such as greater transportation costs which are not strictly speaking costs of production but do influence the make/buy decision.

The degree to which transaction costs of these various types are present helps to determine the actual value of competences to a firm. Superior competences, in the sense of being able to invent, produce or distribute a good or service more cheaply than can competitors,[9] can be eroded if there are unfavourable transaction costs.[10] In addition, in order to exploit its current competences, a firm may have to develop new competences which do not exist elsewhere in the economy or cannot be purchased because the firms that do have them are unwilling or unable to supply them. In either case, a firm may as a result be obliged to internalize production of an input even though the relevant competences that it possesses are inferior to those of other firms. Similarly, firms with superior competences may find that they are unable to compete successfully because of transaction costs. In other words, when the total cost situation is considered, the possession *per se* of superior competences or resources may not be the overriding factor in formulating strategy.

Morris Silver (1984) has used concepts of Schumpeter (1934) as the inspiration for a theory of vertical integration that is based on the costs of coordination. He begins by observing that innovation often involves the qualitatively new. Entrepreneurs who attempt something that is qualitatively new frequently encounter strong opposition. As Schumpeter stressed, this opposition may be cultural and psychological, but more interestingly it may also be informational. If an innovation is to succeed, the adaptation of complementary activities may also be needed. Many of these complementary activities will also be qualitatively new if the innovation itself is indeed qualitatively new. The problem for the entrepreneur is to generate these new specialized activities. To accomplish this through market transactions, the entrepreneur would have to inform and persuade those with the necessary competences, which may not be an easy task since the innovative vision is untried and idiosyncratic virtually by definition. Moreover, the innovator's potential contracting parties may need to invest in specialized assets, and it may be very costly to persuade them to bear the risk of an irreversible investment under such novel conditions. As a result, it may be cheaper for an innovative firm, itself, to invest in the co-specialized activities and to employ directly parties with the relevant competences than to contract with them through the market.

In Silver's view the benefits to internalization are primarily informational since innovators can communicate new procedures and directly supervise their own employees more easily and cheaply than they can explain to a contractor the detailed specifications of the end-product. There are also governance costs to such internal organization: the innovative firm will probably be integrating into areas to which its own competences are less well adapted than they are to manufacturing the main product. An example is the way in which the Ford Motor Company was forced to make many of its own prototypes of machine tools when the assembly line was being developed because specialist machine-tool manufacturers did not believe that the tools could be made to Ford's specifications (Langlois and Robertson 1989).

Vertical integration is also a means of redressing adverse power relationships. Innovation may entail drawing upon competences at more than one stage in the chain of production. When ownership is decentralized, innovation may never occur if some of the existing asset-holders, or suppliers of complementary competences, have the power (for example through trade unions) to block innovation in order to protect their existing rent streams (Robertson and Alston 1992). Thus if innovation does take place, it may be elsewhere in the economy (or perhaps even elsewhere in the world) under the direction of a single asset-holder and decision-maker who is able to ignore existing task boundaries. Under such unified ownership, the owners or their managers can reorganize competences because they have ultimate control. When a single firm is both the developer and the user of an innovation, the benefits are internalized and appropriability is no longer a problem.

The problems of adverse power relationships have attracted far more attention than the problems of coordination that Silver has highlighted. In particular, Teece (1986b) has stressed the importance of appropriability and asset specificity. Appropriability refers to the capacity of one party to the production process to appropriate the rents or quasi-rents arising from an innovation. The extent to which the innovator is directly able to appropriate these rents helps to determine the degree of internal organization. This ability depends both on the degree of complementarity between competences and on the 'regime of appropriability', that is, on the practical and legal ability of an innovator to create and enforce property rights in the innovation (Teece 1986a). An entrepreneur only needs to take a position in, and not to control, all complementary assets to profit from an innovation. When the competences involved are co-specialized, however, the transaction costs generated by asset-specificity will predominate. This implies that innovators must have enough hands-on control to allow their ownership stakes to overcome transaction costs between cooperating stages.

Innovators may wish as well to integrate into competences that are not co-specialized if innovators might otherwise enter quickly and bid away the quasi-rents of innovation. Licensing of an innovation may be sufficient when, as is arguably the case in pharmaceuticals (Levin *et al.* 1987), the knowledge involved can be easily protected by patents. When this is not true, as perhaps in the case of some process technologies, internal organization may be necessary to protect the quasi-rents.

Much of the story told here involves 'bottlenecks' in the innovation process. According to Teece, bottlenecks generate transaction costs because they pose the threat of strategic expropriation of rents. 'The owner of the bottleneck resource, realizing its strategic importance to the innovator, is in a position to threaten to withhold services, causing the price of its services to be raised' (Teece 1986a: 188).

The sustainability of transaction costs

The scenarios of both Silver and Teece may create circumstances in which informational or other varieties of transaction costs cause firms to ignore certain superior competences held either internally or externally in order to gain a better outcome from the use of all competences. Except when it incorporates unbreakable monopoly control over a vital resource, however, no combination of competences is likely to lead to a permanent, or even a long-run, strategic advantage. This is because both transaction costs and competences, themselves, are essentially short-run phenomena.

Transaction costs[11] may be viewed as a type of 'friction' that impedes firms from gaining the full value from their competences. Transaction costs, however, derive from informational problems that (a) make it difficult for firms to enter into meaningful contracts, (b) increase governance costs, or (c), in the case of the extended definition employed here, involve barriers to efficiency in areas such as transportation and distribution. According to Hayek (1945: 523), 'economic problems arise always and only in consequence of change'. Thus any sort of innovation may lead to increased transaction costs because it increases uncertainty and renders existing knowledge less relevant. But the converse also holds: as particular changes age, the problems initially associated with them can be expected to diminish because of increased opportunities for learning. As time passes, contracting parties learn more about each other's behaviour and develop (consciously or inadvertently) institutional arrangements that weaken the sources of transaction costs.

For example, 'bounded rationality' occurs when an agent's knowledge and decision-making ability are so limited that complete contracts cannot be specified. But when similar transactions occur repeatedly, agents will learn progressively about the typical results of those transactions and will therefore be in a position to insert more specific clauses in contracts. This may be reinforced by the prospect of repeated transactions which, because of reputation effects, lessen the scope for hold-up and other moral hazard problems. Similarly, governance costs may be expected to decrease with learning.

The sorts of problem described by Silver (1984) should also decrease as external holders of competences learn how to use them better, thereby freeing former innovators to concentrate on their main operations. The result might be that operations that had been internalized initially because willing suppliers were unavailable could now be delegated to firms with superior specialist capabilities, as Ford in fact did with machine-tool production. Secondly, follower firms that were founded after external competences had been fostered might be less highly integrated vertically than were first-movers. This again occurred in the automobile industry, where a late-comer like Chrysler was able to rely much more heavily on outside suppliers than Ford had (Langlois and Robertson 1989).

Finally, the development of better technology in transport and distribution would be expected to allow firms with superior competences to serve wider markets. As a consequence, firms that had been supplying themselves internally despite inferior competences could then take advantage of cheaper inputs by switching to external sources. For instance, Chandler (1977) attributes much of the industrial development in the United States in the second half of the nineteenth century to the growth of transport and distribution networks that widened markets and encouraged the consolidation and rationalization of firms in order to take advantage of superior manufacturing competences. The resulting economies of scale in input production made external supply more attractive.

Competences in the long run

Access to competences, like transaction costs, alters as time passes. To the extent that competences are based on knowledge, they can also be expected to become more widespread as others have an opportunity to acquire the necessary learning. Competences may spread very rapidly when the underlying knowledge is well known, but even tacit knowledge can be duplicated (and perhaps improved upon) with practice.

A further encouragement to dispersion occurs when competences gain multiple uses. For example, innovative techniques may spread from industry to industry as analogous uses are recognized. This process, which may take decades to work its way fully through the economy in the case of a truly systemic innovation such as electrification, eventually leads to a position like the one in Figure 5.1, with two firms, A and B, that are in different industries. Each firm has its own distinct competences (1, 2, 3 and 4, and 5, 6, 7 and 8, respectively), but both draw on the common competence 9. Initially, use of the common competence may have been confined to only one of the firms, but as its use spreads the possibility of vertical disintegration grows. In this case, either the second firm may purchase competence 9 from the initiator, or a common independent supplier or group of suppliers of the competence may develop to sell to both groups.[12]

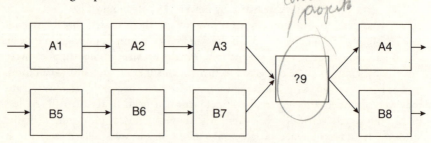

Figure 5.1 Two firms drawing on a single competence
Source: Inspired by Leijonhufvud (1986)

Moreover, the possibility that tacit knowledge might spread as time passes means that the core attributes of a firm might break down as inimitability of competences decreases. As this occurs, idiosyncratic synergy is converted into contestable synergy; transaction costs both become relevant in areas where they previously had no importance and lose their relevance in areas where they had previously been important; and the possibility of vertical disintegration grows.

The short- and long-run boundaries of the firm

It is now possible to bring together the competences approach and the transaction cost approach to specify how the characteristics of a firm may change as time passes (Table 5.2).

As has been shown, in the *short run* the core of a firm comprises those assets that are synergistic and idiosyncratically related to each other. In addition, because these intrinsic competences are inimitable and not contestable, the rents that flow from their value creation are not simply transitory. As most physical

Table 5.2 The effects of spreading knowledge on the use of competences

	Degree of idiosyncracy	Transaction costs	Availability of particular competences	Uses for particular competences	Relative cost of internalization	Degree of vertical integration
Short run	High	High	Thinly distributed	Few	Low	High
Long run	Low	Low	Widespread	Many	High	Low

assets are contestable in theory, the intrinsic competences of a firm consist primarily of knowledge and patterns of behaviour such as routines[13] that are not readily communicated to outsiders, and in the people that embody them.

The addition of further competences to the core depends on the relative transaction costs of internalizing the activities or purchasing them on the market. In many cases, as Chandler (1977, 1990) has noted, the decision to internalize an activity is defensive and designed to protect firms against hold-up or agency problems that cannot be adequately handled by contracts. In other cases, however, internalization can be a positive strategic decision if a firm wants to add new competences to its core in a way that will develop new forms of idiosyncratic synergy (Prahalad and Hamel 1990). In this way, a firm can hope to collect future rents by creating new combinations of inputs that, in the short run at least, are inimitable. Some of these rent-generating competences may be especially useful at the design phase in providing inspiration for new products and processes, but others are part of the ongoing activities of the firm.

In the *long run*, the spread of knowledge should lead to a *tendency* towards the generalized spread of competences that both breaks down idiosyncrasy and reduces transaction costs. As this happens, it is possible that the core of the firm will erode because competences that were once based on tacit knowledge and therefore inimitable become more common as other organizations devote the time necessary to replicate knowledge that has not hitherto been contestable.

For competences that have always been contestable, the spread of knowledge over time should reduce transaction costs and make it more attractive in some cases for firms to buy inputs rather than produce them internally. Over the long run, we might therefore expec t to find vertical disintegration as products mature, technologies spread by analogy to other industries, and competences become generally more contestable at reduced transaction costs. This, of course, is not inevitable, and the exact course of events necessarily varies from industry to industry, or even from firm to firm within an industry.

As this story emphasizes, one implication of this dynamic theory is that the desirability of vertical integration may depend on the existing array of competences available in the economy. When the existing arrangement of decentralized competences is very different from that required by a major systemic innovation, vertical integration – which permits a quicker and cheaper creation of new competences – may prove superior. This may indeed help explain the prevalence of large vertically integrated companies in the historical periods that Chandler chronicles. The major rearrangements of competences enabled by rapid economic growth and the rapid decline of transportation and communications costs in the nineteenth century were refractory to the existing system of decentralized competences. Change came from large integrated firms that could sweep away ill-adapted structures in a wave of 'creative destruction'. But, in other times and in other places, entrenched vertical integration can prove just as refractory to change by freezing competences in institutional patterns that are not suited to new conditions.

The dynamics of firm and industry evolution

When viewed from a broader perspective, there is continual flux in the relationship between firms and products, as firms form and re-form depending on changes in relative competences and transaction costs. As is shown in Figure 5.2, the pattern of change is not invariable, however, because the firm-specific nature of both production and transaction costs will render integration (or disintegration) desirable in some cases but not in others. Thus Firms 4 and 8 remain specialists throughout the period, but Firms 1, 2 and 3 first merge and subsequently spin off some activities, a pattern that is also followed by Firms 10, 11 and 12. The merger of Firms 5, 6 and 7, on the other hand, leads to no spin-offs.

But this is by no means the end of the story since subsequent technological change may be expected to upset existing relationships. In Figure 5.3, Firms 15, 16 and 17 produce innovative outputs that complement or replace the output of established firms. Whereas Firms 16 and 17 merge with older firms, Firm 15 remains independent. Moreover, as products become obsolete, firms or whole industries may die. Thus, the products B and E are no longer needed and are discontinued.

The fact that the argument is couched in terms of *tendencies* and *varieties of experience*, however, does not imply randomness. On the contrary, the options for change at any given point are constrained by the nature of the environment at that point. Whether there is continuity, merger, or disintegration is a function of the cost structure at that time, which in turn depends on the existing distribution of competences throughout the economy and the degree of efficiency of markets. Hence change at the level of the economy as a whole is evolutionary, even when the effects of innovation on particular firms and industries may be revolutionary, because innovation has to fit within a functioning environment which can change only gradually as a response to stimuli.[14]

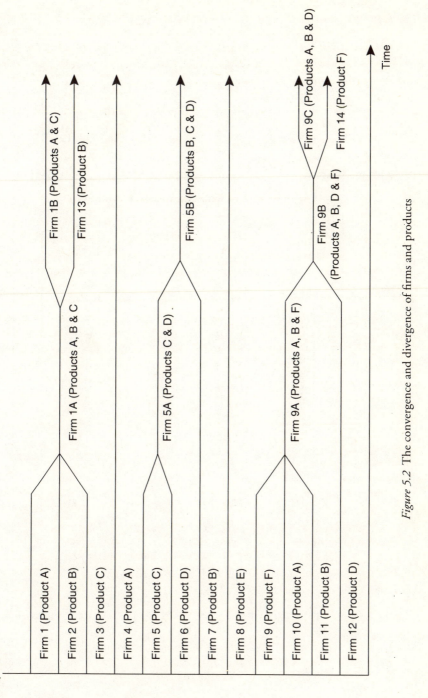

Figure 5.2 The convergence and divergence of firms and products

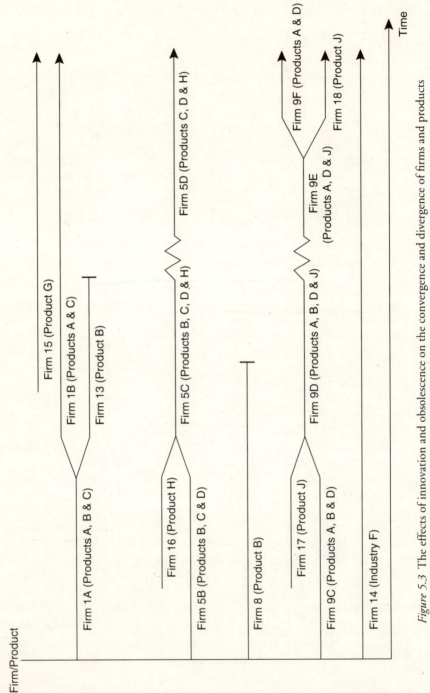

Figure 5.3 The effects of innovation and obsolescence on the convergence and divergence of firms and products

TRANSACTION COSTS, COMPETENCES AND FIRM STRATEGY

The first important message to be derived from the model is that resources must be viewed in their context when formulating strategy. With very few exceptions, competences are only useful because they can be combined with other competences. Thus an outstanding competence may be devalued if a particular firm can only combine it with other competences, be they intrinsic or ancillary, that are inferior to those of competitors or potential competitors. Furthermore, the value of competences also depends on internal and external transaction-cost relationships.

Firms in search of competitive advantage must therefore focus on their entire range of competences and not just on the outstanding ones. The most vital areas for attention may well be those that are weakest or where transaction costs impede efficient use of existing competences. When viewed in this way, a tool such as Porter's value chain can be valuable in identifying areas of weakness or friction if it is employed in sufficient depth and detail (Porter 1985). Firms must not only ask which components of their operations are of the greatest importance to their businesses, but should look into actual or potential factors that influence the successful delivery of these components. It is only at this level of investigation that many problems will reveal themselves.

Strategy implementation then requires attention to the factors that prevent firms from gaining the greatest impact from their competences. The action to be taken depends on the position of both strong and weak competences within their operations. If an outstanding competence cannot be used efficiently because the firm does not currently have access to strong complementary competences, the best course of action might be to develop the needed resources in-house. Should this be beyond the ability of the firm, however, the licensing of its outstanding competence or selling out to another firm with better complementary competences may be the best way of appropriating rents.

Transaction-cost barriers may take two forms. In some instances, as emphasized by Silver (1984), firms may be obliged to use inferior competences because the transaction costs involved in tapping better ones held by other firms are too high. The converse of this is that other firms may find that high transaction costs prevent them from using their superior competences. In both cases, a successful strategic policy might focus on reducing transaction costs. In practice, this could entail finding ways of limiting such factors as opportunism, excessive asset specificity or bounded rationality. Alternatively, improved transport or distribution networks could be the key to making better use of competences. In this latter case, firms might seek to benefit from external economies by clustering in an industrial district such as Silicon Valley, or southeast Michigan in the first half of the twentieth century, where propinquity allows firms to concentrate on their superior competences and delegate other functions through markets to firms that are better equipped to undertake them. Alertness can be especially valuable for supplier firms, such as Firm ? in Figure 5.1, that position themselves to take over activities that other firms had been undertaking with inferior resources when the number of customers reaches an adequate level.

The fragility of transaction costs and competences also has a significant impact on firm strategy. While the 'long run' may last many years in some cases, it can come quickly in others, depending in part on the degree of ease of imitability. Recent Japanese initiatives provide excellent examples. Through organizational changes centring on just-in-time and other quality-control techniques, Japanese firms were able in the 1970s and 1980s to erode the value of the long standing competences of Western manufacturers in home electrical goods, automobiles and many other products. The Japanese were also able to use their superior manufacturing competences to take the initiative in new areas such as semiconductors in which Western firms that had pioneered in their development found that they could not gain sustained rents. However, in contrast to the American automobile industry in which superior competences provided fifty years or more of competitive advantage, the Japanese edge seems more transitory as US firms have been able to fight back and regain at least a portion of their losses in automobiles and semiconductors after only a few years. The principal difference seems to be that the organizational and manufacturing competences of the Japanese have been easier to imitate than earlier American competences were. In part, this reflects cognitive differences, but it is also the result of different circumstances. The early American lead in cars and electrical appliances led to economies of scale that the potential competitors in Europe or Japan were not able to match until the late 1960s because their home markets were much smaller. It took decades for the establishment of the European Community and greater prosperity in Western Europe and Japan to give firms in those countries a better foundation from which to launch an attack on American markets. American firms, however, have not been handicapped by an inadequate domestic base in imitating their new rivals. Thus it again appears that the value of competences is contextual rather than absolute.

The formulation of sound competitive strategy when competences and transaction costs are of transitory value requires two types of alertness. First, firms with established superior competences should whenever possible attempt to protect themselves by erecting strategic barriers as Porter (1980) suggests. In addition to barriers of entry and exit, which may be difficult to build, firms can protect their competences by developing a stream of subsidiary competences that can still be protected, perhaps by patents, after the original competence has lost its uniqueness. Polaroid's defence of its instant photography process against Kodak is a good example of the use of improvements to protect an aged and imitable original competence.

Secondly, firms without superior competences but with strong capacities for imitation should look for opportunities in areas in which competitive advantage can be destroyed because the competences on which it has been based are no longer sufficient. This may occur when pioneering firms have become too complacent and have not bothered to protect themselves adequately. Such firms often establish price umbrellas under which smaller competitors can shelter while improving their own competences.

Finally, it should be noted that superior competences and competitive advantage may be vulnerable for other reasons. 'Improvements' in exchange rates can present formidable problems, as they have for Japan recently or for Italy in the 1920s and the United States at several points since the late 1950s. Seemingly random fluctuations in exchange rates can also discourage firms from making investments to capitalize on superior competences if they fear that future revaluations will erode the value of their advantages.

CONCLUSION

Although the possession of superior competences is of course desirable, it does not guarantee that a firm will gain a competitive advantage. Superior competences in themselves rarely confer such a great edge that other factors are insignificant. In fact, when complementary competences are vital, the firm that owns a particular superior competence may find that it has very little capacity to appropriate the rents arising from its advantage. In other cases, because of transaction costs, firms possessing inferior competences may be forced to produce a good or service while firms with superior competences are unable to compete successfully.

The formulation of competitive strategy therefore requires that firms take a broad look at what their markets require and at their own capacity to meet those needs. The exploitation of a superior competence may well mean that the greatest amount of attention should be given to dealing with inferior complementary competences that are preventing the superior competence from being well used. Strategic attention may also be devoted to transaction costs that are either preventing the full exploitation of a superior competence or forcing a firm into areas in which its competences are inferior.

NOTES

1 For a survey of relevant articles, see e.g. Peteraf (1993).
2 Kay (1993) characterizes strategies based on competences that a firm does not yet possess as 'wish-driven'. See Section IV of his book, particularly pp. 125–6.
3 There is some terminological variation in the literature. Amit and Schoemaker (1993), for instance, distinguish between 'resources' and 'capabilities' but do not define 'competences' and 'routines', although they cite authors who use all of these terms. Here, I follow the more traditional practice of using 'resources', 'capabilities' and 'competences' interchangeably. They all include the current and potential ability to perform operations as well as the possession of material inputs. 'Routines', however, are practices developed by organizations for the use of their resources or competences. 'Distinctive' competences or capabilities are those possessed solely by one organization. Depending on the strategy that the organization has in mind, distinctive competences may or may not also be 'core' competences.

4 For a more detailed statement of this model, see Langlois and Robertson (1995), chs 2–3.

5 Gilson and Roe (1993) apply a similar perspective to Japanese firms by arguing that the *keiretsu* form has been chosen as an efficient way of producing goods and services as well as being an efficient form of corporate governance.

6 Mahoney and Pandian actually refer to 'idiosyncratic bilateral synergy', which they define as 'the enhanced value that is idiosyncratic to the combined resources of the acquiring and target firms' (1992: 368). It is consistent with the remainder of their discussion, however, to extend the term to refer to the combination of any number of resources that are already under common ownership.

7 Teece (1986b) discusses 'co-specialized' assets, which are the same as assets bound by contestable synergy. To use his example, the innovation of containerized cargo required the coordination of both containerized ships and specialized equipment. However, co-specialization (which resembles Richardson's (1972) concept of 'close complementarity') does not require idiosyncrasy, and co-specialized assets may therefore belong to separate organizations and be obtained on the market. Indeed, if individual container ships and port facilities were idiosyncratically related to each other, both would lose their value. Similarly, 'core competences' (Prahalad and Hamel 1990) belong to a firm's core in the sense that they provide a competitive advantage because the firm performs these activities better than other firms do, but they may be contestable and therefore not part of the core as it is defined here.

8 Note that *ancillary*, as used here, means competences that are not part of the firm's idiosyncratically synergistic core, and not competences that are ancillary to the production of a particular good or service. Competences that are central to the production of a given good or service might nevertheless be ancillary to any firm, or indeed, to all firms.

9 Either as an input or as a final product.

10 But, as will be shown, transaction costs that are unfavourable to one firm may be advantageous to other firms.

11 Langlois (1992) provides a more extensive explanation of dynamic transaction costs.

12 Of course, it is also possible that the outcome may be the development of two vertically integrated firms if the second firm to use a competence decides to develop its own internal capacity because the transaction costs of purchasing from outsiders outweigh the costs of duplicating the competence.

13 'Routines', as Nelson and Winter put it (1982: 124) 'are the skills of an organization'. In the course of its development, a firm acquires a 'repertoire of routines' that derives from its activities over the years. These skills refer to the abilities of the workforce and of the firm's physical capital, but they also include its organization – how the activities of the machines and people are linked together. Indeed, 'skills, organization, and technology are intimately intertwined in a functioning routine, and it is difficult to say exactly where one aspect ends and another begins' (Nelson and Winter 1982: 104).

14 The effects of technological change on an existing environment are discussed in Saviotti and Metcalfe (1991) and Dosi and Metcalfe (1991).

REFERENCES

Alchian, A. and Woodward, S. (1988) 'The Firm is Dead; Long Live the Firm: A Review of Oliver E. Williamson's *The Economic Institutions of Capitalism*', *Journal of Economic Literature* 26: 65–79.

Amit, R. and Schoemaker P. J. H. (1993) 'Strategic Assets and Organizational Rent', *Strategic Management Journal* 14: 33–46.

Barney, J. (1991) 'Firm Resources and Sustained Competitive Advantage', *Journal of Management* 17: 99–120.

Chandler, A. D. (1977) *The Visible Hand: The Managerial Revolution in American Business*, Cambridge, Mass.: The Belknap Press of Harvard University Press.

Chandler, A. D. (1990) *Scale and Scope: The Dynamics of Industrial Capitalism*, Cambridge, Mass.: The Belknap Press of Harvard University Press.

Cheung, S. N. S. (1983) 'The Contractual Nature of the Firm', *Journal of Law and Economics* 26 (April): 386–405.

Conner, K. R. (1991) 'A Historical Comparison of Resource-based Theory and Five Schools of Thought within Industrial Organization Economics: Do We Have a New Theory of the Firm?', *Journal of Management* 17: 121–54.

Dosi, G. and Metcalfe, J. S. (1991) 'On Some Notions of Irreversibility in Economics', in P. P. Saviotti and J. S. Metcalfe (eds) *Evolutionary Theories of Economic and Technological Change: Present Status and Future Prospects*, Chur, Switzerland: Harwood Academic Publishers.

Gilson, R. J. and Roe, M. J. (1993) 'Understanding the Japanese Keiretsu: Overlaps between Corporate Governance and Industrial Organization', *Yale Law Journal* 102: 871–906.

Hart, O. D. (1989) 'An Economist's Perspective on the Theory of the Firm', *Columbia Law Review* 89: 1757–74.

Hayek, F. A. (1945) 'The Use of Knowledge in Society', *American Economic Review* 35: 519–30.

Kay, J. (1993) *The Foundation of Competitive Success*, Oxford: Oxford University Press.

Lancaster, K. (1971) *Consumer Demand: A New Approach*, New York: Columbia University Press.

Langlois, R. N. (1992) 'Transaction-Cost Economics in Real Time', *Industrial and Corporate Change* 1: 99–127.

Langlois, R. N. and Robertson, P. L. (1989) 'Explaining Vertical Integration: Lessons from the American Automobile Industry', *Journal of Economic History* 49: 361–75.

Langlois, R. N. and Robertson, P. L. (1992) 'Networks and Innovation in a Modular System: Lessons from the Microcomputer and Stereo Component Industries', *Research Policy* 21: 297–313.

Langlois, R. N. and Robertson, P. L. (1995) *Firms, Markets, and Economic Change: The Dynamics of Institutional Transformation*, London and New York: Routledge.

Leijonhufvud, A. (1986) 'Capitalism and the Factory System', in R. N. Langlois (ed.) *Economics as a Process: Essays in the New Institutional Economics*, New York: Cambridge University Press.

Levin, R. C., Klevorick, A., Richard, R., Nelson, R. R. and Winter, S. G. (1987) 'Appropriating the Returns from Industrial R&D', *Brookings Papers on Economic Activity* 3: 783–831.

Mahoney, J. T. and Pandian, J. R. (1992) 'The Resource-based View within the Conversation of Strategic Management', *Strategic Management Journal* 13 (June): 363–80.

Moore, J. (1992) 'The Firm as a Collection of Assets', *European Economic Review* 36: 493–507.

Nelson, R. R. and Winter, S. G. (1982) *An Evolutionary Theory of Economic Change*, Cambridge, Mass.: Harvard University Press.

Peteraf, M. A. (1993) 'The Cornerstones of Competitive Advantage: A Resource-based View', *Strategic Management Journal* 14: 179–91.

Porter, M. E. (1980) *Competitive Strategy*, New York: The Free Press.

Porter, M. E. (1985) *Competitive Advantage*, New York: The Free Press.

Prahalad, C. K. and Hamel, G. (1990) 'The Core Competence of the Corporation', *Harvard Business Review* May–June: 79–91.

Prescott, E. and Visscher, M. (1980) 'Organizational Capital', *Journal of Political Economy* 88: 446–61.

Richardson, G. B. (1972) 'The Organisation of Industry', *Economic Journal* 82: 883–96.

Robertson, P. L. and Alston, L. J. (1992) 'Technological Choice and the Organization of Work in Capitalist Firms', *Economic History Review* 45: 330–49.

Saviotti, P. P. and Metcalfe, J. S. (1991) 'Present Development and Trends in Evolutionary Economics', in P. P. Saviotti and J. S. Metcalfe (eds) *Evolutionary Theories of Economic and Technological Change: Present Status and Future Prospects*, Chur, Switzerland: Harwood Academic Publishers.

Schumpeter, J. A. (1934) *The Theory of Economic Development*, Cambridge, Mass.: Harvard University Press.

Silver, M. (1984) *Enterprise and the Scope of the Firm*, London: Martin Robertson.

Teece, D. J. (1986a) 'Firm Boundaries, Technological Innovation, and Strategic Management', in L. G. Thomas (ed.) *The Economics of Strategic Planning*, Lexington, Mass.: D. C. Heath.

Teece, D. J. (1986b) 'Profiting from Technological Innovation: Implications for Integration, Collaboration, Licensing, and Public Policy', *Research Policy* 15: 285–305.

Williamson, O. E. (1985) *The Economic Institutions of Capitalism*, New York: The Free Press.

6

STRATEGIC IMPLICATIONS OF BUSINESS PROCESS RE-ENGINEERING

Bo Eriksen and Raphael Amit

INTRODUCTION

While business process re-engineering (BPR)[1] has received substantial attention from management practitioners (Hammer 1990, Hammer and Champy 1993), its effectiveness remains unclear. A recent article in *The Economist* (2 July 1994, p. 6) suggests that up to 85 per cent of the attempts to re-engineer fail. The causes for this failure include organizational resistance to BPR, management's non-commitment to BPR, and the failure to implement proper incentive systems.

In contrast to the more common functional organization in which tasks are carried out sequentially by separate functional units, BPR emphasizes work in cross-functional teams which handle a variety of tasks within a given business process, concurrently. Proponents of BPR suggest that organization in cross-functional teams delivers radical improvements in productivity and in the ability of firms to customize their offerings to specific customer needs. These improvements arise because cross-functional teams are able to achieve better communication, cooperation and learning.

Compaq Computer's move from assembly-line production into manufacturing by three-person multi-task teams (or work cells) illustrates the benefits of BPR. Each work cell prepares the subassemblies (motherboard, disk drives, etc.), assembles and tests the computers. Whereas production-line problems slow down work for everyone on the line, a cell problem affects only that team's production, thereby improving the firm's level of overall productivity. This move has resulted in a 23 per cent increase in worker productivity and a 16 per cent increase in output per square foot of factory floor as compared to assembly-line production (Levin 1994).

Further, production in work cells allowed Compaq to move towards 'made-to-order' manufacturing: the ability to customize each computer to the buyer's exact needs. Such a move increases profitability because of: the reduction of inventory holding costs; the elimination of product obsolescence (crucial in an industry with product life-cycles as short as six months); the reduction of retailers' returns of unsold merchandise; improvement of the firm's responsiveness to changing

97

market conditions; and the increased product demand due to the firm's ability to offer an infinite variety of computer configurations at rock-bottom costs.

A re-engineered organizational form contributes to cost reduction and reduced cycle time. For example, instead of subdividing work into specialized tasks for its invoice maintenance system, the Ford Motor Company simplified its system by merging a number of tasks and thereby reducing its costs dramatically (Davenport and Short 1990, Hammer 1990). Chrysler's new-product development is now done by cross-functional teams, instead of dividing this process into several separate phases carried out in sequence by design, engineering, manufacturing and marketing functions (*Business Week*, 20 December 1993). The designers, industrial engineers, and production and marketing professionals now work together to solve problems concurrently, and the new-product development cycle has dropped from five years to three years, thereby reducing the market uncertainty faced by Chrysler. The new Chrysler models, such as the Neon, are of a higher quality and better match consumer demands.

While the internal benefits of BPR are indeed very substantial, there is a range of strategic issues that relate to identifying the circumstances whereby the benefits of BPR exceed the costs associated with such a management system. Thus, we begin in the next section of this chapter by clarifying what business process re-engineering actually means, by comparing it to the traditional functional organization.

In the following section, we proceed to examine a range of issues related to identifying and exploiting the core business processes of the organization. It is important to identify the factors that determine the dimensions of competition at the industry level, and to identify what differentiates an individual firm from its competitors. We argue that organizing around business processes should exploit and enhance the firm's existing competitive advantage and create a new source of competitive advantage for the firm – its organizational form. Because the process of accomplishing this change is costly, the benefits of re-engineering have to exceed the costs.

Since business process re-engineering relies heavily on cross-functional teamwork, the incentive and monitoring instruments are likely to change character. With a more complex work process comes an increase in the difficulty of monitoring and in the cost of providing efficient incentives. We will address the incentive and monitoring problems through the lenses of organizational economics in a third section.

In the last section of the chapter, we draw some implications for the formulation and implementation of business strategies. We argue that business process re-engineering may add value if the firm's key strategic assets are enhanced.

DIFFERENCES BETWEEN FUNCTIONAL AND BPR ORGANIZATIONS

A functional structure and a re-engineered organization differ considerably in their approaches to a sequential production process. In a functional organization, each function carries out tasks separately. Cooperation between functions is difficult because only one function can work effectively on a problem, which may also influence other functions. A good metaphor for this issue is that of 'throwing the work over the wall'; a function completes its task, then throws the intermediate product 'over the wall' to the next function (e.g. in designing a new car, the designers throw their blueprints over to engineering). If a problem is found with the intermediate product, it is 'thrown back over the wall' to the previous function. Under some circumstances, this may be highly inefficient as compared to a cross-functional team which might have cooperatively solved the problem in the first place.

Since the re-engineered organization solves problems concurrently, there is minimal loss of information as compared to the more traditional functional organization, where communication must cross departmental boundaries. Adjustments are made faster in the BPR organization because it is easier for employees to cooperate with each other; such cooperation can increase each team's efficiency by eliminating costly errors and increasing the rate of intra-organizational learning.

In a typical functional organization, each major activity is grouped separately,[2] usually composed of specialists: a product development department might consist solely of industrial designers, and a marketing department might consist solely of MBAs with marketing majors. However, the re-engineered organization carries out business processes with cross-functional teams. A team consisting of people from marketing, production, industrial engineering and industrial design might carry out new-product development.

A BPR organization reduces, or even eliminates, the traditional hierarchy, because vertical transmission of information is no longer required. The BPR organization is therefore flatter than traditional organizations, as each team is empowered to handle all tasks previously handled by middle managers. There are fewer controls in a BPR organization, since there are fewer measurable outputs in the value chain; less monitoring is exercised, because it is more difficult to identify each individual's contribution to the value-added process. Essentially, it is up to the team members to monitor each other.

In designing the functional organization, the focus is on specialization and efficiency rather than coordination.[3] It is more difficult to coordinate activities as an organization becomes more specialized, and the loss of (potentially valuable) information reduces the effectiveness of the functional organization. Even without loss of information, the increased complexity of the information reduces the effectiveness of a specialized structure, because the cost of communicating such information rises.[4]

The different ways in which BPR and functional organizational modes produce and process information account for much of the difference between them. Business processes can be viewed as firm-specific, *information-based* modes of deploying resources; BPR's value, partially, lies in the fact that specialized information may be used more effectively, thereby increasing productivity and profitability.

Activity coordination, problems of standardization, and BPR

Organizations may coordinate activities in a number of ways. Mintzberg (1983: 5) lists five coordinating mechanisms: mutual adjustment, direct supervision, standardization of input skills, standardization of work processes and standardization of outputs. The more differentiated an organization is, the more it needs to rely on standardization as a central design parameter. If standardization is not adopted, the costs of coordination are likely to increase faster than linearly as the number of activities increases.[5]

However, a more standardized organization loses more in terms of flexibility and adaptability.[6] Standardizing input skills leads to lost abilities in tasks outside the area of specialization and an inability to adapt to changing circumstances.

Standardization of work processes leads to information losses, because the organization will fail to capture certain types of information (mostly non-standard information). An example of this is when an organization has a routine that says: if X_i happens, then do Y_i. However, if X_i is a weak or complex signal about what is happening, the bureaucratic routine will be an inadequate response, and may lead to the wrong action.

The standardization of outputs is the sacrifice of variety for low-cost production. This may be appropriate in some cases, but increasingly, variety *and* low cost seem to be what consumers demand. For example, the Italian clothing firm Benetton has managed to achieve variety at low cost through close integration of sales, logistics, design and production in a flexible manufacturing and distribution system (see e.g. Baden-Fuller and Stopford 1992).

Mutual adjustment is relied on more greatly where an organization's functions become more interdependent, as in a BPR organization. The work processes are based on teamwork, and employees' skills need to be more general. Workers spend more time communicating with each other; this decreases the need to standardize work processes, since each worker knows more about what the others are doing. This makes the team more adaptable, and, consequently, their output can be customized to a greater degree.

Costs of BPR

It is not without costs to adopt BPR. In particular, the costs associated with the BPR form of organization relate to:

(a) *The resource constraints.* Individuals have a limited amount of available time (or effort). They must choose either to work on a particular task and increase output, or communicate with others and devote their effort to teamwork (cooperation). This reality will likely increase the number of functions and activities that need to be coordinated. Further, it is a cost in itself for individuals to switch between teamwork and individual work; it is analogous to the set-up cost incurred each time a machine tool must be reprogrammed.

(b) *Sunk costs.* These costs associated with BPR include: computer hardware and software, cross-functional training of employees, and investments in changing production equipment. Re-engineering may demand the development of new complementary resources and capabilities, a process both costly and irreversible, as well as commitment.

(c) *Agency costs* that emerge from moral hazard in teams. These will be discussed in the next section.

Table 6.1 sums up the key differences between traditional types of organization and the BPR organization.

Table 6.1 Comparison between the BPR organization and traditional types of organization

	Principal coordination mechanisms	Effects	Costs
'Traditional' organization	Standardization of skills, work processes or outputs	Low flexibility	Lost information (opportunity costs)
		Slower reaction to external changes	
		Little adaptability	
		Low production cost	
'BPR' organization	Mutual adjustment	High flexibility, adaptability and faster reaction	Sunk costs
			Resource constraints
		Cost savings due to leveraging of complementary assets	Switching costs
			Moral hazard costs

IDENTIFYING AND EXPLOITING CORE BUSINESS PROCESSES

What are business processes?

We will define business processes as organizational routines, procedures and mechanisms that transform a set of inputs into outputs. Examples include new-product development, manufacturing and customer service. A firm may consist of any number of such distinct processes, each of which may incorporate several different activities: product development, for example, can be divided into market research, product design, product testing, prototype manufacturing, production engineering, and so on. Business processes can be thought of as a set of 'intermediate goods' generated by the firm in order to:

(a) increase productivity of resources;
(b) reduce uncertainty in production and marketing;
(c) save time;
(d) reduce costs; and
(e) improve product quality.

Business processes are developed over time and are often referred to as 'organizational capabilities'.

How do managers decide which processes are important in their business? Clearly these depend on industry characteristics and the firm's overall market strategy. Davenport (1993) suggests that the relevant business processes should match the organization's resources and capabilities. This suggestion would associate business process re-engineering with the literature on the core competence of the firm (Prahalad and Hamel 1990) and the strategy literature known as the resource-based view of the firm (e.g. Wernerfelt 1984; Amit and Schoemaker 1993; Schoemaker and Amit 1994; Dierickx and Cool 1989, 1990).

Strategic industry factors (SIFs) and strategic assets (SAs)

Business processes represent an approach to *organizing* the deployment of the firm's resources. They do not in and of themselves provide information about which resources the firm should develop, and how and where they should be deployed. We argue that managers need to identify the *strategic industry factors* (SIFs) of the industries where it competes and the firm's *strategic assets* (SAs), in order to identify and define key business processes. Then, the problem becomes one of identifying how *the mode of organization* can *enhance* the productivity of the firm's SAs.

SIFs and SAs as concepts were first suggested by Amit and Schoemaker (1993). Due to sunk costs, first-mover advantages, economies of scale, scope, experience, small numbers, bounded rationality and other friction forces, industries may exhibit, at any point in time, uneven distributions of economic rent (see Williamson 1975 or Yao 1988). To outside observers, the industry in question exhibits *strategic industry factors*. These factors (required resources and capabilities that are subject to market failures) are determined at a market level, as the result of complex interactions between competitors, exogenous shocks, customer preferences, regulators, technological innovation, and so on. When examined *ex post*, they have become the prime determinants of economic rents for industry participants. This view is consistent with Ghemawat (1991) who suggests that one may classify industries in terms of the 'strategic factors that drive competition in them by virtue of dominating the structure of sunk costs incurred in the course of competition'. SIFs, in this context, are characterized by their proneness to market failures and subsequent asymmetric distribution over firms. It is important to recognize that SIFs are industry-specific, and that the relevant set of strategic industry factors changes and cannot be predicted with certainty *ex ante*.[7]

The existence of SIFs implies that firms cannot instantly adjust their stocks of *strategic assets*. These assets are firm-specific resources and capabilities that (a) are difficult to trade and imitate; (b) are scarce, durable, and have few substitutes; (c) have returns that are appropriable to the firm, they complement each other, they are specialized to the firm, and (d) exhibit overlap with present and future SIFs. These necessary (but not sufficient) characteristics may confer a firm with a sustainable competitive advantage (see Dierickx and Cool 1989, 1990; Amit and Schoemaker 1993). SAs are more difficult to identify than SIFs because they are idiosyncratic to the firm and often hidden deeply in the firm's administrative systems, culture, and technological and market know-how.

The challenge facing a firm's managers is to identify, *ex ante*, a set of strategic assets as grounds for establishing the firm's sustainable competitive advantage, and thereby generate *organizational rents*. These are economic rents that stem from the organization's resources and capabilities, and that can be appropriated by the organization (rather than any single factor). This requires managers to identify the present set of strategic industry factors as well as to assess the possible sets of SIFs that may prevail in the future. Also, decisions on the further development of existing and new strategic assets – those that are most likely to contribute to the creation and protection of economic rents – need to be made. Not every firm will succeed with its targeted set of *SAs*, as their applicability and relevance ultimately hinges on the complex interaction referred to above. Examples of possible SAs include: technological capability; fast product-development cycles; brand management; control of, or superior access to, distribution channels; a favourable cost structure; buyer–seller relationships; the firm's installed user base; its R&D capability; the firm's service organization; its reputation; its information technologies and so forth.

SIFs are those factors which are required to 'play the game' in the industry at any given point in time, roughly analogous to the Caves and Porter (1977) concept of mobility barriers. SIFs are industry-specific factors characterized by their proneness to market failure. Firms in the industry vary in their stocks of SIFs; such variations could occur if, for instance, a firm has some kind of first-mover advantage, well illustrated in games of sequential entry.[8]

Many possible sources of SIFs have been suggested by the literature on mobility barriers (McGee and Thomas 1986). These include such factors as market strategies (e.g. specialization to specific users and user technologies; choice of distribution channels; geographic coverage), industry supply characteristics (e.g. manufacturing technology; R&D expenditure) and firm characteristics (e.g. degree of vertical integration and diversification).

Investments in SIFs are (at least partly) irrecoverable, and therefore have an entry deterring value. This is a collective stock of capital for incumbents, and makes for increased returns to investment in the industry. Such returns are distributed unevenly between industry firms, depending on each firm's individual stocks of SIFs and the degree of overlap between SIFs and a firm's SAs.

As already noted, strategic assets are usually more difficult to identify than SIFs because they are idiosyncratic to the firm and often manifested as capabilities, 'hidden assets' deeply embedded in the firm's administrative systems, culture and technological and market know-how. They take time to develop, often emerging through complex processes of deploying the firm's resources. True SAs are scarce, durable, difficult to trade or imitate and strictly firm-specific; SAs must overlap with SIFs, as well. Furthermore, SAs often complement each other. Finally, the firm must be able to appropriate the returns from its SAs if economic rent is to be earned.

Resources and capabilities are sources of strategic assets. SAs can be found in resources such as brand names, proprietary technological knowledge and patents on products or processes. SAs can also be found in capabilities such as effective inventory management, adaptability to changing markets or technologies, rapid new-product development cycles and R&D capabilities.

Because each firm has access to a different set of resources and capabilities, differences in economic rent arise between firms in an industry. Although the strategic group in which a firm competes dictates the SIFs, each firm has some degree of freedom in choosing the SAs on which to base its competitive strategy. The managerial task of identifying, developing and deploying an appropriate mix of strategic assets is difficult, due to uncertainty in the industry and the complexity of all relevant factors.

Turning business processes into strategic assets (SAs)

Business process re-engineering can be viewed as a way to improve the productivity of a firm's resources. Effective BPR requires the identification of different business processes, or functional areas. To integrate these business processes effectively, an organizational form must be found so that SAs are being deployed effectively. The focal point of business process re-engineering is in the way that the firm's internal organization and product-market strategy are linked, which turns business processes into SAs.

Timeliness of designs, efficient distribution and retailing channels, and cost-effective, high-quality manufacturing are key SIFs in the fashion industry. The Benetton system meets these demands for effective competition in the fashion industry.

The Italian clothing manufacturer Benetton is organized around a few core business processes in a vertically disintegrated manufacturing and distribution system (see e.g. Jarillo and Martinez 1988). Although the firm does not manufacture anything itself, it chooses the manufacturing technology its suppliers use. Among Benetton's eighty or so suppliers, around 10 per cent are discontinued each year for failure to live up to expectations. By using a large number of suppliers, Benetton becomes more flexible, and is able to make changeovers quickly.

The key business processes in the Benetton system are manufacturing, logistics/distribution and clothes design. The design activities are integrated with manufacturing by extensive use of CAD–CAM technology.[9] Benetton is able to keep up with the latest trends by monitoring sales in selected stores around the world through point-of-sale registration systems. This allows for better matching of production plans with demand conditions. At the same time, the firm maintains only a few places of inventory which are completely automated. Goods are shipped directly from the central warehouses to shops around the world. This makes the system effective in terms of low inventory costs and timeliness of delivery. The software Benetton uses to manage sales, inventory and production is a strategic asset, since it is all proprietary.

The Benetton system is a good example of both a 'virtual corporation' (Davidow and Malone 1992) and a re-engineered firm. The three business processes are each supported by the proper information technology and organizational structure, the focal point being the integration of the functional areas of design, manufacturing and logistics/distribution. The key to the system is the extensive use of information technology to integrate different functional areas; information technology is what links the firm's internal organization to its product-market strategy.

The organizational form of the Benetton system *enhances* SAs. The point-of-sale registration systems allow the firm to make use of timely market information, and thus better keep up with consumer trends. By integrating design, manufacturing and logistics, and by using high-tech production, distribution and design equipment, the firm lowers its inventory cost and speeds up delivery. By substituting labour with capital, the firm thus makes production costs less sensitive to labour costs (in an industry where low-cost production in the Third World is the norm). In a sense, each business process becomes a core capability for Benetton, and thereby the business processes become strategic assets.

The key to identifying the firm's core business processes is understanding, *ex ante*, the strategic industry factors and the firm-specific strategic assets. Core business processes should be designed to enhance existing SAs. Thus, business process re-engineering *leverages* complementary resources and capabilities.

One firm's risky structure

The hearing-aid industry is a relatively research-intensive industry, dominated by large firms such as Siemens from Germany. In this industry, R&D capability and technological knowledge are required to compete effectively. A key strategic asset is differential R&D capability. The Danish firm Oticon, which develops and manufactures hearing aids, has been quite successful at this in recent years. Oticon's managers found that the firm could not match the financial resources of the industry's giant firms. These could easily out-spend the comparatively small Danish firm. Therefore, they needed to identify a way to increase their differential R&D capabilities; that is, they had to become more innovative than their competitors.

Oticon has adopted what it calls a 'spaghetti-organization' (named after the look of apparent chaos that cooked spaghetti has). At its headquarters, there are no functional departments and employees are fully empowered to decide upon the work they wish to undertake and in what team they wish to work. This has boosted not only innovation, an example of which is the introduction of a line of brightly coloured children's hearing aids, but has also increased profits substantially. Consequently, Oticon is now considered to be one of the leading producers of hearing aids worldwide.

For outsiders, Oticon's organization is extremely difficult to understand and, by implication, even more difficult to copy since many of its competitors are large, diversified businesses where decisions follow bureaucratic routines. The Oticon example shows how the organizational form can enhance a strategic asset, and become a strategic asset in and of itself due to competitors' inability to imitate the organizational form.

However, Oticon has chosen a very risky strategy: the apparent chaos may be more than apparent. Management could easily lose control of its strategic direction as well as its day-to-day operations. Secondly, it becomes more difficult to implement strategy due to the moral hazard problem that may arise in team-work situations.

THE INCENTIVE PROBLEM IN IMPLEMENTING BPR

When managers have identified the key business processes in the firm, and have decided on how to structure the organization around these, to leverage complementary resources and capabilities, they are faced with the challenge of actually implementing BPR.

There are several problems to implementing BPR, such as training and overcoming organizational resistance and fear. A principal difficulty, however, is the need to redesign incentive systems that will induce employees to provide their best effort once the systems and procedures are in place. This task is by no means trivial. Since direct supervision and other forms of monitoring become more difficult, managers have to rely upon more efficient incentive mechanisms (see also Holmström 1982).

Designing efficient incentives in an organization that emphasizes work in cross-functional teams is challenging since it is very difficult to obtain meaningful measures about individual performance. Unlike the functional structure, there are few intermediate outputs that can be measured (such as number of units produced in department X by worker i). The only measurable output is that of the team, and individual performance cannot be deduced from this statistic. Employees find it easier to free-ride on each other when their actions become less observable; this results in agency costs emerging from moral hazard in teams. For example, if an employee receives an incentive bonus which is a fixed proportion of the team's output, a shirker will still earn the same *proportion* of the team's smaller output; since he or she exerts no effort by shirking, that shirker's earnings increase in net utility terms.

Team theory and principal-agent literature stress the design of incentive mechanisms and the monitoring of employees as important concerns. However, little attention has been given to the design of incentive schemes for teams. In an early contribution, Alchian and Demsetz (1972) asserted that employees have an incentive to shirk where each employee's contribution is difficult to observe, and that the solution is to appoint an employee to monitor team production. In order to ensure a proper incentive to monitor the other workers, the monitor should also be the residual claimant of the firm.

However, this model does not inform us about what to do when monitoring becomes less effective, as with re-engineering. As monitoring becomes less effective, the principal must rely more on providing the proper incentives; Holmström (1982) argued that the principal's role, rather than monitoring, involves enforcing and making credible the incentive contracts.

In his analysis of the free-rider problem, Holmström (1982: 325) showed that, 'under certainty group incentives alone can remove the free-rider problem', and further noted that 'group incentives can also work well under uncertainty, but their effectiveness will be limited if there are many agents and if the agents are risk averse'. Here, Holmström accordingly suggests competition among agents so that the principal can extract the free-rider rents.

The merging of different functions significantly alters the firm's information, and accordingly, its incentive structure.[10] As the work process grows more complex, difficulties will arise in ascertaining the efforts of individual employees; this also holds for monitoring within a team, as individual members will have difficulty identifying who works hard and who shirks. Thus, employees on teams can free-ride, and must either be monitored more or given effective incentives not to shirk. This situation is true in the functional organization also; however, the potential effects in the BPR organization are much larger, and incentives based on individual effort are ineffective here.

Employees' incentives must be based on the output of the team; such payment schemes are incentive-compatible. This will likely be more costly, because under such a scheme, employees must be compensated not only for their private information on the team's effort, but also their information about their own individual contribution. Each employee takes on a risk under such a scheme because their salary depends in part on their fellow team members, and for this it costs more to compensate them.

In summary, we find that in order to implement BPR successfully, managers must offer incentive contracts based on team productivity. Employees must be compensated for the additional risks they run, thereby making BPR more costly for owners. Thus, the benefits of implementing a BPR organization must be weighed against the additional costs necessary to provide employees with greater incentives.

The point of adapting the incentive systems to match a team-based structure is to *augment* the team's activities. By tying individual pay to the team's performance, it is expected that employees will be motivated to provide extra effort towards improving the team's performance.

CONCLUSION

In this chapter, we have discussed business process re-engineering and attempted to link it to formulation and implementation of business strategies. We argued that business processes should be centred on the strategic industry factors (SIFs) and the firm's strategic assets (SAs) that the firm controls. The central aspect of BPR is to leverage the firm's portfolio of SIFs and SAs by taking advantage of complementarities between these. Effective management of these complementarities will enhance the firm's competitive advantage.

By focusing on the firm's SAs as the key to understanding its competitive advantage, and on business processes as ways of linking the firm's SAs in a more effective way, we have developed a new insight on core competences. We understand core competences as business processes that link SAs.

We propose that managers first analyse the industry and the firm in order to determine the past, present and future SIFs and SAs. Next we propose that linkages between SIFs and SAs be identified in order to reveal how the firm can get the most leverage out of its portfolio of SAs. Such an analysis may, for example, reveal linkages between product design, manufacturing and distribution, which could become the bases of the firm's core processes. The Benetton system is a good example of an organizational structure linked to its competitive strategy.

We argued that a central implementation problem is designing new incentive systems. As the information structure in the firm changes as a consequence of the redesign of work, the incentive systems must also be changed. Emphasis should be placed on team-based incentives instead of incentives that compensate only individual effort. If incentives are directed towards individual performance, cooperation and coordination in the team structure may be severely constrained.

If managers are able to link the internal organization of the firm effectively to the competitive strategy of the firm, it may indeed improve performance substantially. However, the process is difficult, and the costs and benefits are not always apparent.

NOTES

1 Business process re-engineering is known under many synonyms. Examples include: *organizing around core business processes, the re-engineered organization, process innovation, business process redesign.*
2 By major activity, we mean a basic organizational unit, such as marketing, manu-facturing or R&D.
3 This 'Ford mass-production' approach to organization design refers back to Alfred Taylor's time and motion studies, and argues that a task should be broken down to its smallest possible sub-tasks, i.e. maximum specialization.
4 In fact, the information costs are one of the major causes of declining returns to scale in specialized organizations.
5 For example, if each function in a functionally organized firm communicates through the top manager, the communication costs are likely to rise $n-1$ times the number of functions, equal to the number of bilateral communication lines. In the BPR organization, if each function communicates directly with the others, commu-nication costs are likely to rise by $(n-1)n/2$ times the number of functions, equal to the number of bilateral communication lines.
6 In evolutionary economics, a standard way of representing this trade-off is as a trade-off between static and dynamic efficiency (Nelson and Winter 1982). In resource-dependency theory, the terms 'efficiency' and 'effectiveness' are usually employed (Pfeffer and Salancik 1978), the former being equal to static efficiency and the latter being equal to dynamic efficiency.
7 As Dierickx and Cool pointed out, even though it may not be possible to identify *ex ante* the relevant set of *SIFs*, one can usually screen out those factors that are *not* strategic.
8 For example, in a duopoly Stackelberg game with competition in quantities, the first mover sets a higher output (corresponding to the monopoly output), and earns higher profits than the second mover.
9 CAD–CAM stands for computer-aided design and computer-aided manufacturing.
10 The costs of *monitoring* the workers' effort are likely to increase when the re-engineered organizational form is adopted. Monitoring costs increase because individuals performing increasingly interdependent and non-standardized tasks are more difficult, and hence more costly, to monitor.

REFERENCES

Alchian, A. A. and Demsetz, H. (1972) 'Production, Information Costs and Economic Organization', *American Economic Review* 63: 777–95.
Amit, R. and Schoemaker, P. (1993) 'Strategic Assets and Organizational Rent', *Strategic Management Journal* 14: 33–46.
Baden-Fuller, C. and Stopford, J. M. (1992) *Rejuvenating the Mature Business*, London: Routledge.
Business Week (1993), 'The Horizontal Corporation', 20 December.
Caves, R. and Porter, M. E. (1977) 'From Entry Barriers to Mobility Barriers', *Quarterly Journal of Economics* 91: 241–61.

Davenport, T. H. (1993) *Process Innovation*, Cambridge, Mass.: Harvard Business School Press.

Davenport, T. H. and Short, J. E. (1990) 'The New Industrial Engineering: Information Technology and Business Process Redesign', *Sloan Management Review* Summer: 11–27.

Davidow, W. H. and Malone, M. S. (1992) *The Virtual Corporation*, New York: Harper Business.

Dierickx, I. and Cool, K. (1989) 'Asset Stock Accumulation and Sustainability of Competitive Advantage', *Management Science* 35: 1504–14.

Dierickx, I. and Cool, K. (1990) 'A Resource-based Perspective on Competitive Strategy', Mimeo, INSEAD, September, Paris.

Ghemawat, P. (1991) 'Resources and Strategy: An IO Perspective', Mimeo, May, Harvard Business School.

Hammer, M. (1990) 'Reengineering Work: Automate, Obliterate', *Harvard Business Review* July–August: 104–12.

Hammer, M. and Champy, J. (1993) *Reengineering the Corporation*, New York: Harper Business.

Holmström, B. (1982) 'Moral Hazard in Teams', *Bell Journal of Economics* 13: 324–40.

Jarillo, J.-C. and Martinez, J. I. (1988) 'Benetton Spa', Harvard Business School Case 9–389–074.

Levin, D. (1994) 'Compaq Storms the PC Heights from its Factory Floor', *New York Times*, 13 November: 5.

McGee, J. and Thomas, H. (1986) 'Strategic Groups: Theory, Research and Taxonomy', *Strategic Management Journal* 7: 141–60.

Mintzberg, H. (1983) *Structures in Fives*, Englewood Cliffs, NJ: Prentice-Hall International.

Nelson, R. R. and Winter, S. G. (1982) *An Evolutionary Theory of Economic Change*, Cambridge, Mass.: The Belknap Press of Harvard University Press.

Pfeffer, J. and Salancik, G. (1978) *The External Control of Organizations*, Homewood, Ill.: Irwin.

Prahalad, C. K. and Hamel, G. (1990) 'The Core Competence of the Corporation', *Harvard Business Review* (May–June): 79–91.

Schoemaker, P. and Amit, R. (1994) 'Investment in Strategic Assets: Industry and Firm Level Perspectives', *Advances in Strategic Management* 10: 3–33.

Wernerfelt, B. (1984) 'A Resource-based View of the Firm', *Strategic Management Journal* 5: 171–80.

Williamson, O. E. (1975) *Markets and Hierarchies: Analysis and Antitrust Implications*, New York: The Free Press.

Yao, D. A. (1988) 'Beyond the Reach of the Invisible Hand: Impediments to Economic Activity, Market Failures, and Profitability', *Strategic Management Journal* 9: 59–70.

7

ANALYSING THE TECHNOLOGY BASE OF THE FIRM

A multi-dimensional resource and competence perspective

Jens Frøslev Christensen

INTRODUCTION

This chapter attempts to clarify the concept of the technology base of the firm (or, what may also be called the firm portfolio of assets for technological innovation) by bringing together two so far rather separated research traditions, the competence-based strategy literature and the literature on the dynamics and management of innovation and technical change.

The competence approach to analysing the firm and its potential competitive advantage has in recent years become a 'focusing device' for much of the strategy literature to change the primary focus of analysis from the product-market positions of the firm to the internal assets (resources, capabilities and competences) of the firm. The efforts, originally pioneered by Edith Penrose (1972), to develop a competence-based theory of the firm have explicitly addressed what has largely remained a 'black box' in conventional economic theory, namely the resources and capacities that constitute the quasi-stable basis of the firm's economic performance and direction of development. From her perspective 'a firm is more than an administrative unit; it is also a collection of productive resources the disposal of which between different uses and over time is determined by administrative decision' (p. 24). Thus, she sets the agenda for analysing the role and distinctive features of firm resources and competences as the foundation of firm growth. The competence literature from recent years has further penetrated the implications for the theory of the firm and strategic management (see especially Lippman and Rumelt 1982; Wernerfelt 1984; Barney 1986, 1991; Dierickx and Cool 1989; Conner 1991; Mahoney and Pandian 1992; Peteraf 1993), and empirical analysis from a competence perspective has been particularly occupied with the question of diversification (Chatterjee and Wernerfelt 1991, Montgomery and Hariharan 1991, Montgomery and Wernerfelt 1988, Teece *et al.* 1994).

The literature on *innovation and technical change* has shown a growing interest in studying the innovative dynamics at the level of the firm, focusing on path-dependent technological trajectories, learning and searching heuristics and the management of technology (for a broad overview see Adler 1989; Coombs, Saviotti and Walsh 1987; Dosi 1988; Freeman 1982; Tushman and Moore 1988). Much of this literature has directly or indirectly challenged the one-dimensional R&D perspective that for too long has dominated the academic and public conception of technical change. Within this perspective R&D is uncritically recognized as *the* functional and purely technical capacity for producing techno-logical innovation. The purpose of this chapter is to propose a framework for analysing the base of assets for technological innovation that is consistent with a Penrosian view of the firm and that draws on recent contributions from both the more general competence perspective and the innovation and technology perspective of the firm.

The argument of the chapter is based on the following premises. First, I make a distinction between resources that may be accessed at factor markets, and (technical) capabilities and (managerial) competences that have to be accumulated in-house. Second, I reject the one-dimensional view that identifies innovative assets with the level of R&D. There is not one but several generic categories of innovative assets which differ with respect to functional orientation, distinctive skills, organizational locus and strategic importance in a given context. Finally, these assets may be complementary and more or less co-specialized in the sense that the process of technological innovation requires the activation and coupling of different types of innovative asset, not just the mobilization of R&D resources in general. The technology base of the firm can be analysed as including not only a portfolio of innovative or technological capabilities (and resources), but also the competences in managing these capabilities (and their services) and developing new ones to assure the production of competitive new products and processes.

In the next section, I try to clarify the central analytical building-blocks in the competence theory of the firm: the firm assets as constituted by resources, capabilities and competences. The section furthermore discusses two central features of assets that have tended to be played down within the competence literature: the external (versus in-house) dimension, and the dynamic features of firm assets. In 'Assets for Technological Innovation' (p. 118), the more general conceptual framework is specified with respect to the technology base of the firm. Different categories of technological and innovative assets are identified, and the central role of inter-asset couplings in technological innovation is underlined. In 'The Strategic Significance of the Technology Base' (p. 124), important strategic dimensions of the technology base – especially its 'external fit' and coherence – are addressed. Finally, I provide a summary.

FIRM ASSETS:
RESOURCES, CAPABILITIES AND COMPETENCES

Resources and capacities

I shall suggest a distinction between resources, capabilities and competences. This subsection discusses the analytical distinction between resources and capacities (capabilities and competences); subsequently the distinction between capabilities and competences will be specified.

Usually, three general types of firm resources are identified: physical resources, financial resources and intangible resources. Physical resources (the firm's plant, its physical technology, raw materials, etc.) tend to have more limited flexibility with respect to use than the two other types. In contrast, financial resources are generally the most flexible of all resources, since they can be used to buy other types of resources. Intangible resources are much more difficult to delimit and value than physical and financial resources. Following Barney (1991) they include both *human resources* (training, experience, judgement, intelligence, relationships and insight of managers and workers in the firm) and *organizational capital resources* (a firm's reporting structure, planning, controlling and coordination systems, as well as informal relations within a firm and between a firm and its environment). These resources are dependent on specific people and their skills, but intangible resources may also include 'property assets' that are independent of specific people and may be (more or less) subject to legal protection (i.e. trade marks, reputation, patents, contracts and trade secrets) (see Hall 1992, 1993). Moreover, the existing products in the product portfolio of the firm constitute important resources which embody elements of both physical resources and intangible resources (as well as capabilities and competences, see below).

The present distinction between resources and capacities (competences/ capabilities) is similar to the distinction between resources and capabilities suggested by Grant (1991: 118–19):

> Resources are inputs into the production process – they are the basic unit of analysis . . . But, on their own, few resources are productive. Productive activity requires the cooperation and coordination of teams of resources. A capability is here taken to be the capacity for a team of resources to perform some task or activity. While resources are the source of a firm's capabilities, capabilities are the main source of its competitive advantage.

Competences/capabilities constitute the 'experience base' of the firm – and therefore have to be accumulated internally, whereas individual resources tend to be tradable at 'strategic factor markets' (Barney 1986). I shall use the term 'asset' to comprise both resources and competences/capabilities that possess strategic value to the firm.

To clarify the distinction on the basis of the tradability criteria, the conceptual delimitation suggested by Barney and Grant should be somewhat modified. First, the conception of intangible resources should only include resources which in principle are tradable, and that is clearly not the case with much of what Barney terms 'human resources' and 'organizational capital resources'. The team-based and experience-based human and organizational 'capital' I shall preferably consider part of the competence or capability concept, while individual skills and formal organizational procedures (but not informal relations) are tradable resources. Thus I stick to a narrower conception of resources than Barney's in order to discriminate between resources and competences/capabilities (which Barney does not). With respect to Grant's concept of resources, I disagree with his assertion that 'resources are inputs into the production process', and agree with Penrose's (1972: 25) formulation that only the services that the resources can render (and not the resources themselves) provide inputs into the production process. Finally, I disagree with the tendency in Grant's formulation to understand capabilities in terms of aggregated resources (a capability as a 'capacity for a team of resources'). A competence or capability cannot be reduced to a given number or combination of resources.[1]

Competences/capabilities are capacities for structuring and orienting clusters of resources – and especially their services – for productive purposes that potentially provide the firm with a competitive advantage. As Loasby (1994: 253) puts it, 'a collection of highly talented individuals does not automatically constitute an effective organization'. It must also involve a distinct capacity to set these resources in motion and direct their services for productive purposes. This capacity has two central features. First, it involves the internally accumulated 'stock' of experience in mobilizing (and possibly acquiring) and orienting these or similar resources for productive purposes. Such an experience-based capacity is precisely what makes the difference between a cluster of resources *per se* and a capability or competence. Second, this experience-based capacity is embedded in social teams (or networks of people) and not in discrete individual skills, even if individuals as entrepreneurs or 'champions' may be prime movers in building competences/capabilities.

The firm's products and their market positions are mostly much more visible and clearly identifiable than the resources and (especially) the capabilities and competences on which the product market positions are based. More generally, the competence view suggests that the firm's economic performance, its market orientation and its probable direction of diversification to a large extent are based on its resource and competence/capability profile (or, in short, asset profile).

Capacities: capabilities and competences

So far I have discussed competences and capabilities under a common heading as reflecting a capacity to structure and orient a cluster of resources for productive purposes. This capacity must integrate two constituent and complementary capacity dimensions, an organizational/managerial dimension (henceforth *managerial*) and a functional/technical dimension (henceforth *technical*).[2] The one cannot do without the other. Technical capacities necessarily involve managerial capacity to work, and likewise, managerial capacities cannot be thought of as existing *per se*, that is, as disconnected from one or more technical capacities. However, the trade-off balance between the two dimensions may vary greatly and this is underlined in the suggested distinction between capabilities and competences.

A capability is here defined as a lower-order functional or inter-functional, technical capacity to mobilize resources for productive activities. It reflects a team-based or sometimes network-based capacity, and the social context of co-operating people tends to be primarily located within the firm or a department within the firm. The boundary of a capability may sometimes, however, reach beyond the firm boundary and into inter-firm or other types of external relations. Capabilities, thus, refer to specialized capacities in which the technical dimension is dominating, while the managerial element is narrow in scope, in the sense that it deals exclusively with managing the particular capability and the services it can render (for example, project management and team-building).

A competence is a higher-order managerial capacity of the firm or corporate management to mobilize, harmonize and develop resources and capabilities to create value and competitive advantage. This involves an administrative dimension (designing and managing proper organizational structures and processes), an allocative dimension (deciding what to fund, develop and produce and how to price it) and a transactional dimension (deciding whether to 'make or buy', 'use or sell', or work in partnership).[3] Compared to the more specialized capabilities competences refer to more global domains (i.e. overall corporate management) in which the managerial dimension dominates relative to the technical dimension.

In the following I use the term 'asset' as a common denominator for resources (including products), capabilities and competences. Thus, the term 'asset' is used when it is indefinite, or not critical to the argument, whether the focus is on resources, capabilities or competences. Moreover, I use the term 'capacity' as a common denominator for capability and competence.

The internal and external dimensions of assets

Within the competence perspective it is mostly implicitly assumed that firm capacities not only are accumulated internally but also have a distinct introvert orientation. It should, however, be stressed that assets are the combined result of internal learning and 'absorptive learning' or import, that is, learning and buying in from external sources. Firms may possess a more or less elaborate capacity to absorb knowledge (about resources and capacities on the one hand, and opportunities on the other) from external sources (Cohen and Levinthal 1990). This 'absorptive capacity' represents the bridging between internal and external resources and capacities.[4]

The strength of a firm's absorptive learning capacity depends on (a) the strength of the firm's internal capacities, (b) the quality and relevance of the external knowledge or competence environment, and (c) the structure of relations between the firm and the external environment. One part of this structure concerns the firm's gatekeeper function that not only involves the scanning of relevant knowledge from data bases, the literature, conferences, and so on, but also the importing of knowledge of who has relevant capacities or knowledge, as rivals or partners. Another part of the external relations concerns the organization and management of formal or informal network relations.

Absorptive learning that adds strategic value to the firm may depend on privileged network relations to high-quality external knowledge sources such as lead-users or centres of excellence in relevant research fields. Capabilities which transcend firm boundaries are generally linked to network relations. The risk of breakdown in absorptive capacity is likely to be greater if it is based on privileged external relations rather than on gatekeeper scanning of 'public knowledge', since control over the external knowledge-suppliers tends to be weaker than control over the internal gatekeepers. On the other hand, absorptive capacity based on privileged external relations may provide knowledge of more strategic value than absorptive capacity based exclusively on 'public-knowledge' scanning since the former may provide access to critical external capabilities while the latter provides access to more codified and generally more widely or easily diffused knowledge.

Mostly, however, it would be wrong to assume that absorptive capacity is a distinct form of capacity that can be isolated from 'internal' capacities. In real life it is probably more relevant to assume that capacities possess more or less elaborate absorptive dimensions, and a very elaborate absorptive capacity presupposes strong 'internal' capacity (Cohen and Levinthal 1990).

The dynamics of assets

Within the 'standard' competence view it is generally assumed that distinctive firm capacities are given and that firm strategy should deal with the exploitation of these given capacities rather than with the creation of new ones (for an explicit example, see Kay 1993: 125–6). Recently, a 'dynamic capabilities approach' has been proposed that focuses attention on the mechanisms by which firms accumulate new assets and the forces that influence the rate and direction of these learning and searching processes (Markides and Williamson 1994; Sanchez, Heene and Thomas 1995; Teece and Pisano 1994; Teece et al. 1994).

The insights from both the 'dynamic capabilities' literature and the broader literature on organizational learning tend to be presented in quite robust – but also simplistic and too sharp – conceptual dichotomies of learning and competence dynamics: generally we see a distinction between reproductive dynamics and explorative dynamics.[5]

The reproductive dynamics of assets imply that given resources, capabilities and competences are exploited in such ways that these assets are basically reproduced or only developed incrementally within limited margins and a relatively short-to-medium time-horizon. Reproductive dynamics may either be replicative (corresponding to the notion of 'static routines' suggested by Teece *et al.* 1994) and serve to increase efficiency in existing trajectories and patterns of routines (i.e. in conventional experience-curve economies), or they may be incrementally innovative (i.e. in product or process development). The scope for innovation and improvements, however, remains limited and declining within a relatively short time-horizon. Reproductive dynamics tend to be based on *experiential (or experience-based) learning* that is strongly path-dependent. Learning by doing (Arrow 1962) and learning by using (Rosenberg 1982) are two articulations of such experiential learning.

The explorative dynamics of assets provide the long-term basis for competitive advantage by promoting innovation and creating new routines and capacities. Successful exploration presupposes competence (or powerful skills or luck) not only in mobilizing resources and capabilities for specific productive purposes, but also for learning and searching at the longer term which gives rise to new strategic options for the firm. This learning capacity is especially important with respect to strategic assets for innovation which we shall turn to in the next section. Compared to reproductive (or experiential) learning, explorative (or experimental) learning reflects a less path-dependent – and mostly also more chaotic – search process based on trial-and-error and characterized by the building of new competences and routines.

Managerial capacities involved in reproductive dynamics are likely to be more mechanistic, routine-based and narrow in scope than the managerial capacities involved in explorative dynamics (cf. the recent discussion under the heading of 'the learning organization' and the distinction between single-loop and double-loop learning, Agyris and Schön 1978). Moreover, while reproductive dynamics (and especially the replicative variant) may do without or have only weak absorptive capacity (including the ability to exploit existing external relations, such as user-relations), explorative dynamics generally depend strongly on elaborate absorptive capacity (including the ability to build new external relations).

Let me briefly sum up the conceptual reflections on capabilities and competences. Firm capacities constitute the firm's experience-based capacity to structure and orient a cluster of resources for productive services, and that may provide the firm with a competitive advantage. This capacity must integrate both a technical dimension and a managerial dimension. Two subcategories of capacities can be distinguished, capabilities in which the technical/functional element dominates and competences in which the organizational/managerial element dominates. While capabilities reflect more specialized functional domains, competences reflect broader managerial domains in the firm. Even if capabilities and competences may for some time rest on purely internal learning, mostly absorptive learning, possibly in partnership with external parties, is required to maintain, improve or create capacities. Finally, firm assets may be subject to different kinds of dynamics, from reproductive or incremental learning dynamics to explorative learning and searching dynamics.

ASSETS FOR TECHNOLOGICAL INNOVATION

To delimit more precisely the concept of assets for technological innovation, the present use of the notions of technology and technological innovation should first be explained. Following Metcalfe and Gibbons (1989: 154) technology signifies two complementary phenomena: first, products and production processes as artifacts or embodied knowledge and second, the corresponding knowledge, capability or competence (theoretical knowledge, practical skills, procedures and routines) which is directly or indirectly applied in the creation of products, services and production processes. Product and process technologies are the technologies that contribute directly to the development and production of products and services, while other technologies such as office, planning and budgeting technologies that are primarily linked to the broader firm infrastructure, may be termed 'support technologies', since they only indirectly contribute to product and process development.

Moreover, to identify what is here meant by 'technological innovation', I have to distinguish between 'technological resources' that are – more or less easily – accessible at the market or from the stock of public knowledge, and capacities for technological innovation that have to be developed internally and – to some extent – through privileged network relations with external parties. Technological resources that are easily accessible at the market (or from the stock of public knowledge) and at a competitive price are generally well documented and embodied in 'package solutions', licensed patents, components, machinery or software programs. Innovative capacities comprise technical capabilities and skills that are more 'tacit' and linked to internal experiential and experimental learning and searching. Only firms that possess a capacity for autonomous technology development can be technologically innovative *and* have a potential for earning above-normal returns on their innovative assets (cf. Barney 1986). That does not, however, imply that innovation is exclusively based on in-house knowledge-accumulation and problem-solving, only that innovation requires some internal innovative capacity (i.e. for product development) even if much of the knowledge and material resources required for implementing the innovation may be accessed from the market place. Generally a firm's technology strategy is strongly focused on acquiring or accumulating the technologies that have a direct bearing on the development of new products or processes. Thus, assets for technological innovation here refer to resources, capabilities and competences required for producing new or improved technologies and ultimately new products and processes.

The technology base of the firm

The resource and competence perspective on technological innovation has primarily been addressed in the management-of-technology literature, often under the heading 'the technology base of the firm'. To those who believe that the term 'technology base' is of recent date and exclusively linked to the management-of-technology literature, it may come as a surprise that Penrose (1972) had already coined the term in 1959:

> Each type of productive activity that uses machines, processes, skills, and raw materials that are all complementary and closely associated in the process of production we shall call a 'production base' or 'technological base' of the firm, regardless of the number or type of products produced. A firm may have several such bases.
>
> (p. 109)

> The significance of distinguishing such groupings lies in the fact that a movement into a new base requires a firm to achieve competence in some significantly different area of technology.
>
> (p. 110)

More recently Adler and Shenbar (1990: 26) have proposed a somewhat more elaborate definition of the technology base as reflecting an organization's

> ability to develop new products that meet current market needs, to manufacture these products using the appropriate process technologies, to develop or adapt new product and process technologies to meet projected future needs, and to respond promptly to unexpected technology moves by competitors and to unforeseen opportunities.

Compared to the early Penrose definition, Adler and Shenbar's definition recognizes the role of product technology and not only the production-related side of technology, and moreover they stress the *dynamic* competence dimension and not exclusively, as Penrose does, the resource and activity dimension of the technology base.

The recent revival of the 'technology base approach' has focused on the internal building and commercial exploitation of technological capacities defined in terms of 'technical disciplines', 'strategic technological areas', 'core skills' or 'technology–product portfolios' (Adler and Shenbar 1990, Frohman 1985, Grant 1991, Link and Tassey 1987, Mitchell 1985, Prahalad and Hamel 1990, Meyer and Utterback 1993). The product-market orientation of the firm is perceived at least partly as springing from the technology base of the firm rather than vice versa (see especially Link and Tassey 1987, Prahalad and Hamel 1990), that is, technology-related diversification is considered a decisive form of strategic renewal and a test of the long-term viability of the technology base.

Like other assets, assets for technological innovation must be conceived in terms of clusters of resources and the capacity for activating these resources and promoting learning. Technological resources comprise physical resources (technical equipment, machinery, etc.), intangible resources (technical skills and experience, patents, documents containing codified knowledge, relations to external sources of knowledge, organizational routines, and reputation as related

119

to the quality of the technology base), and financial resources dedicated to technology development. Intangible technological resources do not exclusively comprise codified, technical knowledge as stored in the heads of particular individuals, and technical recipes written down in documents, articles and patents. As Nelson and Winter (1982) have argued – and more recently further developed (Nelson 1992, Winter 1987) – innovative resources are just as much linked to tacit knowledge as to articulable knowledge and recipes. However, consistent with the conceptual distinction between resources and capacities, intangible innovative resources of this more tacit nature are embodied in skills. Sometimes technological innovation may be primarily driven by individual entrepreneurs, but most innovation, I suggest, is likely to require team-based capabilities and managerial competence as linked to firm-specific experience-building.

In the same vein Adler and Shenbar (1990) conceive an organization's technology base in terms of four asset categories that elaborates on the distinction between technological and organizational assets:

1   Technological assets (the specific technologies in which the organization can claim competence).
2   Organizational assets (broken down into five key elements: skills;[6] procedures for assessing, selecting, planning and controlling new projects; the organizational structure; the strategy to guide action; and the culture that shapes the assumptions and values in the organization).
3   External assets (the external relations that can fuel the development of internal technological assets).
4   Project management assets.

This conceptual delimitation of the technology base fits quite well to the delimitation of the asset concept outlined in the section on 'Firm Assets: Resources, Capabilities and Competences'. Technical capabilities and associated (technological) resources correspond to Adler and Shenbar's 'technological assets' and 'project management assets'; managerial competences correspond to 'organizational assets' in Adler and Shenbar's terminology. Finally, the absorptive capacity which is here considered part of the general capacity concept corresponds to their 'external assets'. To some extent there may be trade-off effects across these dimensions. For instance, a comparatively weak internal technical capability may be compensated for by strong absorptive (learning) capacity; or powerful capability may be more or less nihilated due to poor managerial competence and cross-functional communication.

While academics and managers sometimes tend to assume that the internal technical skill resources and capabilities are the most critical and the others (the absorptive and managerial dimensions) will automatically follow in their wake, Adler and Shenbar (1990) suggest that it is usually the organizational assets – or in our terminology, the managerial competences – and the skill base that prove to be the limiting elements. Moreover, absorptive capacity – including network relations – may tend to be a more important part of the technology base than generally recognized by much of the competence literature. This implies that privileged access to critical external capabilities and know-how may be just as vital for the creation of competitive advantage as internal capabilities (Foss and Eriksen 1995).

Identifying assets for technological innovation

How do we delimit the notion of innovative assets, and especially the distinct capabilities associated with technological innovation? Two approaches to this issue can be identified: a 'technical functionality' approach (also sometimes termed 'technology mapping' or 'technology audit') and an 'innovative functionality' approach (for an extensive discussion, see Christensen 1995, 1996).

Technology mapping in a firm perspective (e.g. Jasper 1980, Frohman 1985, Mitchell 1985) as well as in a macro-level perspective (Engelsman and van Raan 1994) mostly involves distinguishing technological assets in terms of 'fields' or 'disciplines'. To be well suited for strategic discussion in the firm the technology-mapping procedure must operate on a very disaggregate level of 'fields' that may be iteratively adapted to the specific reality of the firm and its competitive environment (Adler and Shenbar 1990: 27). Such a technology-mapping procedure does not, however, by itself provide any insights into the innovative potential for the firm of the technological assets identified.

Therefore technological assets should also be analysed as *'innovative assets'* that reflect the different roles or functions involved in producing technological innovation. The R&D rubric may be said to reflect the 'function' in the firm that is specialized to produce technological innovation, and R and D represent two sub-functional categories of innovative assets. Elsewhere (Christensen 1995) I have proposed a more differentiated 'innovative asset' framework that distinguishes four generic categories of innovative assets: scientific research assets (corresponding to the R in R&D), process-innovative assets, product-innovative application assets (subdivided into technical and functional application) and aesthetic design assets (the last three are specifications and elaborations of the D). *Scientific research assets* involve both basic research of a pre-competitive nature and applied or industrial research that provide direct inputs into process development and new-product application. *Process-innovative assets* both comprise capacity for 'hardware' process innovation, and the more 'systemic' competence involved in developing the production system, the inbound and outbound logistics, quality control and plant layout. *Product-innovative application assets* are the resources and capacities required to deal with product development (apart from the possible scientific research and aesthetic design): product engineering, instrumentation and software development. This asset category can be further divided into technical and functional applications. *Technical application* deals with 'purely' technical issues in order to reduce technical uncertainty from the engineering and economic perspective of the firm, while *functional application* is directed towards reducing functional uncertainty with respect to the user-interface (Lotz 1992). *Aesthetic design assets* are mostly thought of as part of the marketing attributes of the product, but aesthetic design is also a distinct part of or has a close physical relationship to the product, which makes it a bridge between technical and functional features of the product and the marketing features.

This taxonomy, I believe, is better able to grasp the multi-dimensional asset base for technological innovation than the R&D rubric. The technology-mapping procedure may help to specify the technical dimension of the three most 'technical' innovative asset categories (scientific research assets, process-innovative assets and product-innovative assets), and the aesthetic design category may likewise be specified in terms of 'design fields' (Walsh *et al.* 1992). On the other hand, exclusively analysing the technology base according to conventional technology or R&D mapping techniques systematically fails to see the innovative potential of the firm and especially the potential significance of aesthetic design assets.

Inter-asset linkages and organizational design

Technological innovation may sometimes require the activation of only one of the asset categories, but more often a specific constellation of asset types has to be mobilized. A very important aspect of innovative competences deals with the building, coordination and co-specialization of different innovative skills and capabilities as delimited in the previous subsection.

The accumulation of innovative assets as well as decisions concerning their funding, strategic orientation and management may take place at different organizational levels or at different functional or hierarchical interfaces. In large innovative corporations the generic assets have generally been subject to increasing division of labour, professionalization, cultural segregation and rivalry over financial resources. This development reflects differences between the asset categories, not only with respect to the professional functions and skills involved but also with respect to organizational culture, management traditions and relative prestige and power allocated within the company (Christensen 1995). Parallel to this 'balkanization' process, coordination and integration problems have become more complex and urgent, and this development tends to increase the importance of managerial competences in technological innovation, as has been reflected in recent literature on management of technology (see for example Coombs and Richards 1993, Rubenstein 1989).

A critical test of excellence in management of technology and innovation is, of course, its ability to create competitive advantage from new products and processes. This reflects a competence in acquiring technological resources, creating or improving innovative capabilities, and mobilizing these assets for innovative activities. At least in larger firms with a differentiated technology base this implies the building of inter-asset specificity (or co-specialization) across different categories of innovative assets (for example, between product and process application or between different technologies such as mechanical engineering and software engineering), and between innovative assets (or innovations) and complementary assets.

The level of inter-asset specificity refers to the degree to which innovative activities based on one asset category implies idiosyncratic activities based on other asset categories. Generally it can be suggested that a strong competence in building and exploiting high degrees of inter-asset specificity provides greater scope for innovation, makes higher demands on the management of the technology base, and provides a more powerful appropriability regime (Teece 1986) than low degrees of inter-asset specificity (Christensen 1996). Moreover, the question of inter-asset specificity reaches beyond the narrow scope of distinct assets for technological innovation. Building and exploiting inter-asset coupling between innovative assets (or a particular innovation) and complementary assets (such as marketing, after-sales service and user-knowledge) can in two ways contribute to strengthening the appropriability conditions associated with technological innovation: either through mobilizing complementary assets for 'complementary innovations' which fit the innovation in question, or by adapting the innovation to the existing operational assets of the firm as well as to externally located complementary assets such as supplier input or user know-how (Christensen 1996).

The organizational governance structure should reflect these inter-asset constellations. Thus, the room for 'balkanization' and externalization (into arm's-length market relations) is greater when inter-asset specificity is low, while some kind of integrative organizational structure or elaborate interorganizational competence is needed when inter-asset specificity is high. Inter-asset specificity may be the result of strategic choice and idiosyncratic competences to handle such couplings rather than the result of objective criteria.

The dynamics of innovative assets

Excellence in management of technology and innovation also implies the capacity to assure a proper balance between reproductive or incremental dynamics on the one hand and explorative dynamics on the other.

The dynamics of innovative assets may be reproductive or explorative (or more or less so). Reproductive innovative dynamics serve to maintain or improve existing innovative capabilities and generate incremental innovations in terms of new or improved products or processes. Reproductive dynamics involve strongly path-dependent experiential learning and searching. Given innovative assets are exploited and improved within well-defined technological trajectories (Dosi 1982). Explorative innovative dynamics may not only produce more radical innovations,[7] they also pave the way for the building of new innovative assets in the firm – both technical capabilities and managerial competences. Sometimes opportunities for radical innovation 'spring up' as a side-effect of building new capabilities, sometimes the new capabilities accumulate as a side-effect of specific innovative activities that turn out to be more radical than initially expected.

Generally, reproductive innovative dynamics tend to be linked to a relatively narrow or 'local' asset base that may, however, be very 'deep' in terms of capability and competence. Explorative innovative dynamics, on the other hand, tend to be more 'open-minded' in the sense that they explore into a more diverse asset base, and this will mostly imply a more complex learning organization in which external (absorptive) learning plays a significant role.

In the previous subsection the issue of inter-asset couplings was argued to be of critical importance for the successful management of innovation. It is, however, important to underline that this issue has a fundamentally dynamic character. The dynamics of evolving co-specialization across individual assets may be incremental or more radical in nature, corresponding to the difference between maintaining and improving inter-asset specific relations and building new examples of such relations; and the building of inter-asset specificity may be more difficult if it combines with the building of new capabilities.

A firm's R&D activities tend to be thought of as predominantly explorative – perhaps even as *the only* 'explorative function' in the firm. However, there is need for care here. It may very well be that R&D activities are often dominated by reproductive efforts such as incremental product application and process development, routine tests of components and materials, and so on, and evaluation – and usually rejection – of innovative ideas. In large industrial corporations in which innovative activities take place both at the centre (i.e. in central R&D laboratories) and in different divisions (i.e. divisional engineering departments), the centralized R&D activities tend to place stronger emphasis on explorative efforts targeted at competence building (rather than at specific process- or product-innovative activities), while the decentralized activities tend to focus relatively more on reproductive and incremental efforts targeted at product or process development (and only secondarily – or as an unintended side-effect – at capability or competence-building). Moreover, the centre may focus relatively more attention at managerial competences (in technology management and strategic planning), while the divisional level may direct more attention directly at the distinct technical capabilities and the services they can render.

THE STRATEGIC SIGNIFICANCE OF THE TECHNOLOGY BASE

In order to judge the strategic potential of technological or innovative assets (and the associated complementary assets) these should be analysed along four dimensions:

1 the 'external fit' of the technology base, i.e. its actual and potential competitive significance and comparative strength,

2   the appropriability conditions,
3   the factor market conditions, and
4   the 'internal coherence' of the technology base.

The role of a firm's technology assets in providing and sustaining competitive advantage first of all depends on its relative importance for the competition at the level of product markets and technology regimes, and the firm's technology position vis-à-vis competitors (Welch and Nayak 1992). This is the question of the 'external fit' of the technology base. A strong external fit means that the firm possesses or has the capacity (and luck) to build superior innovative assets that are the most decisive for the competition at the targeted product markets, and that provide the firm with favourable options for technology-related diversification in the longer term. Analysing the actual and potential competitive significance of the technology base and its most promising course of direction involves both an introvert evaluation and a much broader external focus on industry trends, technological opportunities, competitor moves, customer priorities, regulatory measures, and so on. While it may be relatively straightforward to judge the short-term external fit, it is generally much more difficult to predict the requirements for the more distant future.

The second strategic dimension on which to judge the technology base is the conditions for appropriability, that is, the ability to monopolize innovative assets and prevent decisive knowledge diffusing to potential rivals. The ease with which critical innovative knowledge may diffuse to external parties depends on the characteristics of the knowledge in question and measures to prevent imitation. Winter (1987) has proposed a relevant typology of knowledge dimensions that can provide a basis for appraising the ease of knowledge diffusion. Thus, the more tacit, the less observable in use, the more complex, and the more systemic the knowledge is, the more difficult is the transference of the knowledge from one firm to another. Winter's criteria should (and can) be aligned with the fundamental distinction between resources and capacities (capabilities and competences) suggested in the section 'Firm Assets: Resources, Capabilities and Competences'. If tacit and complex knowledge is embodied in a single individual it may in one sense be easily transferable: the individual can leave the firm and get hired by a rival. Even if some of the individual's knowledge can be considered part of the 'property asset' of the firm, its ability to exert legal protection of this asset is usually difficult. In this case, knowledge is to be considered a resource. However, if the knowledge in question reflects a team-based and experience-based capacity accumulated within the firm, this kind of knowledge transfer is either not possible or very difficult.[8] In this case the knowledge is to be considered a capability or competence.

The firm may also pursue various measures to prevent knowledge diffusion or prolong the possible lead time (such as patent protection, secrecy measures, building switching costs through sales and service efforts or continuously creating lead time by offensive R&D). Complementary assets that are co-specialized with the innovative assets and the products and processes they give rise to may form an important second line of defence (Teece 1986, Christensen 1996).

The third strategic dimension to take into account is the factor-market conditions of the resources and capacities which constitute the technology base. These conditions are likely to be substantially related to the question of the appropriability conditions and involve more or less the same analysis, even if the normative viewpoint differs. The appropriability question asks: how can our assets be protected from involuntary diffusion or transfer to competitors? The factor-market question asks: how can assets best be acquired or used? This involves the options of in-sourcing knowledge and other resources from outside (e.g. from rivals or suppliers) or transferring (selling) assets to external parts.

Thus, while the appropriability issue is concerned with preventing asset transfer, the factor-market issue is concerned with the options for voluntary asset transfer and, thus, deals with the transactional dimension of management. This includes both a 'make or buy' and a 'use or sell' problem. The former deals with the question of how to get access to the relevant resources, capabilities and competences. Can or should they be accessed from 'strategic factor markets' or accumulated internally (Barney 1986, Dierickx and Cool 1989)? The second problem deals with the question of how to exploit maximum benefits from existing firm resources and capacities. Are there favourable trading alternatives to internal use? In 'Firm Assets: Resources, Capabilities and Competences' I maintained that an important difference between resources and capabilities or competences is that resources can be traded while the latter usually cannot and therefore have to be both accumulated and used in-house. Thus, the factor-market issue refers to the following sorts of questions. What type of capabilities or competences should the firm build *and* use? Which resources are required to build these capacities, and which of these resources can favourably be accessed in the market place? Can excess resource capacity be favourably sold or licensed to external parties without undermining the competitive strength of the firm, or should they be reserved for the creation of new growth options?

The final dimension on which to judge the technology base concerns its coherence. The coherence of the technology base may be viewed as part of a broader coherence concept that focuses attention on internal consistency and interrelationship between elements of the firm or the corporation.[9] The coherence of the technology base may apply to two levels: coherence between the elements of the technology base ('local coherence') and coherence between the technology base and the broader firm or corporate context ('contextual coherence').

The local coherence perspective focuses on the degree of integration and interrelatedness within the technology base between the different technological and innovative assets. A strong local coherence reflects a highly integrated technology base comprising a varied portfolio of technologies and innovative assets characterized by the exploitation and exploration of a high level of inter-asset specificity and synergy in innovative efforts. The local coherence is *not* a reflection of the diversity of the technology base (i.e. the more diverse the less coherent). To exhibit coherence in a highly diverse (multi-asset) technology base in a diversified corporation is much more demanding than to exhibit coherence in a specialized firm with a narrow technology base.[10] Thus local technology base coherence only gives sense in a diverse multi-asset context.[11]

The contextual coherence concept focuses attention on the correspondence between the technology base and the broader firm or corporate context (the complementary assets, the operational and infrastructural firm context, business and corporate level strategy and culture). Also this coherence problem is much more complex in large diversified corporations than in small firms. A 'bad fit' may be characterized by 'balkanized rivalry' over resources and mutual mistrust between the 'innovative asset agents' and the 'operational asset agents'. A 'good fit' is not necessarily marked by harmonic relations and agreement between parties. But these tensions and conflicts are dealt with in ways that promote synergy and a common sense of contributing to the same general course of direction. Part of the contextual coherence issue can be analysed in terms of couplings between innovative and complementary assets (Teece 1986, Christensen 1996).

CONCLUSION

This chapter has proposed a framework for analysing the technology base of the firm from a resource and competence perspective. The framework is intended to contribute to the creation of a more richly faceted conception of the technology base than the one provided by the formal R&D rubric or by conventional technology-mapping procedures.

Initially the chapter attempts to clarify the central building blocks in the competence theory of the firm: the firm assets as constituted by resources, capabilities and competences. While resources tend to be tradable at 'strategic factor markets', competences and capabilities constitute the 'experience base' of the firm. They reflect the firm's capacities for structuring and orienting clusters of resources (and their services) for productive purposes that potentially provide the firm with a competitive advantage. A capability is a lower-order functional or technical capacity, while a competence is a higher-order managerial capacity. Two features of assets are discussed: the external or absorptive (versus internal) dimension and the dynamic dimension. Two broad categories of asset dynamics are identified: reproductive and explorative dynamics.

Under the heading 'Assets for Technological Innovation' a framework is developed for analysing assets for technological innovation that is consistent with the general conceptual framework. Assets for technological innovation are defined as resources and capacities for developing new products and processes. The total portfolio of such firm assets constitutes the technology base of the firm.

Capacities for technological innovation comprise a functional dimension (the technologies in which the firm can claim competence), an organizational or managerial dimension (technology management skills and procedures, organizational structure and culture), and an absorptive dimension (capacity for scanning public knowledge and external relations that can fuel the internal technological competence). While it is often taken for granted that the technical capabilities are the most critical part of the technology base, there are good reasons to suggest that the managerial and absorptive capacities may often tend to be at least as important.

A taxonomy of innovative assets is proposed that distinguishes four generic categories of innovative assets: scientific research assets, process-innovative assets, product-innovative application assets and aesthetic design assets. These categories differ with respect to type of knowledge and competence, functional role within the innovation process, organizational locus and strategic significance. It is believed that this taxonomy of innovative assets (in combination with some form of technology mapping) is better able to grasp the multi-dimensional competence base for technological innovation than the conventional R&D conception or technology-mapping procedure.

It is suggested that most industrial innovation requires the combination of two or more asset types. Thus, innovative assets are generally more adequately characterized in terms of 'inter-asset' linkages than in terms of either one asset category or a portfolio of asset categories. High degrees of inter-asset specificity provide greater scope for innovation and make higher demands on the technology base and its organizational coordination than low degrees of inter-asset specificity. This implies that core competences tend to involve elaborate technical, managerial and absorptive capacities as related to several innovative assets and technical fields as well as the capacity to exploit specific couplings between them. Moreover, by exploiting inter-asset specificity between innovative assets and complementary assets, core competences may become more robust and thereby strengthen the appropriability conditions surrounding technological innovation.

Finally, the chapter discusses four strategic dimensions that should be analysed in order to judge the strategic potential of the technology base: the 'external fit' of the technology base (its relative importance for the competition and its comparative strength); the appropriability conditions; the factor-market conditions; and the 'internal coherence' of the technology base.

Within the competence literature the internal coherence problem has so far primarily been addressed empirically in terms of product-portfolio coherence and its implications for strategic diversification. The competence theory of the firm and its strategic ramifications need a better understanding of asset or competence coherence along the lines proposed in this chapter, and future research should be directed towards this issue.

NOTES

1 A minor point of criticism concerns Grant's term 'team of resources' which I find somewhat misconceived. I prefer to use the term 'team' in its normal context, that

is, as referring to small social groups or networks. Instead of 'teams of resources' I prefer to speak of clusters of resources.

2 Functional/technical capacity does not necessarily correspond to the conventional functional areas of the firm. Rather it signifies the ability to perform any relevant technical function or value activity within the firm, including the ability to develop new products and processes and to operate facilities effectively. It corresponds to the notion of technical competence suggested by Teece et al. (1994).

3 This distinction between capabilities and competences draws on Sanchez, Heene and Thomas (1995) and the conception of competences is inspired by Doz (1994). The distinction between two economic dimensions of competence (the allocative and transactional) draws on Teece et al. (1994).

4 External assets have been discussed under various headings such as 'external economies' or 'industrial districts' and only recently been more consistently related to the resource-based approach (Foss and Eriksen 1995).

5 The terminological variation is great, while the substantial difference may be marginal between the following pairs of concepts proposed in the literature: 'static routines' versus 'dynamic capabilities' (Teece et al. 1994), 'competence maintaining and leveraging' versus 'competence building' (Sanchez, Heene and Thomas 1995), 'exploitation' versus 'exploration' (March 1991, Levinthal and March 1993), 'single-loop learning' versus 'double-loop learning' (Agyris and Schön 1978). These dichotomies are here generalized into a distinction between reproductive and explorative dynamics.

6 Under the heading of organizational assets they include two categories of skills, technical skills and technology-management skills, and they suggest that these skills constitute the single most important element in the technology base. Although we may agree to that, it seems more appropriate to place technical skills as a critical resource within their technological asset category than within the organizational asset category.

7 Radical innovation includes radically new end-products or process technologies as well as radically new components, materials, etc. which may feed into incremental innovation with respect to the system architecture of products.

8 This is most obvious when the knowledge structure is contextualized not only within the team (the knowledge of different individuals within the team is highly co-specialized) but also between the team and the firm's other assets (including other teams). If the team-based knowledge is not strongly contextualized to the particular firm, the option may be open that a whole team moves to another context (a rival firm or some other organization) which can benefit from the team's knowledge or capability.

9 While most of the traditional strategic management literature focuses on the congruence or fit between firm strategy and its environment, a more internal conception of congruence or 'fit' has recently been emerging under the heading of 'coherence'. Teece et al. (1994) use the term 'corporate coherence' to focus on the relatedness among the businesses in multi-product corporations: 'A firm exhibits coherence when its lines of business are related, in the sense that there are certain technological and market characteristics common to each' (p. 4). Nath and Sudharshan (1994) use the notion of coherence to signify consistency of strategic choices across business and functional levels of strategy (p. 44).

10 Coombs and Richards (1993) provide some illustrative evidence on the complexity of promoting strategic technology-base coherence in large diversified companies.

11 Teece et al. (1994) similarly define corporate coherence in a multi-product sense.

REFERENCES

Adler, P. S. (1989) 'Technology Strategy: A Guide to the Literatures', *Research in Technological Innovation, Management and Policy* 4: 25–151.

Adler, P. S. and Shenbar, A. (1990) 'Adapting Your Technological Base: The Organizational Challenge', *Sloan Management Review* 25: 25–37.

Agyris, C. and Schön, D. (1978) *Organizational Learning*, Reading, Mass.: Addison-Wesley.

Arrow, K. J. (1962) 'The Economic Implications of Learning by Doing', *Review of Economic Studies* 29: 155–73.

Barney, J. (1986) 'Strategic Factor Markets: Expectations, Luck and Business Strategy', *Management Science* 42: 1231–41.

Barney, J. (1991) 'Firm Resources and Sustained Competitive Advantage', *Journal of Management* 17: 99–120.

Chatterjee, S. and Wernerfelt, B. (1991) 'The Link between Resources and Type of Diversification: Theory and Evidence', *Strategic Management Journal* 12: 33–48.

Christensen, J. F. (1995) 'Asset Profiles for Technological Innovation', *Research Policy* 24: 727–45.

Christensen, J. F. (1996) 'Innovative Assets and Inter-Asset Specificity – A Resource-based Approach to Innovation', *Economics of Innovation and New Technology* (forthcoming).

Cohen, W. M. and Levinthal, D. A. (1990) 'Absorptive Capacity: A New Perspective on Learning and Innovation', *Administrative Science Quarterly* 35: 128–52.

Conner, K. R. (1991) 'A Historical Comparison of Resource-based Theory and Five Schools of Thought within Industrial Organization Economics: Do We Have a New Theory of the Firm?', *Journal of Management* 17: 121–54.

Coombs, R. and Richards, A. (1993) 'Strategic Control of Technology in Diversified Companies with Decentralized R&D', *Technology Analysis and Strategic Management* 5: 385–96.

Coombs, R., Saviotti, P. and Walsh, V. (1987) *Economics and Technological Change*, London: Macmillan Education.

Dierickx, I. and Cool, K. (1989) 'Asset Stock Accumulation and Sustainability of Competitive Advantage', *Management Science* 35: 1504–11.

Dosi, G. (1982) 'Technological Paradigms and Technological Trajectories. A Suggested Interpretation of the Determinants and Direction of Technical Change', *Research Policy* 11: 147–62.

Dosi, G. (1988) 'Sources, Procedures, and Microeconomic Effects of Innovation', *Journal of Economic Literature* 26: 1120–71.

Doz, Y. (1994) 'Managing Core Competency for Corporate Renewal: Towards a Managerial Theory of Core Competencies', Working Paper, INSEAD, Paris.

Engelsman, E. C. and van Raan, A. F. J. (1994) 'A Patent-based Cartography of Technology', *Research Policy* 23: 1–26.

Foss, N. J. and Eriksen, B. (1995) 'Competitive Advantage and Industry Capabilities', C. A. Montgomery (ed.) *Evolutionary and Resource-based Approaches to Strategy*, Boston: Kluwer.

Freeman, C. (1982) *The Economics of Industrial Innovation*, 2nd edn, London: Frances Pinter.

Frohman, A. L. (1985) 'Putting Technology into Strategic Planning', *California Management Review* 27: 48–59.

Grant, R. M. (1991) 'The Resource-based Theory of Competitive Advantage: Implications for Strategy Formulation', *California Management Review* 33: 114–35.

Hall, R. (1992) 'The Strategic Analysis of Intangible Resources', *Strategic Management Journal* 13: 135–44.

Hall, R. (1993) 'A Framework Linking Intangible Resources and Competencies to Sustainable Competitive Advantage', *Strategic Management Journal* 14: 607–18.

Jasper, D. P. (1980) 'Inventory Your Technology for Increased Awareness and Profit', *Research Management* 4: 16–20.

Kay, J. (1993) *Foundations of Corporate Success. How Business Strategies Add Value*, Oxford: Oxford University Press.

Levinthal, D. A. and March, J. G. (1993) 'The Myopia of Learning', *Strategic Management Journal* 14: 95–112.

Link, A. N. and Tassey, G. (1987) *Strategies for Technology-based Competition*, Lexington, Mass: Lexington Books, D. C. Heath.

Lippman, S. A. and Rumelt, R. P. (1982) 'Uncertain Imitability: An Analysis of Interfirm Differences in Efficiency under Competition', *The Bell Journal of Economics* 13: 418–38.

Loasby, B. (1994) 'Organizational Capabilities and Interfirm Relations', *Metroeconomica* 45: 248–65.

Lotz, P. (1992) *Demand-side Effects on Product Innovation*, Frederiksberg, Denmark: Samfundslitteratur.

Mahoney, J. and Pandian, J. R. (1992) 'The Resource-based View within the Conversation of Strategic Management', *Strategic Management Journal* 13: 363–80.

March, J. G. (1991) 'Exploration and Exploitation in Organizational Learning', *Organization Science* 2: 95–112.

Markides, C. C. and Williamson, P. J. (1994) 'Related Diversification, Core Competences and Corporate Performance', *Strategic Management Journal* 15: 149–65.

Metcalfe, J. S. and Gibbons, M. (1989) 'Technology, Variety and Organization: A Systematic Perspective on the Competitive Process', *Research on Technological Innovation, Management and Policy* 4: 153–93.

Meyer, M. H. and Utterback, J. M. (1993) 'The Product Family and the Dynamics of Core Capability', *Sloan Management Review* 34: 29–47.

Mitchell, G. R. (1985) 'New Approaches for the Strategic Management of Technology', *Technology in Society* 7: 227–39.

Montgomery, C. A. and Hariharan, S. (1991) 'Diversified Expansion by Large Established Firms', *Journal of Economic Behavior and Organization*: 71–89.

Montgomery, C. A. and Wernerfelt, B. (1988) 'Diversification, Ricardian Rents, and Tobin's q', *Rand Journal of Economics* 19: 623–32.

Nath, D. and Sudharshan, D. (1994) 'Measuring Strategy Coherence through Patterns of Strategic Choices', *Strategic Management Journal* 15: 43–61.

Nelson, R. R. (1992) 'The Roles of Firms in Technical Advance: A Perspective from Evolutionary Theory', in G. Dosi, R. Gianetti and P. A. Toninelli (eds) *Technology and Enterprise in a Historical Perspective*, Oxford: Clarendon Press.

Nelson, R. R. and Winter, S. G. (1982) *An Evolutionary Theory of Economic Change*, Cambridge, Mass.: The Belknap Press of Harvard University Press.

Penrose, E. T. (1972) *The Theory of the Growth of the Firm* (originally published 1959), Oxford: Basil Blackwell.

Peteraf, M. A. (1993) 'The Cornerstones of Competitive Advantage: A Resource-based View', *Strategic Management Journal* 14: 179–91.

Prahalad, C. K. and Hamel, G. (1990) 'The Core Competence of the Corporation', *Harvard Business Review* May–June: 79–91.

Rosenberg, N. (1982) *Inside the Black Box: Technology and Economics*, Cambridge: Cambridge University Press.

Rubenstein, A. (1989) *Managing Technology in the Decentralized Firm*, New York: Wiley.

Sanchez, R., Heene, A. and Thomas, H. (1995) 'Towards the Theory and Practice of Competence-based Competition', in R. Sanchez, A. Heene and H. Thomas (eds)

Theory and Practice in Competence-based Competition. From Industry Studies to a New Theory of Competitive Dynamics, London: Elsevier Pergamon Press.

Teece, D. J. (1986) 'Profiting from Technological Innovation: Implications for Integration, Collaboration, Licensing and Public Policy', *Research Policy* 15: 285–305.

Teece, D. J. and Pisano, G. (1994) 'The Dynamic Capabilities of Firms: An Introduction', *Industrial and Corporate Change* 3: 537–56.

Teece, D. J., Rumelt, R., Dosi, G. and Winter, S. (1994) 'Understanding Corporate Coherence. Theory and Evidence', *Journal of Economic Behavior and Organization* 23: 1–30.

Tushman, M. L. and Moore, L. (eds) (1988) *Readings in The Management of Innovation*, 2nd edn, Cambridge, Mass.: Ballinger.

Walsh, V., Roy, R., Bruce, M. and Potter, S. (1992) *Winning by Design. Technology, Product Design and International Competitiveness*, Oxford: Blackwell.

Welch, J. A. and Nayak, P. R. (1992) 'Strategic Sourcing: A Progressive Approach to the Make-or-Buy Decision', *Academy of Management Executive* 6: 23–31.

Wernerfelt, B. (1984) 'A Resource-based View of the Firm', *Strategic Management Journal* 5: 171–80.

Winter, S. G. (1987) 'Knowledge and Competence as Strategic Assets', in D. J. Teece (ed.) *The Competitive Challenge. Strategies for Industrial Innovation and Renewal*, New York: Harper & Row.

8

STUDIES OF KEY FACTORS OF PRODUCT-DEVELOPMENT SUCCESS

A resource-based critique and reinterpretation

Kirsten Foss and Hanne Harmsen

INTRODUCTION

In recent years, scholars within the area of product development have shown a growing interest in the determinants of product success. This interest is motivated by the commonplace observation that some products are more successful than others, and that some firms over a period of time seem to have more success than other firms with the products they develop.

What is it that the more successful firms do? This is the research question posed by a number of scholars interested in finding the key factors of product-development success. Since the mid-1950s this line of research has resulted in the publication of a large and continuous number of studies probing into the factors of success or failure for new products or product-development programmes.[1] The studies are conducted at different levels of analysis (product, product-development project or firm), but their overall aim is to understand the determinants of product-development success.

The methods used in this type of research are primarily *inductive*: managers are asked to identify a number of the factors underlying *success* or *failure* of product-development programmes or products. Generally the results of the empirical studies with normative implications are lists of *key factors of success* in order of priority. The main conclusion that can be drawn from this literature is that there is no single magic formula for success. Rather there seems to exist a large number of factors that influence success or failure.

Why some firms are persistently more successful than others is also the research question guiding much of the theoretical work within the *resource-based perspective* in strategic management. This perspective is an important part of the more overarching competence perspective that is the core theme of the present book. However, there are deep differences in the research styles and methods of the product-development research tradition and the resource-based perspective. Most importantly, the resource-based approach is strongly *deductive*, not least because it is so largely based on economic theory.

133

The basic tenet of the resource-based perspective is that successful performance depends on obtaining access to undervalued rent-yielding resources. When access to such resources is secured – for example, through acquisition – the rents they yield may in principle be captured in numerous ways, such as selling the resource on a market, leasing it or deploying it to a product market through using the resource in-house (Dierickx and Cool 1989). In practice, it is the latter option that has primarily interested resource-based researchers. Moreover, much attention has been devoted to examining the characteristics that make this rent-yielding capacity possible. Like the empirically oriented product-development tradition, the resource-based perspective also concludes that there is no – and cannot be any – magic formula for success. But this conclusion is derived in an entirely different way, namely by arguing that only private information and knowledge can be the ultimate foundation of competitive success. As we shall see, this is a simple conclusion with profound implications, not least with respect to the soundness of the normative implications of the product-development tradition.

While both the resource-based perspective and the empirical studies of key factors of success stress the importance of firms' resources, they disagree about what distinguishes the sources of success. The empirical studies search for a number of factors that are common to identified successful firms (or products) across firms and industries. From many sides it has been emphasized that because results from the different studies are consistent, even across industries, there are indeed a number of fairly general success factors (Cooper 1990, Lilien and Yoon 1989).

In the resource-based literature, it is argued that only the unique aspects of a company's resources can be the sources of long-lasting success. More precisely, resources have to be valuable, rare and inimitable in order to be sources of sustained competitive advantage (Barney 1991). Thus, from a resource-based perspective one would be led to doubt whether the success criterion derived from identifying factors common to most successful firms is really a sufficient or even a necessary criterion for identifying the true sources of success.

The question we raise in this chapter is precisely concerned with this issue. To be more precise, we argue that the identification of the sources of success hinges on the causal relation between success and success factors – a relation that is unaccounted for in the empirical studies of key factors of success within the product-development literature. However, the resource-based perspective provides – at least to some extent – an account of this causality. An analysis of the circumstances under which resources can generate long-lived rents indicates that there is a more subtle causal relation than what is implicitly assumed in the empirical studies. Moreover, if a number of resources are common to many successful firms, they will at the most constitute the *necessary* conditions – but never the *sufficient* – conditions for success (Amit and Schoemaker 1993).

By discussing the empirical results of key-factors-of-success studies in the context of the theoretical framework of the resource-based perspective, a more precise picture of the nature of the results may be reached. Once the nature of the results is determined, the resource-based perspective can also provide insights on how the results may in fact be used by firms. We realize that while the empirical studies we are discussing are concerned with explaining the differences between product-development success and failure, the resource-based perspective is concerned with the explanation of long-lived profitability differences between firms – a much 'grander' question. The resource-based perspective might therefore be considered more directed towards the under-standing of successes or failures of whole firms than towards single-product successes or failures. In spite of this difference, we believe that the theoretical framework developed in the resource-based perspective can equally well be applied at the level of product development.

We have chosen to exemplify the reinterpretation of key factors of success by two specific studies, which we find represent the research area particularly well. The two studies are Cooper's 'NewProd IIII' (1990), which is an analysis of the successes and failures of 203 new products, and Edgett, Shipley and Forbes's (1992) 'Japanese and British companies compared', which is a study of factors contributing to new-product success and failure in 202 British and Japanese companies.[2]

KEY FACTORS OF SUCCESS: DEFINITIONS AND RESEARCH STRATEGIES

The concept of 'key factors of success' within the area of product development and the related concept of 'key success factors' within the area of strategic management have attracted much interest. Consequently, precise definitions of these concepts as well as clarification of the ways of identifying the sources of success are issues of great importance.

In the context of product-development studies, key factors of success may on a general level be defined as those factors which contribute to the success of a product or a firm in most of the identified successful cases. The usual procedure in the studies is to identify a number of successful, and sometimes also un-successful firms, and ask managers to indicate which of a number of factors in their opinion have significantly contributed to product success or failure. The factors most often indicated as important are called 'success factors'.

The empirical identification of specific key factors of success is of course very much dependent on the measures of success used, as well as on the general design of the studies. Research designs and statistical methods used to identify the key success factors often differ among the studies. Also, some studies use very broad categories like 'industrial products' (e.g. Hise *et al.* 1989, Cooper 1990), includ-ing a number of different industries and identifying success factors across these industries. Other studies narrow their search for determinants of success down to one or a few industries (e.g. Zirger and Maidique 1990, Ayal and Raban 1990), perhaps in an acknowledgement of situation-specific key factors of success.

However, recent studies have emphasized the generality of the results across industries. Based on an examination of a number of earlier empirical studies, Lilien and Yoon (1989) conclude that 'the findings of these studies are often similar and consistent' (p. 4) (including studies in different industries). Cooper (1990) agrees when he states that 'the results remain remarkably consistent across studies, regardless of the study's context' (p. 27) (including industry and firm size). In fact, the very existence of such general factors has been taken as an indication that there do exist a number of factors which are positively correlated with success in most firms across industries.

Critiques of key factors of success studies

The major part of the critique raised from within the area of key-factor-of-success studies[3] is concerned with problems such as the reliability and comparability of the studies. A lack of precise definitions, specified conceptual models[4] or representative samples have been used as arguments against their reliability and consequently their comparability (e.g. Hart and Craig 1992).

Some criticism has also been raised against the use of financial measures of success. It has, for example, been emphasized that a project, though a failure from a financial point of view, may contribute to organizational learning in a way which makes it an advantage in the long run or that a high success rate may be explained in relation to very low-risk incremental product innovations, which are not sufficient for the firm's long-run survival (Cooper 1984). This criticism is primarily directed towards understanding the most appropriate measures of success, whereas others question the possibilities of identifying any *single* factors behind success, claiming that synergistic effects and configurational efficiency may explain much more of the variance in performance than single factors.[5]

When it comes to the *normative advice* on how to use the results of the empirical studies criticisms have been raised concerning the possible implementation of the results (Ghemawat 1991). In Ghemawat's opinion, identifying the factors behind success does not solve the managerial problem of what to do about it. This is because no mechanism 'that is supposed to mediate between the organization's stock of success factors and its performance' is spelled out (Ghemawat 1991: 7). Moreover, the success factor approach 'does not adequately account for the constraints imposed both by past decision on current ones, and by current on those yet to come' (p. 7).

On a more general level, Camerer and Fahey (1988) have argued that 'Any advice [on what strategies to follow] must rest on an assumption about whether the industry is in equilibrium or not . . . and on the expectations and knowledge of others' (p. 446). By 'equilibrium' they mean that firms maximize profits and that they do it on the basis of knowledge of the 'relevant economic theory'.[6] The relevant theory could be firms' knowledge of the relation between superior returns and the key factors of success. Under this assumption, firms know what researchers know and use this knowledge in making investment decisions. But if firms know the key factors of success the empirical studies hold no advice to managers because firms will already have arrived at an equilibrium in which investments in key factors of success yield marginal benefits no larger than marginal cost. Thus, any gains to the 'discovery' of key factors of success will have been competed away already.

However, if the industry is *not* in equilibrium – for example, because not all firms know about the key factors of success, and those that do know suffer from imperfections in capital markets which makes them unable to take over the less knowledgeable firms – *then* the normative advice may have a positive impact on some firms' performance. But in that case, key factors of success may disappear, once they become known to all companies, as pointed out by Amit and Schoemaker (1993). Firms taking advice from the empirical studies of key factors of success will then not be able to earn more than the average return. This is clearly something which may reduce the normative value of the studies.

As we shall argue below, this conclusion is closely related to the general tenor of the resource-based literature, where much attention is directed towards identifying the mechanisms that will hinder valuable rent-earning resources from becoming dissipated to all companies through imitation (Barney 1991). However, bringing knowledge to the industry about the key factors of success may not always lead to an erosion of the competitive advantage stemming from these factors. This would be the case if there exist sustainable asymmetries within an industry which are not overcome by reducing the information asym-metries. For example, firms may suffer from time-compression diseconomies[7] (Dierickx and Cool 1989) in accumulating the assets identified as key factors of success. This could imply that bringing perfect knowledge to firms about the factors behind success may not alter the competitive ranking of firms within the industry, since the firms that are late to know about the factors may never catch up. In other words, the industry will be in an equilibrium in which differences between firms' performance will prevail.

In our opinion the arguments of Ghemawat (1991), Amit and Schoemaker (1993) and Camerer and Fahey (1988) indicate that an understanding of phenomena such as successes and failures of firms strongly depends on the assumptions regarding the causal relations between success (measured as an economic return) and key factors of success. We believe that some of the critical comments that have been directed towards empirical studies of product-development successes and failures may be addressed in a more concise manner within the resource-based perspective. By relating the research tradition of key factors of success to the resource-based perspective, it becomes possible to address more explicitly the limitation of the concept of key factors of success. More precisely, the question posed is this: is it the case that the key factors of success possess the characteristics necessary to be sources of long-lasting superior performance? The conclusions drawn from the resource-based perspective would seem to exclude many of the factors identified in the empirical studies as factors of long-lasting success.

KIRSTEN FOSS AND HANNE HARMSEN

THE RESOURCE-BASED PERSPECTIVE: THE CAUSAL LINK BETWEEN RESOURCES AND RETURNS

Within the area of key factors of success as well as within the resource-based perspective, it is argued that differences in firms' resources and capabilities are the underlying causes of differences in profitability and that those firms which possess superior resources will earn a greater than average return. But whereas the central issue within key-factor-of-success studies is *the identification* of the relevant factors of success, the central issue within the resource-based perspective is *what characterizes* the factors behind long-lasting superior performance. The resource-based perspective approaches the underlying causes of superior profitability from the perspective of economic theory and it is the rent-generating characteristics of resources that – at least to some degree – provide this causal link.

The causal relation between key factors of success and returns

With the term 'resource-based perspective', we shall associate a number of recent publications in strategic management, taking their lead from Wernerfelt (1984) and Rumelt (1984). The resource-based perspective is primarily a theory of company-specific resources as sources of competitive advantage. Focus is on the specific characteristics of firms rather than on the market conditions which are common to all firms in an industry (such as the degree of competitiveness). The analysis of resources and their rent-generating potential has implications for firms' product-development strategies as resources and products are seen as, in a sense, two sides of the same coin: knowing the optimal product mix may allow one to specify the optimal resource portfolio and vice versa (Wernerfelt 1984).

Barney (1986, 1991) presents five sufficient conditions which will ensure the firm sustainable economic advantages from its resources. These are that the resources:

1 have to be valuable,
2 have to be rare,
3 have to be imperfectly imitable,
4 are not substitutable by other resources, in order to be sources of rent, and
5 have been obtained at a price below their value.

In the following three subsections we will more thoroughly examine these conditions. On the basis of this discussion, it appears that the idea that success is based on factors which are common to a large number of firms is very much questionable. As a consequence, the results from the empirical studies of key factors of success should be reinterpreted as valuable resources that are necessary but not sufficent for success. We now turn to the question of how valuable resources are identified.

138

Valuable resources

Resources are *valuable* to a firm if they enable the firm to implement strategies that exploit opportunities or neutralize threats in its environment (Barney 1986, 1991). Apart from this general statement, scant attention is given to the problem of how firms identify valuable resources. It may be assumed that whenever resources produce successful products they are valuable. The results of the empirical studies of key factors of success can therefore be interpreted as a list of valuable resources/capabilities. Taking the existence of valuable resources for granted, there are two important theoretical as well as normative questions in the resource-based perspective. When do firms earn *long-lived rents* from their valuable resources? When are rent-generating resources likely to have productive *value in excess of their hire-price* (Conner 1991)? These questions are the subjects of the following two subsections. The discussion will show that it is only certain types of valuable resources that can be key factors of success and that such valuable resources are not common to a large number of firms.

The sources of rent

The central assumption in the resource-based perspective is that returns are linked to resources through their rent-earning potential. Whenever firms possess scarce and heterogeneous resources,[8] some of them may earn Paretian or Ricardian rent because their resources are superior.

Ricardian rent is the rent earned due to efficiency differences in the same type of resource. It is therefore a requirement that resources of different efficiencies are scarce factors.[9] A central idea in the resource-based perspective is that some general types of resources are likely to have firm-specific variants. The general types of resources can be culture, reputation, technology, and so on, and the firm-specific variants can be the specific character of a firm's culture, its unique reputation and idiosyncratic technology. It is on the basis of efficiency differences in those firm-specific variants that firms earn Ricardian rent. *Paretian rent* or quasi-rent is the difference between a resource's payment in its best use and the payments it would receive in its next best use. When firms vary with respect to their factor-endowments, some firms will be able to find a better use for a certain resource than other firms.[10]

Once a firm is endowed with valuable rent-earning resources, its ability to sustain its rent hinges on how easily the relevant resources can be replicated. The concepts of 'isolating mechanisms' and 'resource-position barrier' (see Rumelt 1984 and Wernerfelt 1984, respectively) are the essential theoretical concepts for explaining the sustainability of rent. An isolating mechanism/resource-imitation barrier may make the sources of rent strictly inimitable or uncertainly imitable. Resources such as a patent on an invention or the ownership of a rich mineral deposit are protected by isolating mechanisms of enforceable rights to the exclusive use of the unique resource – such isolating mechanisms make the resource *strictly inimitable*. Other resources, such as production or market experience, or organizational capabilities and routines, are protected by isolation mechanisms which make them *uncertainly imitable*. The isolating mechanisms of uncertainly imitable resources may be grouped as:

1 cognitive constraints to imitation of success,
2 time disadvantages to imitators, or
3 economic disadvantages to imitators.

For the the first mechanism, the cognitive constraints of *causal ambiguity* act as a powerful blockage to imitation. Causal ambiguity is 'the basic ambiguity concerning the nature of the causal connections between actions and results' (Lippman and Rumelt 1982: 420). Thus, the ambiguity disguises which factors are responsible for superior performance (Reed and DeFilippi 1990).

As regards time disadvantages, these can be caused either by the history-specific and path-dependent resource accumulation or by time-barriers to resource accumulation. Some resources, such as a culture, are intrinsically bound up with a firm's unique history and heritage (Barney 1991). Because history cannot be copied, the resource will be inimitable. Time disadvantages have other faces, such as time-compression diseconomics, asset mass efficiencies and interconnectedness of asset stocks (Dierickx and Cool 1989). These disadvantages to imitators arise because it takes time to accumulate such resources as knowledge and because the efficiency in the accumulation depends on prior accumulated resources or the stock of complementary resources.[11]

With respect to the third mechanism, what we have called 'economic disadvantages to imitators', Wernerfelt (1984) focuses on resource-position barriers as isolation mechanisms. These barriers protect the kind of resources where a first-mover advantage translates into a cost advantage in resource acquisition. An example may be having a large production capacity, which in Wernerfelt's reasoning can be a source of sustained advantage – not because it is inimitable, but because it will be economically irrational for competitors 'to buy the resource necessary to compete in a market where excess capacity would lead to cut-throat competition and low returns' (p. 174). That is to say, entry-deterrence may be an important aspect of protecting resources.

The costs of valuable rent-earning resources

When firms have valuable rent-earning resources they have a comparative advantage over competitors but not necessarily an absolute advantage in terms of high profits. According to Barney, the unique and valuable resources also have to be under-evaluated (acquired at a price below their value).

Firms may possess under-evaluated resources to the extent that the strategic factor markets[12] on which they are acquired are *imperfect*. Resources obtained in perfect strategic factor markets – that is to say, factor markets in which the price and the discounted present value of a resource coincide – will not earn an above-normal return, even if the implemented strategies create imperfect product markets. The firms that are either lucky or have superior insight may gain a competitive advantage by obtaining valuable resources at a price below their value. It is argued that all apparent sources of rent, such as rent earned on control of resources or on co-specializations of resources, ultimately boil down to either superior information or luck in obtaining under-evaluated resources.[13]

Lippman and Rumelt (1982) argue that markets for factors will be imperfect under conditions of *uniqueness*, under *enforceable property rights* to special factors and by *ambiguity*. In general it may be assumed that all resources that are stepwise *internally accumulated* are more likely to be under-evaluated. Because of these characteristics it may be very difficult to identify the under-evaluated rent-earning resources or to assess their true value.

To recapitulate, the resource-based perspective argues that if there is a causal relation between company resources and superior return, the resources in question have to be valuable, scarce, non-imitable, non-substitutable and acquired at a price below their value. *Key factors of success should therefore be defined as such resources*. It is likely that it is easiest to find the key factors of success among the internally accumulated resources because they are most likely to possess all of the necessary characteristics (Dierickx and Cool 1989).

Key factors of success as sources of sustained competitive advantage

It can be inferred from the discussion above that only factors that are valuable, rare, etc. resources possess the kind of characteristics which make them both necessary and sufficient sources of success. It can therefore be argued that the strategy for identifying success factors really should be to look for internally accumulated firm resources with certain specific characteristics, rather than general classes of success factors. However, it is true that the researcher may encounter deep problems because some key factors of success are hidden by causal ambiguity.

The requirement that rent-earning resources have to be inimitable and in scarce supply in order to be sources of lasting superior performance may also reduce the normative value of identifying such firm-specific key factors of success. The firms late to realize the profit potential of the empirically identified key factors of success may simply never be able to acquire these factors.

If we take a look at the 'key factors of success' identified in some of the empirical studies, it is clear that these are most often general types of resources and competences. The empirically identified key factors of success may therefore in a sense be sources of success as defined within the resource-based perspective, since it may be that the successful firms control specific variants of the general resources and competences identified as key factors of success, and on which they earn Ricardian or Paretian rents. An example is 'good marketing research' (Edgett, Shipley and Forbes 1992). The general act of marketing research may be carried out in all firms, but marketing research is only a source of advantage if the firms have developed adequate and firm-specific procedures that are difficult for other firms to copy.

But is it likely that a large number of firms earn rent on variants of the same general type of resource? An analysis of rent, costs of resource acquirement, and competitive imitation and asset-accumulation demonstrates that this central assumption in the empirical studies is likely to be wrong. Let us assume that marketing capabilities have been identified as a key factor of success ranking high among factors listed as contributing to above-normal returns in the successful firms. The question then is whether the marketing capabilities will also be undervalued in all these firms. According to Barney (1991: 107),

> it may be possible for a small number of firms in an industry to possess a particular valuable resource and still generate a competitive advantage. In general, as long as the number of firms that possess a particular valuable resource (or bundle of valuable resources) is less than the number of firms needed to generate perfect competition dynamics in an industry . . . that resource has the potential of generating a competitive advantage.

However, if marketing capabilities are ranking high as a source of success in most successful firms, it is likely that competition over inputs needed to create even the firm-specific variant of such a resource is stronger than over some of the factors which are not so often mentioned as a source of success by the successful firms. Therefore, it is likely that marketing capabilities – even if they are valuable, scarce and rent-earning – are not the prime source of superior return in the successful firms. To summarize, it does not seem likely that a factor is undervalued when all firms with above-normal returns possess it, unless of course the 'inputs' needed to create the unique variants of marketing capabilities are in plentiful supply; but if that is the case the successful firms will most likely not earn rent on the factor.[14]

There are also other kinds of problems regarding the empirical identification of success factors. Specifically, temporary imperfections in some firms' knowledge may result in other firms being more successful than their competitors, even if they do not possess any valuable and rent-earning resources. For example, high profit on a product may stem alone from under-evaluated resources that in no other respect are valuable resources. Firms simply may have acquired some of their standard input at a very low price due to a price war between suppliers. The economic benefit of these resources will not be long-lasting ones, however, because the input can be available to a large number of firms.

Yet another problematic aspect of identifying the sources of success may be ascribed to the possibility that some firms possess a number of rent-earning resources that are not under-evaluated and a number of non-rent-earning under-evaluated resources. A snapshot of the firm's situation reveals that it earns high profit, but the success may be ascribed to the wrong factors. Finally, financial measures in themselves are uncertain because of the great difficulties in measuring the exact cost of a single product.

The conclusion on all this is the following: the lists of key factors of success identified in empirical studies should be interpreted as some of the minimum required resources or competences for product success. We might also say that the studies come up with a list of different kinds of valuable resources.

IMPLEMENTING KEY FACTORS OF SUCCESS

While an earlier section was devoted to a discussion of the definition and identification of key factors of success, this section is devoted to a discussion of the *implementability* of the valuable factors identified in the studies. In a resource-based perspective, 'key factors of success' are the resources and competences that give a firm long-lasting superiority in product development. Within this perspective, the problems of implementing such factors in other firms are irrelevant, simply because they are defined as inimitable resources and therefore not implementable in other firms. But what happens when – as we have argued they should be – the empirical results are interpreted as consisting of lists of valuable resources or competences? To what extent can firms make use of the results to ensure that they at least will possess the necessary conditions for product success?

In the empirical studies, recommendations often amount to such statements as 'careful attention to the areas that our extensive research has identified will lead to enhanced probabilities of success for new product developers' (Zirger and Maidique 1990). The question – how do firms go about doing it? – is not really answered. The resource-based perspective does not provide a clear-cut answer to this question either; however, the insights gained from this perspective on the characteristics which make imitation of capabilities and resources difficult may enable us to provide a more detailed view on the issue of implementation.

We shall discuss the implementability of key factors of success identified in two representative studies, namely Cooper (1990) and Edgett, Shipley and Forbes (1992). Table 8.1 summarizes the two studies.

In the following, these key factors of success (or rather, valuable assets) will be classified into resources and competences, because it reveals something about the ease with which the results can be implemented in firms.

However, let us begin by noting that the resource-based perspective reveals some uncertainty about what to include in the definition of resources (Foss and Eriksen 1995). One position is to define resources as assets owned and controlled by a firm (Wernerfelt 1984, Peteraf 1990). A second position is to distinguish between competences and resources (Penrose 1959, Grant 1991). Thus, Grant (1991) defines resources as the inputs to the production process, such as items of capital equipment, skills of individual employees, patents, brand names and finance. Competences,[15] in contrast, refer to the 'capacity for a team of resources to perform some task or activity' (p. 119). Thus, competences are not just bundles of resources; they are, rather, complex patterns of coordination between people and between people and other resources. It is not always easy to distinguish

Table 8.1 Key factors of success identified in two studies

Key factors underlying success: Cooper	Success factors of product: Edgett, Shipley and Forbes
1 A superior product that delivered unique benefits to the user	1 Well matched to customer needs
2 A well-defined product and project prior to the development phase	2 Superior to competition in quality
	3 Superior to competition in reliability
3 Quality of execution of technological activities	4 Superior to competition in value for money
4 Technological synergy	5 Superior to competition in design
5 Quality of execution of pre-development activities	6 Highly price-competitive
	7 Well matched to company objectives and image
6 Marketing synergy	8 Unique
7 Quality of execution of marketing activities	9 Skilfully marketed
	10 Based on good marketing research
8 Market attractiveness	11 Launched on large markets
9 Other factors	12 Created synergy in production or marketing
	13 Avoided competitive markets with satisfied customers

between resources and competences. Management, for example, may in itself be interpreted as a resource while the act of managing and the quality of actions taken by management can be defined as competences (cf. Penrose 1959).

In general, however, competences are usually created within the firm, while resources are assets which are either acquired in the market or which are internally accumulated under the influence of the firm's competences. In practice the implementation of resources and competences cannot be treated separately, because there is a dual relation between them. On the one hand, the implementation of efficient competences depends on the stock of resources; for example, marketing capabilities may depend on the accumulated experience in performing marketing tasks. On the other hand, the acquisition of resources depends on the firms' capabilities: for example, how good firms are at accumulating market knowledge depends on their procedures for information-gathering.

What is of importance when discussing the implementability of valuable assets is the fact that whenever resources are internally accumulated and subject to asset-mass efficiencies or time-compression diseconomies, it takes time and a consistent set of competences to accumulate a desired change in a resource, even when the 'input' needed to accumulate a sufficient stock of the resource is in plentiful supply.

The implementability of the results

As can be inferred from Table 8.1, the empirical results of the two studies encompass resources and competences over which it is assumed that managers possess some control,[16] as well as descriptors of the successful product and the markets in which the product was launched.

Of the thirteen success factors identified by Edgett, Shipley and Forbes (1992), ten are what we call 'descriptors'. The results reveal that the product should be superior to competition in quality, reliability, value for money, design and price. It should also be unique, launched into large non-competitive markets with satisfied customers. Finally, the product has to be matched to customer needs, as well as to company objectives and image. While the descriptors mentioned may be interpreted as the outcome of the two competences (skilful marketing and good marketing research) or the resource (synergy to production and marketing), there has been no attempt to establish such a link.

Not surprisingly, Cooper's study shows that a superior product is the number one key to success. Apart from this almost tautological statement, the only other descriptor is that the market should be attractive. The primary lesson to be learnt from Cooper's study is – according to that author – that the quality of competences or actions taking place from idea to launch are some of the most important success factors. The factors listed are: firm's ability to provide a sharp definition of the product; well-executed technological, pre-development, marketing activities; technological synergy; and marketing synergy (that is, fit between a firm's distribution system and sales force and the product).

The descriptors may be used at the operational level to improve the screening procedures used in the firm. The lists of competences and resources show managers where they should concentrate their efforts in order to raise the rate of successful products. The lists encompass a number of more or less similar activities, which are the outcome of firms' competences. If the firm wants to be able to perform any of the listed activities itself, it will have to build up the competences internally. How easily this is done will depend on the firm's experience and expertise in the area. Depending on the alternative cost the firm may be better off acquiring its services from, for example, consultancies, if possible.

While a number of valuable competences have been identified, the valuable resources seem relatively unaccounted for in the studies. Perhaps that is partly caused by the interlinkedness between resources and competences. If, for example, market knowledge (a resource) is identified as important, it is very likely that the success factor will be formulated as a competence (good marketing research), because the activity is a more operational link to the resource.

Firms that already possess the mentioned competences or resources will find no aid in the results, because they give no hint as to what, for example, 'good' marketing research or 'quality' of pre-development activities might mean at the operational level. Firms that do not currently possess the resources and capabilities mentioned should consider implementing them in their firms if acquiring the assets does not involve time or economic disadvantage to imitators.

Finally, a word of caution. Not all the key factors of success identified over large samples of firms and industries may be useful in all firms. Because there are situation-specific conditions, not all results will be appropriate in all situations.

Again, this is in conformity with the resource-based view that strategy is essentially situational.

CONCLUSION AND IMPLICATIONS

The empirical findings of key-factor-of-success studies hinged on two important implicit assumptions: namely, first, that there is a causal relation between the factors identified and success, and, second, that there is a number of general key factors of success. From a resource-based perspective, it can be inferred that long-lasting returns endure only from valuable rent-earning and under-evaluated resources and therefore that the 'strategy for identifying' success factors really should be to look for internally accumulated firm-specific resources with the above-mentioned characteristics, rather than for the factors common to most successful firms.

The resource-based perspective implies that the existence of a causal link between above-normal return and resources common to a large number of firms is unlikely, since such resources would either be in plentiful supply, which would make it impossible to earn rent on these resources, or they would be in scarce supply, but not be undervalued because of the competition over these resources. In either case, firms would not be able to earn sustainable above-normal returns on the resources. As a consequence, we argue that the list of key factors of success should be interpreted as a list of valuable resources representing some of the necessary resources and competences for product success.

When the lists of key factors of success are interpreted as valuable resources and competences, we have shown that some implications for implement-ability might be deduced from the resource-based perspective. Categorizing the results of the empirical studies of key factors of success into resources, competences and descriptors serves as the first step towards a better understanding of the implementability of the results. Due to the lack of detail in the results, they can only serve as a checklist encompassing the necessary activities and resources for product success. The results uncover nothing about how to acquire superiority in the activities.

APPENDIX: A BRIEF DESCRIPTION OF SOME CENTRAL STUDIES

Cooper's NewProd is a series of research studies into the factors that underlie new-product success and failure. The results of this study build on 203 new projects (123 successes and 80 failures) in 125 firms located in Canada. In these studies, performance is defined from a financial standpoint (four measures). Using personal interviews, information on forty variables (covering product factors, market factors marketing factors, synergy factors, and management factors) was gathered. The results have been published in a number of articles, for example, Cooper and Kleinschmidt (1987a), 'What Makes a New Product a Winner', and Cooper and Kleinschmidt (1987b), 'New Products: What Separates Winners from Losers ?'

Edgett, Shipley and Forbes made a comparative study of success and failure factors for British- and Japanese-owned companies in the United Kingdom. The study included 202 firms (mailed questionnaire) with a response rate of 54.5 per cent for the Japanese firms and 38.2 per cent for the British firms. The study included both programme- and project-level questions covering types of new-product introductions within the previous five years, reasons for introducing new products, success rate of new products, and factors contributing to new-product success. Results were presented as percentages for British and Japanese firms, with a note on significant differences.

NOTES

1 For an overview of these studies, see, for example, Schewe (1991), Hauschildt (1992), or Hart and Craig (1992), and see also the appendix to this chapter.

2 The studies are briefly described in an appendix to this chapter.

3 Much of the argument presented is directed towards the studies of 'key success factors', but it can equally well be used against the studies of 'key factors of success'.

4 Exceptions include Cooper (1980) and Zirger and Maidique (1990), who develop explicit conceptual models.

5 We note in passing that this is an important point within the competence-based perspective, which tends to emphasize clusters of resources and competences rather than individual resources. See, for example, Eriksen and Mikkelsen (chapter 4).

6 This is essentially the concept of rational expectations equilibrium.

7 Time-compression diseconomies mean that there are diminishing returns from accelerating the accumulation of an asset by investing more in accumulating it.

8 Lippman and Rumelt (1982) and Dierickx and Cool (1989) are among the few who have addressed the question of how firms acquire their uniqueness. For example, Dierickx and Cool state that: 'Central to our argument is the notion that "success breeds success": historical success translates into favourable initial asset stock positions which in turn facilitate further asset accumulation' (Dierickx and Cool 1989: 1507).

9 Ricardo noted that land varied in fertility, so that when demand was sufficient to make it economic to grow corn on less fertile land, high profits were earned by any-one owning very fertile land. This extra profit was called rent because it ultimately accrued to the owners of the land.

10 Penrose (1959) implicitly identified firms' rent-generating potential from resources as the Paretian rent earned on resource-productive services due to the specific way in which they are deployed. As she explained: 'The services yielded by resources are a function of the ways in which they are used – exactly the same resource when used for different purposes or in different ways and in combination with different types or amounts of other resources provides a different service or set of servces . . . it is largely in this distinction that we find the source of the uniqueness of each individual firm' (p. 25).

11 'For example, to the extent that new product and process developments find their origin in customer requests or suggestions, it may be harder to develop technological know-how for firms who do not have an intensive service network' (Dierickx and Cool, 1989: 1507).

12 A strategic factor market is defined as a market where the resources necessary to implement a strategy are acquired.
13 Wernerfelt (1984) identified imperfections with the different levels of *bargaining power* possessed by firms. Barney's line of argument also shows that superior bargaining power (as argued by Wernerfelt) can only be a source of above-normal profit if the position is obtained at a cost below its value.
14 The existence of strategic groups within an industry (Porter 1980) is an example of firms competing on different classes of resources. The fact that firms survive within the groups implies that firms can and do earn rent on different types of general resources.
15 Actually, Grant talks about 'capabilities', but to preserve consistency with the terminology used in other chapters in this book, we use the – almost – synonymous word 'competences'.
16 The differences in results may be caused by the differences in design of the investigations and in the samples.

REFERENCES

Amit, R. and Schoemaker, P. J. H. (1993) 'Strategic Assets and Organizational Rent', *Strategic Management Journal* 14: 33–46.
Ayal, I. and Raban, J. (1990) 'Developing Hi-Tech Industrial Products for World Markets', *IEEE Transactions on Engineering Management* 37: 177–84.
Barney, J. B. (1986) 'Strategic Factor Markets: Expectations, Luck, and Business Strategies', *Management Science* 32: 1231–41.
Barney, J. B. (1991) 'Firm Resources and Sustained Competitive Advantage', *Journal of Management* 17: 99–120.
Camerer, C. and Fahey, L. (1988) 'The Regression Paradigm: A Critical Apprasial and Suggested Directions', in J. H. Grant (ed.) *Strategic Management Frontiers*, Greenwich, Conn.: JAI Press.
Conner, K. R. (1991) 'A Historical Comparison of Resource-based Theory and Five Schools of Thought within Industrial Organizational Economics: Do We Have a New Theory of the Firm?', *Journal of Management* 17: 121–54.
Cooper, R. G. (1980) 'How to Identify Potential New Product Winners', *Research Management* September: 10–19.
Cooper, R. G. (1984) 'New Product Strategies: What Distinguishes the Top Performers?', *Research and Technology Management* Nov.–Dec.: 27–31.
Cooper, R. G. (1990) 'New Products: What Distinguishes the Winners?', *Journal of Product Innovation Management* 1: 27–31.
Cooper, R. G. and Kleinschmidt, E. (1987a) 'What Makes a New Product a Winner', *R&D Management* 17: 175–89.
Cooper, R. G. and Kleinschmidt, E. (1987b) 'New Products: What Separates Winners from Losers?', *Journal of Product Innovation Research* 4: 169–84.
Dierickx, I. and Cool, K. (1989) 'Asset Stock Accumulation and Sustainability of Competitive Advantage', *Management Science* 35: 1504–14.
Edgett, S., Shipley, D. and Forbes, G. (1992) 'Japanese and British Companies Compared: Contributing Factors to Success and Failure in NPD', *Journal of Product Innovation Management* 9: 3–10.
Foss, N. J. and Eriksen, B. (1995) 'Competitive Advantage and Industry Capabilities', in C. A. Montgomery (ed.) *Evolutionary and Resource-based Approaches to Strategy*, Boston: Kluwer.
Ghemawat, P. (1991) *Commitment – The Dynamic of Strategy*, New York: The Free Press.

Grant, R. M. (1991) 'The Resource-based Theory of Competitive Advantage: Implications for Strategy Formulation', *California Management Review* 33: 114–35.

Hart, S. and Craig, A. (1992) 'Dimensions of Success in New Product Development', Äarhus (Denmark): EMAC Conference Proceedings.

Hauschildt, J. (1992) 'Determinanten des Innovationserfolges', Working Paper no. 294, Institut für Betriebswithschaftliche Innovationsforschung, Kiel.

Hise, R., O'Neal, L., McNeal, J. and Parasuraman, A. (1989) 'The Effect of Product Design Activities on Commercial Success Levels of New Industrial Products', *Journal of Product Innovation Management* 6: 43–50.

Lilien, G. and Yoon, E. (1989) 'Determinants of New Industrial Product Performance: A Strategic Reexamination of the Empirical Litterature', *IEEE Transactions on Engineering Management* 36: 3–10.

Lippman, S. A. and Rumelt, R. P. (1982) 'Uncertain Imitability: An Analysis of Interfirm Differences in Efficiency under Competition', *The Bell Journal of Economics* 13: 418–39.

Penrose, E. T. (1959) *The Theory of the Growth of the Firm*, Oxford: Basil Blackwell.

Peteraf, M. A. (1990) 'The Resource-based Model: An Emerging Paradigm for Strategic Management', unpublished working paper.

Porter, M. E. (1980) *Competitive Strategy*, New York: The Free Press.

Reed, R. and DeFilippi, R. J. (1990) 'Causal Ambiguity, Barriers to Imitation, and Sustainable Competitive Advantage', *Academy of Management Review* 15: 88–102.

Rumelt, R. P. (1984) 'Towards a Strategic Theory of the Firm', in R. B. Lamb (ed.) *Competitive Strategic Management*, Englewood Cliffs, NJ: Prentice-Hall.

Schewe, G. (1991) 'Key Factors of Successful Innovation Management', Working Paper no. 274, Institut für Betriebswithschaftliche Innovationsforschung, Kiel.

Wernerfelt, B. (1984) 'A Resource-based View of the Firm', *Strategic Management Journal* 5: 171–80.

Zirger, B. J. and Maidique, M. A. (1990) 'A Model of New Product Development: An Empirical Test', *Management Science* 36: 867–83.

9

THE IMPACT OF FOREIGN ACQUISITION ON THE EVOLUTION OF DANISH FIRMS

A competence-based perspective[1]

Torben Pedersen and Finn Valentin

PROBLEM AND MAIN CONCEPTS

The last decade has seen a considerable increase in cross-border acquisition of firms. The tendency has been global, and has most recently also included Denmark. This development is well documented but only a few studies analysing the business economic effects of foreign acquisitions have been conducted so far.

On the basis of a study of Danish firms acquired by foreign firms, conducted at the Copenhagen Business School,[2] this chapter attempts to analyse the business economic effects of such acquisitions. The key questions of the analysis are: are the competences of Danish production firms expanded, reduced or in other ways changed as a result of a foreign take-over and is the position of these firms weakened or strengthened? The analysis focuses on two aspects: the role of the acquired firm within the multinational enterprise (MNE), and its characteristic competences. Both have a significant impact on the way in which the firms develop after acquisition.

Even if pure sales subsidiaries are excluded, the various manufacturing subsidiaries perform considerably different roles in relation to the MNE (henceforth referred to as their 'MNE role'). Some production subsidiaries are oriented towards gaining access to the domestic market, whereas others have a product and development mandate of a specific product line. The MNE's ownership motive and the firm's role are two sides to the same issue.[3] The planned role after take-over of one firm which has been acquired for the purpose of becoming the MNE's Danish sales outlet will play a considerably less prominent role than the firm which has been acquired for its unique firm-specific knowledge. Over time, the ownership motive may shift, with implications for the firm's role within the MNE and for the competences of the firm. Ownership motive and MNE role are thus key factors shaping the firm's development.

Another feature determining the acquired firm's subsequent development con-

150

sists of its characteristic competences. The firm may already possess competences characterized by various growth potentials and thus be predisposed to higher or lower growth. If the firm is to maintain its competitive value, the parent company is required continously to upgrade its competences. Consequently, the firm's competences constitute an independent set of preconditions for its development after the acquisition.

There is an interactive relationship between the two factors: MNE role and firm competences. The MNE role defines the scope and type of competences which the firm is free to develop or to have transferred from the MNE, just as the firm's existing competences are important to the role assigned to it within the MNE.[4]

The structure of the chapter follows this analytical distinction between competences and MNE roles. The first main section explores the acquired firms' MNE role. In a first subsection, theories of MNEs are discussed on the basis of Dunning's Eclectic Paradigm (Dunning 1981, 1988, 1992), examining particularly the motives for acquisition derivable from this paradigm. In a second subsection, on the basis of data on the acquired firms, three essentially different types (clusters) of foreign-owned firms in Denmark are identified and related to the theoretically derived motives for acquisition.

The second main section analyses the firms from a competence perspective. A first subsection summarizes the competence-based theory of the firm (e.g. Barney 1991, Grant 1991, Penrose 1959). A second subsection presents the empirical observations of the competence profile on foreign-owned firms in Denmark. The next main section presents three hypotheses on the MNE role and competence structure of the firms and their bearing on changes related to the acquisition. We attempt to identify which type of specialization and relative shift in competences characterizes the various types of manufacturing subsidiaries, and the type of development and performance linked to these.

A TYPOLOGY OF SUBSIDIARIES BASED ON THEIR MNE ROLES

Theories of MNE activities

Various theories have been proposed to explain the dimensions and nature of MNEs' foreign activities. The prevailing explanation is Dunning's Eclectic Paradigm (Dunning 1981, 1988) which is a taxonomy of the various theories of MNEs. Its basic hypothesis is that three types of advantage constitute the necessary preconditions for direct foreign investment. These are:

- *Ownership-specific* advantages such as patents, brand names; R&D, management or marketing knowledge; or privileged access to natural resources; which can compensate for deficient local knowledge compared with the local producers.

- *Location-specific* advantages relating, for example, to the cost of factors of production, low duty or transportation costs; without these the owner-specific advantage would merely be exploited through export (from the home country).

- *Internalization-specific* advantages achieved, for example, by avoiding negotiation costs and by tighter protection of knowledge; without these it would be more profitable to sell the right to exploit the assets in the market (licensing, franchising, etc.).

Dunning (1988, 1992) has also developed a typology for various types of foreign subsidiary, classifying them primarily according to ownership motives. The ownership motive is seen as the main determinant of the subsidiary's MNE role and of the nature and extent of the activities carried out by the subsidiary. Thus, the typology operates with a connection between MNEs' motives for locating themselves in a certain geographical area and their behaviour in that location.

The typology incorporates four different ownership motives. *Market-seeking* subsidiaries are primarily established in order to overcome various sales barriers. The primary goal is to secure the best possible foreign-sales outlets. *Resource-seeking* subsidiaries are established in order to gain access to low-cost production factors such as natural resources or cheap labour. *Efficiency-seeking* subsidiaries are established as part of a pattern in which global MNEs locate their specialized manufacturing units all over the world to achieve the greatest possible scale and scope advantages. These three types of foreign company are established to exploit some competitive advantages, which the MNE already possesses, whereas *strategic-asset-seeking* subsidiaries are typically acquired for the purpose of obtaining assets in the acquired firm, which combined with the MNE's existing assets have a higher value than in alternative use.

We suggest that Dunning's typology may in fact be reduced to two underlying dimensions – *a location dimension* and *an asset dimension* – which together can be used to classify the individual types of foreign subsidiary. The distinction between these two dimensions is central to the subsequent typologization of foreign-owned firms in Denmark.

The location dimension comprises the concrete advantages which may be exploited by an MNE in a given location. On this dimension a distinction is made between whether the subsidiaries are established to ensure better access to the market and thus fulfil an import-substituting function (the market seekers), and whether they are established for the purpose of exploiting more favourable production conditions in the given location (resource and efficiency seekers). The asset dimension refers to whether a subsidiary has been acquired for the purpose of obtaining assets of some kind which the MNE lacks (strategic-asset seekers); or whether it has been acquired solely to facilitate a better utilization of the MNE's existing assets (the three remaining types).

Dunning's original typology of foreign subsidiaries (Dunning 1988) included only resource-, market- and efficiency-seeking companies. To these, Dunning has recently added the strategic-asset seekers (Dunning 1992). The reason for expanding the typology to include strategic-asset seekers is probably the last ten years' increasing wave of acquisitions. The Eclectic Paradigm focused essentially on the MNE's possession of owner-specific advantages which it attempts to exploit abroad through its own subsidiaries. Clearly, the purpose of acquiring existing firms is not merely to transfer competences from the MNE which can be utilized in the acquired company, but also to secure new competences from the acquired enterprise, which can strengthen the MNE's overall competitiveness.

The empirical study

The empirical analysis is based, in part, on a survey conducted in 1991 of all foreign manufacturing firms in Denmark,[5] and in part on financial statements covering, in most cases, the period from 1974 to 1991. The data base contains detailed information on a total of 141 foreign-owned production companies corresponding to 55 per cent of all foreign-owned manufacturing companies in Denmark with at least 20 employees.[6] Among the 141 foreign-owned firms in Denmark, 40 were green-field investments, whereas 101 represented foreign acquisitions of Danish firms. The present analysis is based exclusively on information on acquired firms.

On the basis of three firm characteristics the firms are separated into three clusters[7] (Valentin and Pedersen 1993). The three characteristics have been chosen on the basis of their theoretical and empirical explanatory value. Theoretically, the three variables constitute an adequate operationalization of the above-mentioned location and asset dimensions. Empirically, a factor analysis of a large number of variables (of which the most important are summarized in Table 9.1) revealed that precisely these three variables most adequately represented meaningful underlying dimensions (i.e. they scored the highest factor-loading on the three factors of the highest explanatory value).[8]

The three variables are: (a) the firm's degree of domestic market orientation; (b) skilled workers' share of the total staff; (c) the share of R&D costs of the total turnover. By means of cluster analysis, the firms are classified into three categories, each including firms with homogeneous scoring on the three variables. Thus each cluster represents one type of role for a subsidiary within the MNE, indicating the degree of local-market orientation (the location dimension) and the nature and extent of the subsidiary's assets (the asset dimension). In conformance with their respective major orientations the three clusters are referred to as the *market cluster, the production cluster* and *the R&D cluster*, respectively. It is important to bear in mind that the study only includes manufacturing firms. Consequently, the three clusters represent different types of manufacturing activity.

In Table 9.1, each of the three types are characterized on the basis of their average score on the three firm characteristics forming the basis of the clusters. The lower part of the table represents some additional characteristics, which vary

Table 9.1 Average values and analysis of variance (ANOVA) of the three clusters related to selected variables describing the firm

Selected structure variables	Average values for the three clusters			
	Market	Production	Research	Average for all 101 firms
% of skilled workers of total staff	13.7 (B)	26.9 (A)	9.2 (B)	16.8
% of sales in Denmark of total turnover	77.3 (A)	25.6 (C)	47.7 (B)	49.7
% R&D of total turnover	0.5 (B)	1.8 (B)	6.7 (A)	3.2
% pure resale of total turnover	18.9 (A)	13.5 (A)	10.6 (A)	14.3
% MNE internal export of total turnover	9.5 (B)	28.3 (A)	18.5 (A,B)	19.0
% export of total turnover	13.2 (C)	46.1 (A)	33.8 (B)	31.3
% salaried staff of total staff	33.1 (A,B)	28.9 (B)	40.5 (A)	34.1
% engineers of total staff	4.6 (B)	7.1 (A,B)	7.9 (A)	6.6
Average number of employees in 1991	136 (B)	301 (A)	265 (A)	236
Average turnover in millions DKr in 1991	157 (B)	325 (A)	281 (A)	257
Characteristic product and task properties	Transport- or service- intensive products	Flexible small-scale production	Research- based large-scale production	

Note: The letters indicate if differences in the average score for a given cluster deviate significantly from the two other clusters. Letters A, B and C indicate averages in declining order. Duncan grouping at the 5 per cent significant level is applied.

systematically between the three clusters. As can be seen from the table each of these different clusters of acquired firms can be characterized according to their specific characteristics.

The market cluster is strongly oriented towards the domestic market, which, on average, receives 77.3 per cent of sales. This cluster also has a high share of pure resale (almost 19 per cent of the total turnover) of products to which the firms have added no new value. Also, this cluster represents comparatively small firms, with the lowest R&D intensity of the three clusters. On average, only 0.5 per cent of the turnover is spent on research and development. The cluster primarily represents industries such as foodstuffs, paper and printing, and non-metal basic materials as well as certain subsectors within the electronics industry and the chemical industry.

The production cluster is primarily characterized by a high share of export (on average 74.4 per cent of the turnover), covering both internal MNE exports and independent exports, and a high share of skilled workers (on average 26.9 per cent of the staff). The R&D level is well below the level characterizing the R&D cluster, but it is still notably higher than that of the market cluster. Most of the firms represent sectors within which flexibility and continuous product development are important: textiles, wood and furniture, metal works, machinery and transport equipment.

The R&D cluster is characterized by a significantly higher R&D intensity than the other two clusters. This cluster is less export-intensive than the production cluster, and its share of exports is very close to the total average of the three clusters. Thus, this cluster represents firms which primarily base their knowledge generation on formal R&D activities. Most firms within this cluster operate within sectors characterized by strong international competition and of which research is a significant competitive parameter, such as telecommunications, measuring instruments, software, and subsectors of the chemical industry.

Based on their empirical characteristics, the three clusters display differences that resemble Dunning's typology. There is a clear similarity between market seekers and the identified market cluster. According to our study, looking more closely into the motives behind individual market cluster acquisitions, many of them are motivated by a desire to capture and protect market shares on the Danish market rather than a wish to obtain more favourable production conditions in Denmark. Some produce goods with extremely high costs of transportation compared to the production price itself (e.g. paper, glass, concrete, metal containers and foodstuffs); others must be capable of servicing their products quickly and efficiently (e.g. elevators). In still other cases, the production facilities have to be located near customers in order to adapt the product to local needs (e.g. software and publishing).

Finally, there is a group of firms that has chosen to place production in Denmark in order to gain access to various public contracts (e.g. producers of electrical installations and of asphalt). It is characteristic of the firms in this cluster that they, for various reasons, are forced to produce in Denmark in order to capture a satisfactory share of the Danish market. Consequently, their Danish production is limited to what is necessary to capture the maximum market share. Consistent with this, a large share of these firms' turnover is pure resale of products produced elsewhere within the same MNE, and their rate of exports is very low (only 22.7 per cent, of which more than 40 per cent are MNE internal exports).

While the distinction between the production cluster and the R&D cluster is not immediately evident in Dunning's typology, it can be interpreted as a differentiation of Dunning's strategic-asset seekers, which acquire firms to provide new assets for the MNE – assets being in the form of knowledge, technology or market shares. The firms in the production cluster are aquired primarily for their product or process know-how, probably especially the latter. These characteristics are reflected in the share of skilled labour combined with the relatively lower share of salaried staff and engineers. At the same time, the unique competence of these firms is reflected in the export share, which represents three-quarters of the turnover; most of this export is independent of the MNE.

Firms in the R&D cluster are primarily acquired on account of their R&D capacity, achieved through more formally organized R&D activities. Some of these firms have certain features in common with the firms in the market cluster: relatively large sales in Denmark and a relatively large resale of the MNE's other products. What is acquired in these firms is thus a combination of R&D capacity and market shares in Denmark.

Based on the acquired firms' role in relation to the MNE, the analysis shows the following points.

1 Danish manufacturing subsidiaries primarily perform three types of role in relation to the parent company: they enhance access to the Danish domestic market and strengthen the MNE strategically in that they represent two types of asset – production and R&D – in a form the MNE does not already possess.
2 These three types of role correspond to the motives for ownership of foreign subsidiaries as specified by the present MNE theory: market access, and acquisition of strategic assets in terms of R&D and production.
3 The three types of role are represented in the firms as follows. The domestic-market motive appears to be the single most dominant role of a specific type of firm: 'the market cluster'. The acquisition of product/production assets is the single most dominant role of another type of firm, those in the 'production cluster'. The acquisition of R&D assets corresponds to the type of firm found in the 'R&D cluster' but this type of acquisition to a certain extent also includes the domestic-market motive.

This three-way distinction between different roles for subsidiaries within MNEs is based solely on simple statistical indicators such as trade within and outside the MNE, the export share of sales, industrial sector affiliation, R&D intensity and the profile of staff skills. The following section examines whether each of the three types of firm is characterized by specific competences.

DIFFERENCES IN COMPETENCE BETWEEN THE TYPES OF FIRM

Dunning's Eclectic Paradigm explains why MNEs acquire firms for the purpose of performing different roles. In itself, the paradigm says nothing about how such different roles can be expected to predispose the firms to different subsequent patterns of development and growth. A basic condition for understanding firms' long-term patterns of growth is to examine the competences underlying the firms' characteristics and actual competitiveness. The competence-based theory of the firm is discussed in detail elsewhere in this volume (Eriksen and Mikkelsen, chapter 4). The following is a short summary.

The competence-based theory of the firm

Originating with Penrose's (1959) seminal work, the competence-based theory of the firm emphasizes the process by which firms transform resources purchased on factor markets into a set of specialized services. These services are the actual inputs into the production process, and it is by virtue of them that the firm develops its unique configuration of production, products and market services. Thus, the firm can be viewed as the bundle of competences inherent in these services. The competences of a firm are by nature collective to the organization and are primarily maintained in the form of routines (Nelson and Winter 1982). To the company they represent an organizational and social capital (Eriksen and Mikkelsen, chapter 4). Since this bundle of competences is created through a sequence of prior choices and decisions, it becomes path-dependent in a form which is *distinct* for each firm. Unlike resources, such competences cannot be traded in markets.

Path-dependence defines the limitation of the firm's future strategic options. It also includes the possibility of achieving a higher rate of value creation at relatively lower costs or of higher quality than the competitors (Teece, Pisano and Shuen 1990). This possibility for additional profit (in the forms of Ricardian or Schumpeterian rent) is sustainable as long as the competences are *imperfectly imitable*. A number of competence properties provide such barriers to imitation. In our context, three types of imitation barrier are particularly important:

1 *Asymmetric information.* The internal and cumulative nature of the competences imply that the firm possesses more information about them than the
   imitators can obtain (Grant 1991).
2 *Causal ambiguity.* Even though the firm possesses more information about
   its own competences than its imitators, the causal relations behind the
   competences' creation of value are rarely exhaustively understood. The concept of causal ambiguity (Lippman and Rumelt 1982, Reed and DeFilippi
   1990) emphasizes that the most effective barrier to imitation is that no one
   – not even the firm subject to imitative efforts – fully comprehends the causal
   relationships that must be understood before imitation is possible. In this
   context, it is important whether vital parts of the firm's competences exist as
   'tacit' knowledge: that is, function implicitly and internally in terms of
   routines and local rules of thumb, as opposed to explicitly and formalized in
   terms of unambiguous principles or equations (Barney 1991, Grant 1991).
3 *Synergy competences* are advantageous in that they are of low or no value when
   imitated individually. With their concept of 'interconnectedness of asset stocks'
   Dierickx and Cool (1989) emphasize that when the value of a given firm's
   competences depends on their mutual synergy and indivisibility, competitors
   achieve little or nothing from imitating them individually. Alternatively, if
   the competitors attempt to imitate the total bundle of synergy-producing
   competences, their path-dependent nature, asymmetric information and
   causal ambiguity become all the more effective as imitation barriers.

Apart from being difficult to imitate, competences must be durable (Grant 1991). Such durability may take the form of a well-established trade mark or reputation. However, the firm must additionally possess competences to renew itself at least at the rate of change encountered in its competitive environment. The general technological development, for example, must be matched by the firm's innovative competences.

Finally, the firm must be capable of appropriating the return on its competences by impeding their transfer to other units (Grant 1991). An example is the risk of important competences being transferred to competitors through staff mobility. One way of limiting this risk is to strengthen the collective qualities of competences and make them less dependent on individual employees.

When a firm is integrated through acquisition into a large MNE, the problem of transferability may assume a different form. Through ownership, the parent company obtains access to transfer competences to other parts of the MNE, motivated for instance by its wish to pursue scale advantages. It has been argued, in fact, that access to such transfers is a vital part of the rationale of contemporary MNEs (Kogut and Zander 1992). In contrast to the threat of competitive imitation, a subsidiary is not protected against such transfers by asymmetric information. However, it may be fairly well protected by causal ambiguity and the indivisibility of competences stemming from the synergy benefits. A significant competence synergy between customer service and product development, for example, may imply that the given competences yield the best return within the acquired subsidiary. If the MNE wishes to develop competences in a context of this kind, such upgrading must be linked to the development and growth of the given subsidiary.

The empirical study

Table 9.2 presents the competence profiles of the firms based on the strengths and weaknesses of various firm-specific properties as perceived by the given firms themselves. In order to understand the competence profile of the firms, it is necessary to examine if they differ in the way positively assessed competences are *bundled* within the same type of firm, and if this bundling indicates a synergy effect.

Such differences between the three clusters' bundling of competences are illustrated in Figure 9.1. Within each type of firm the figure shows positive correlations between those firm-specific properties which were assessed as relatively advantageous (the properties on which the cluster in Table 9.2 scored an 'A'). Thus Figure 9.1 shows whether each cluster has positive properties supplementing and reinforcing one another by being present simultaneously, or whether its competitiveness is based on a few isolated advantages. In the figure, knowledge-oriented properties are grouped on the left of the diagram, market-oriented properties on the right, while the remaining firm properties are indicated in the middle column. On the basis of Table 9.2 and Figure 9.1 the characteristic competences of the three types of firm can be described as follows.

Table 9.2 Average values and analysis of variance (ANOVA) of the three clusters related to selected firm properties

Selected firm properties[a] assessed as strengths/weaknesses	Average values for the three clusters			Average for all 101 firms
	Market	Production	Research	
Knowledge-oriented properties				
Technological expertise	1.93 (B)	3.07 (A)	2.67 (A)	2.56
Knowledge among professional staff	1.79 (A)	2.43 (A)	2.37 (A)	2.20
Collaboration with research institutions	0.46 (B)	0.33 (B)	1.22 (A)	0.66
Product development	1.18 (B)	2.50 (A)	2.33 (A)	2.01
Knowledge among skilled staff	1.07 (B)	1.53 (A,B)	1.96 (A)	1.52
Market-oriented properties				
Sales/marketing	2.07 (A,B)	2.60 (A)	1.85 (B)	2.19
Advanced user contact	1.50 (A)	2.17 (A)	1.69 (A)	1.80
Specialized customer insight	2.36 (B)	3.00 (A)	2.74 (A,B)	2.71
Other properties				
Production scale advantage	1.54 (A)	2.10 (A)	0.33 (A)	1.35
Supplier relationships	1.46 (A)	0.93 (A)	1.26 (A)	1.21
Insight into the competitors	1.19 (A)	1.17 (A)	1.26 (A)	1.20

Notes: The letters indicate if differences in the average score for a given cluster deviate significantly from the two other clusters. Letters A, B and C indicate averages in declining order. Duncan grouping of the 5 per cent significant level is applied.

[a] On a scale from –5 to 5 the firms were asked to indicate to what extent the given firm property is a strength (+5) or a weakness (–5).

The firms in the *market* cluster demonstrate values below average on almost all firm properties. Only production-scale advantages and the firm's supplier relationships are assessed as above-average advantageous properties (not significantly higher, however, than the two other clusters). The parent company ranks prominently among supplier relationships (cf. Table 9.1), and in this sense the high score on this property reflects a certain MNE-dependence. In terms of product development, capabilities and specialized knowledge about technology and customers, the cluster comes out with a score significantly below average.

Figure 9.1 shows only few correlations between the various properties, and only one is below the 5 per cent level of significance. However, in those cases where the firm's supplier relationships represent an advantage, it tends to be reinforced by advanced user contact, by professional expertise, and by insight into competitors' know-how. Compared with the two remaining clusters, this pattern of correlations indicates low synergy and integration between the various competences of the firm, and their individual scoring indicates a fairly weak capability for independent technological development. The cluster depends to a very large extent on the framework provided by the MNE. Compared with the

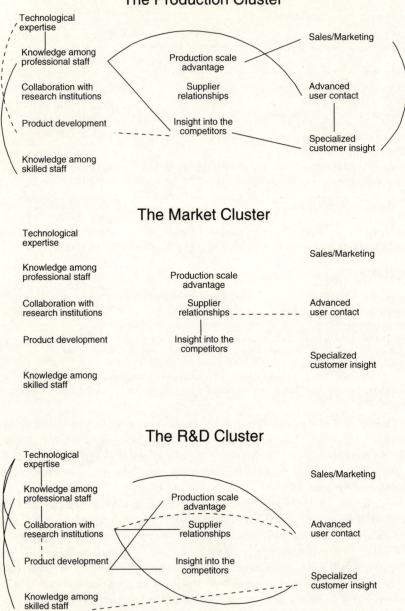

Figure 9.1 Relations between firm properties of the three clusters
Note: The solid and broken lines indicate significance levels of 1 per cent and 5 per cent respectively.

two other clusters, its competitiveness is considerably less grounded in its own internally created competences.

The firms in the *production* cluster demonstrate the highest score on a number of knowledge-related properties such as technological expertise, product development and professional expertise (see Table 9.2). In addition, they score relatively high on issues related to sales/marketing (in export markets where they sell most of their production, see Table 9.1) and specialized customer insight. Figure 9.1 shows a series of correlations (most of which are significant at the 1 per cent level). Knowledge-oriented advantages tend to be combined with more market-oriented advantages, such as the strong relationship between professional expertise and specialized customer insight. The various knowledge-oriented competences are more strongly integrated here than within the market cluster, but more weakly than within the R&D cluster. Thus the firms in the production cluster are oriented towards technology and development, but less on the basis of formal research and more on the basis of specialized product knowledge and learning-related product innovation. The cluster demonstrates significant positive competence synergy.

The firms of the *R&D* cluster demonstrate the highest score on the properties of collaboration with research institutions and expertise among skilled staff. As regards the remaining knowledge-oriented properties linked to product development, technological expertise and professional expertise, their score is also above average, albeit not as high as that for the production cluster. The superiority of the production cluster is even more pronounced with respect to the market-oriented properties. The correlation diagram shows widespread synergy within five knowledge-oriented properties, and a certain synergy between this and some market-oriented properties. Compared with the production cluster, the market-oriented properties seem to be less integrated into one another and into the remaining firm properties. The R&D cluster consists of technologically advanced companies. Compared to the production cluster, there is less emphasis on the specialization of their competences. Their technological and market-oriented aspects seem, furthermore, to be less integrated. But they exhibit a more widespread synergy within their various technological competences.

The above empirical analysis of firm properties of the three clusters of companies corresponds to some of the central concepts of the theory of the competence-based firm discussed in the previous subsection. This applies to the distinction between *resources* and *competences* and to the concepts of *durability, imitativeness and transferability.*

As to the *distinction between competences and resources,* the empirical analysis reveals that the clusters tend to be most homogeneous in terms of those firm properties which are the *least* competence-related. This applies to properties linked to the firm's external relations, such as insight into the know-how of competitors and relations with advanced users. Also, it applies to knowledge-intensive resources when they are immediately accessible on the factor markets in the form of supplier relationships and professional experts. On the other hand, the clusters clearly differ with respect to properties reflecting distinct firm competences. This applies to the firm's level of technological expertise, capability in product development, collaboration with research institutions, sales and marketing, and knowledge among skilled staff (for which *internally* cumulated competences may be strongly differentiated between firms).

In terms of *durability* the clusters appear strongly differentiated. Among the firm properties studied, durability is most directly reflected in product-development competence. Within the production and R&D clusters, this competence is significantly more pronounced than within the market cluster; furthermore, the correlation diagram shows that within the first two clusters this property is more closely linked to those firm properties which signify the depth of the firm's expertise.

As to *imitation barriers* the clusters differ on tacit knowledge. In Table 9.2, the production and R&D clusters demonstrate a higher score on precisely the two properties of specialized customer insight and knowledge among skilled staff, both of which typically appear in tacit and firm-specific forms.

There is, moreover, a pronounced difference between the clusters in the synergy-related indivisibility of competences. Within the market cluster, the correlation diagram shows only a few mutually reinforcing combinations between competences. By contrast, the other two clusters exhibit widespread competence synergy. The R&D cluster is concentrated on the generation of technical knowledge. Synergy within the production cluster, on the other hand, is particularly evident in the integration of market relationships with the internal competences of the firm.

Table 9.3 presents data on *transferability*, referring to the above-mentioned relationship between the subsidiary and its MNE. Transfer of knowledge from a Danish subsidiary to an MNE is most pronounced within the R&D cluster. This cluster differs most significantly from the other two clusters not only in terms of transfer of research and development results but also in terms of patent rights and continual R&D coordination. At the same time, the R&D cluster receives more know-how and patents from the MNE than do the other two clusters.

In the light of the observations presented so far, the relatively weaker exchanges of knowledge between MNE and subsidiaries within the production and market clusters require different explanations. Within the market cluster, firms are in general less knowledge-intensive; firms within the production cluster are characterized by a high intensity of knowledge, the form of which impedes both ingoing and outgoing transfer of knowledge. Several of our observations indicate that the production cluster is characterized by more learning-based technology development. Its more informal, local, tacit and learning-based technology is more difficult to transfer. On the other hand, the R&D cluster is characterized by a more formalized R&D function including, among other things, collaboration with research institutions, and thus by a more codified

Table 9.3 The nature of transfers between an MNE and its Danish subsidiaries

Selected transfers of competence	Average values for the clusters			Average for all firms
	Market	Production	Research	
Transfer of knowledge from the MNE in the form of[a]				
Patents/licences	0.6 (B)	0.8 (A,B)	1.2 (A)	0.9
Research/development results	1.6 (B)	1.5 (B)	2.4 (A)	1.8
Continual coordination and exchange of R&D	1.7 (B)	2.1 (A,B)	2.5 (A)	2.1
Transfer of knowledge from Danish subsidiary in the form of[b]				
Know-how	1.9 (B)	1.8 (B)	2.1 (A)	1.9
Patents/licences	1.1 (B)	1.2 (A,B)	1.4 (A)	1.2
The impact of MNE affiliation in terms of[c]				
Transfer of managerial competences	2.4 (A)	2.4 (A)	2.2 (A)	2.3
Access to financial competences	2.5 (B)	2.8 (A)	2.7 (A,B)	2.7

Notes: For letters A, B, C see note to Table 9.2.

[a] Indicated on a scale from 0 (no importance) to 5 (decisive importance for the technological development of the firm)

[b] Indicated on a scale from 1 (does not occur) to 3 (occurs to a significant degree)

[c] Indicated on a scale from 1 (reduced) to 3 (increased)

and explicit knowledge. Such knowledge draws more easily on external inputs, and it is also much easier to transfer from the subsidiary to other parts of the MNE.

Consequently, the potential rent from the technology developed by a firm within the production cluster must be realized within that firm. Technological capabilities become more directly linked to the development and growth of the given firm. On the other hand, technologies developed within the R&D cluster may be more widely applied, including in other parts of the MNE in question, allowing the generation of rent and derived growth also to become more widely diffused within the MNE.

In addition to this, there are other differences in transfers between MNEs and Danish subsidiaries. Within the market cluster, transfers are primarily dominated by transactions of goods in terms of internal MNE trade (see Table 9.1) and, to a certain extent, by transfer of managerial competences (see Table 9.3). The firms within the production cluster primarily transfer general (and non-product-specific) competences such as managerial and financial competences and access to an international sales organization, whereas the firms within the R&D cluster transfer more product-specific competences such as continual exchange of research and development results.

In sum, the above competence-based analysis shows that:

1 There is greater difference between the three types of firm in terms of competences, and less in terms of resource-inputs from the factor markets.
2 The market cluster demonstrates competences which are relatively weak both individually and in terms of their mutual synergy.
3 Compared with the latter the production and R&D clusters possess more valuable and well-integrated competences as a basis for sustainable, non-imitable competitiveness; the production cluster, in particular, is protected by causal ambiguity and competence synergy.
4 Transfer of competences from subsidiary to MNE is more widespread within the R&D cluster than within the production cluster. Generation of rent and continued accumulation of competences thus seem most directly linked to the long-term growth of the subsidiary itself within the production cluster.
5 The analysis shows that the competence levels and characteristics to a large extent are maintained and developed through mechanisms endogenous to the firm. Thus, differences in the clusters as to these levels and characteristics must be assumed to have been present prior to the acquisition of the firms, perhaps in a less pronounced form (see below).

ADVANCE AND TEST OF HYPOTHESES ON THE DEVELOPMENT OF FIRMS AFTER ACQUISITION

This section presents an operationalization of the analytical model in terms of hypotheses on the impact of two factors: the firm's MNE role and the composition of its competences as they affect the post-acquisition development and change of the firm. The hypotheses are based on the above identification of three types of manufacturing subsidiary with their specific composition of competences and the sustainability of competitiveness generated by that composition.

Hypotheses

Hypothesis on pre-acquisition growth

Compared to the firms of the market cluster, the firms of both the production and R&D clusters (the two strategic-asset-seeking acquisitions) are expected to have a stronger potential for generating growth *independently* of their MNE affiliation since they are based on more valuable and durable competences. The MNE-independent potential for growth is tested by comparing the cluster's growth process prior to acquisition:

H1: During the period prior to foreign acquisition, the firms in the market cluster demonstrate a weaker growth rate than the firms of the remaining clusters.

164

We have chosen employment as indicator of the growth of the individual firm. Among available proxies, employment is the most reliable indicator for the volume of the total activities in the companies of the present sample.[9]

Hypothesis on the post-acquisition changes in competences

The above-mentioned MNE-independent growth potentials of the firm do not disappear after the acquisition, but are mixed with an *MNE-dependent effect*. For two reasons in particular, this MNE influence can be expected to include an emphasis on competences linked to those functions which are central to each of the three types of firm. First, the role ascribed to an acquired firm assigns to it a more specialized strategic objective. Second, the MNE affiliation provides the acquired firm with access to a series of complementary assets (e.g. sales outlets in international markets) which allows it a greater degree of specialization in relation to core competences. To test this MNE dependent effect, the following hypothesis is advanced:

H2:   As an effect of the foreign acquisition, the activities and competences of the firms in the three clusters are expanded differentially; expansion will be most pronounced for the competences representing the particular strength of the companies.

This hypothesis will primarily be tested on the basis of the firms' own perceptions of how foreign acquisition has affected the composition of the firm's activities. In the study, the firms indicated whether seven activities (in the areas of sales, production and research) had been given greater or lesser emphasis after the foreign take-over. On the basis of this information, it is possible to calculate the relative shifts in importance of the individual activities after the take-over.

Hypothesis on post-acquisition growth

One of the conclusions to the previous section was that the production and R&D clusters – but not the market cluster – in terms of their composition of competences have potentials for long-term positive growth. This potential is particularly pronounced for the production cluster, due to the low imitability and transferability of its competences. The following hypothesis will be tested:

H3:   Long-term post-aquisition growth is highest in the production cluster, second highest in the R&D cluster, and lowest in the market cluster.

In the short run, the growth process will depend on the mutual adaptation process between the MNE and the subsidiary. For this reason, it is not possible to advance systematic hypotheses on short-term effects on the basis of the data presented in this chapter. H3 is also tested with reference to employment figures for the individual firm. We also draw upon the firms' own perceptions of how the acquisition has affected their growth and strategic freedom of action.

TESTING OF THE HYPOTHESES

Test of hypothesis on pre-acquisition growth

The analysis of the pre-acquisition growth is based on changes in employment during the period from five years prior to the year of acquisition. This analysis is conducted for firms acquired during the years from 1975 to 1990, excluding cases in which it has been impossible to obtain this information via publicly available financial statements.[10]

To test the hypothesis on the growth process prior to the acquisition the following model is specified:

EMPLOYMENT = $k + A_{cluster}$

of which the response variable is calculated as an index of the employment in the firm for each of the years (from five years to one year prior to the acquisition) compared to the year of acquisition (index = 100). A is a classification variable indicating to which cluster the firm belongs.

The test is made with analysis of variance, the result appearing in Table 9.4 as the average employment index of the three clusters for the period from five years to one year prior to the year of acquisition. As the table shows, pre-acquisition employment levels can be explained by the cluster variable (at a 5 per cent level of significance), thus confirming hypothesis 1. The firms in the three clusters have different competence bases which, even without MNE affiliation, creates different conditions for the firms' competitiveness and growth.

Table 9.4 Analysis of variance of pre-acquisition employment level in each of the three clusters

Average employment index for the period from five years to one year prior to the acquisition (year of acquisition = index 100)			Average for all firms	F-value
Market	*Production*	*Research*		
94.5 (A)	90.0 (B)	79.4 (C)	89.7	3.18**

Notes: For letters A, B, C see note to Table 9.2.
** Indicates that the model has a significance level of 5 per cent.

Firms in the R&D cluster have, in particular, experienced high growth during the years immediately prior to acquisition. Their average employment index is 79.4 during this five-year period, which means that their index on average has increased by 20.6 in order to reach the index for the year of acquisition (100). The index for the firms of the market cluster has, however, only grown by 5.5 in the same period. The firms of the production cluster are in the middle position, with an average increase in the employment index of 10.0 during the five-year period prior to acquisition.

Test of the hypothesis on post-acquisition changes of competences

In the questionnaire, the firms were asked to indicate if each of the seven types of activity listed in Table 9.5 has received increased or reduced emphasis since the acquisition. Indications were given as scores on a five-point Lickert-scale, the five points indicating the values: considerably lower priority, somewhat lower priority, same priority, somewhat higher priority and considerably higher priority.

Table 9.5 Relative shifts in emphasis on seven types of firm activity after the acquisition – analysis of variance

Firm activity	Firm clusters			Average shift	F-value
	Market	*Production*	*Research*		
Manufacturing	1.11 (A)	1.05 (A)	0.99 (A)	1.05	0.85
Assembly	0.83 (A)	0.91 (A)	0.97 (A)	0.91	0.82
Storing	1.00 (A)	0.80 (B)	0.91 (A,B)	0.89	2.60*
Sales	1.26 (A)	1.07 (B)	0.97 (B)	1.09	4.20**
Service	0.96 (A)	1.03 (A)	0.90 (A)	0.97	1.22
Development	0.97 (B)	1.16 (A)	1.18 (A)	1.11	4.41**
Research	0.86 (B)	0.98 (A,B)	1.08 (A)	0.98	1.58*

Notes: For letters A, B, C see note to Table 9.2.
** and * indicate a significance level of 5 per cent and 10 per cent, respectively.

Based on these scores, the relative shifts in the importance of firm activities are calculated for each firm (the stated change in each activity divided by the average change in all seven firm activities; that is, the sum of changes in each firm is 1). When the firm gives a higher ranking to an activity, this is interpreted as an expression that this activity and its underlying competence have been strengthened and upgraded; conversely, if the activity is given a lower ranking, this is interpreted as an expression that the activity and its underlying competence have been weakened and reduced.

Table 9.5 presents the results of an analysis of variance of the relative shifts in the importance of the seven firm activities in three clusters. As can be seen, three firm activities – development, sales and manufacturing – on average have been given a higher ranking after acquisition, whereas the activities storing and assembly on average have been ranked lower. However, the clusters differ strongly as to shifts in emphasis among the various firm activities. Among the three clusters, shifts in four of the seven firm activities differ significantly.

Firms in the *market cluster* give significantly higher ranking to sales and storing activities and lower ranking to development and research activities. Firms in the *production* cluster display fewer shifts in importance ascribed to the individual firm activity. However, the firms of the production cluster have attached relatively greater importance to development activities and less importance to storing and assembly activities. Firms in the *R&D cluster* differ from the other two clusters in that they have ranked research activities significantly higher; like the production cluster firms they have, in addition, further emphasized development activities.

Summarizing Table 9.5, the three clusters tend, after the take-over, further to emphasize exactly those firm activities which prior to the take-over represented the core activities of the various clusters. Firms in the R&D cluster have attached increased importance to research activities; firms in the production cluster have attached increased importance to development activities, and firms in the market cluster have attached increased importance to sales activities. Following the take-over, the firms develop in a way which deepens their fundamental characteristics and further emphasizes their core competence, thus confirming hypothesis 2.

Test of the hypothesis on post-acquisition growth

The growth process after the acquisition will also be examined on the basis of the employment index. Among the 70 firms acquired during the period from 1975 to 1990 it has been possible to collect comparable information on employment for 55 after the acquisition.

The hypothesis on a differential growth process between the three clusters after the take-over is tested on the basis of the following model:

$$\text{EMPLOYMENT} = k + A_{\text{cluster}} + B_{\text{from one year to ten years after acquisition}} + C_{\text{cluster, time}}$$

The response variable employment and the cluster variable A are identical with the above-mentioned variables, while the time variable B is a classification variable indicating the current year (from one year to ten years after the acquisition) and C is a variable indicating the interaction of the two classification variables (cluster and time). The time variable B is included in order to control shifts in firm activities and other changes in the firms resulting from the foreign take-over, but which only become manifest over time (see hypothesis 2); the interaction variable is included in order to control for the interaction between the variables cluster and time (i.e. systematic variations over time which deviate between the three clusters).

This model is tested with a two-sided analysis of variance. Table 9.6 presents test results of the model, and Figure 9.2 illustrates the average employment index of the three clusters covering the year of acquisition and the subsequent ten years. Table 9.6 shows both the cluster variable and the time variable to be significant (at the 1 per cent level) whereas the interaction variable is insignificant. The significance of the time variable means that time is of independent importance to the growth process across the clusters. Correspondingly, the significance of the cluster variable implies that cluster affiliation in itself is important to the firms' post-acquisition growth process.

The analysis thus confirms the hypothesis regarding a rank order of the

Table 9.6 Analysis of variance of the impact of the variables cluster and time on post-acquisition employment level

	F-value
Cluster (A)	7.34***
Time (B)	3.03***
Interplay $_{cluster,time}$ (C)	0.76
Total model	1.65**
R^2	20.4
DF	35

Notes: *** and ** indicate a significance level of 1 per cent and 5 per cent, respectively.

long-term growth level of the three clusters.[11] It appears from Figure 9.2 that the growth process of the R&D cluster does not differ significantly from that of the market cluster until nine years after the acquisition. The figure also demonstrates that the growth processes of the three clusters are relatively similar in the first five years after acquisition. Thereafter the firms of the production cluster in particular stand out. This parallel process during the first five years is the reason why the time variable by itself is also significant. During the first three years after acquisition, all three clusters demonstrate a very limited growth in the employment index, probably due to the fact that immediately after take-over the new owner restructures and rationalizes the firm, upgrading its areas of strength and reducing other activities. During this period, growth is fairly limited since some activities are reduced while new activities are introduced simultaneously.

The three hypotheses have been tested independently. However, they indicate as a whole that there is a mutually reinforcing relationship between developments in competence which are both dependent *and* independent of MNE affiliation. This is perhaps most pronounced in the case of the production cluster's greater ability than the firms of the other two clusters to exploit the foreign take-over. The firms of the production cluster are typically small and medium-sized firms which, in many cases, have developed a unique product or process technology which due to MNE-independent properties represents valuable and durable competences. These firms, however, have difficulties in exploiting their sales potential in international markets. The MNE affiliation strengthens the firm's competitiveness significantly in that the MNE's international marketing division takes over or strongly supports the firm's export activities. General managerial competence is infused into the firm.[12] This makes it possible to concentrate on its strong position, the technical production and development-oriented aspects, while its weak positions are compensated for through the MNE affiliation, which makes it possible to exploit the international marketing potential more optimally.

The somewhat weaker growth among the firms of the R&D cluster is not exhaustively explained by the fact that the competences of this cluster are more formalized and more easily transferable to the rest of the MNE. Several of the

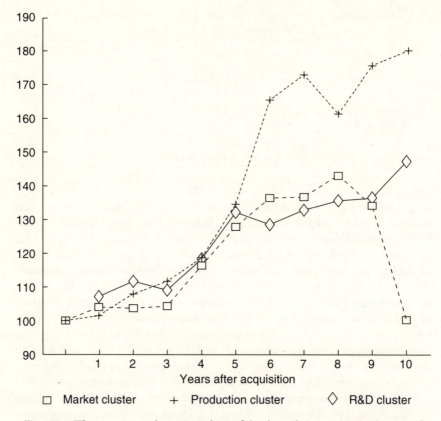

Figure 9.2 The average employment indices of the three clusters covering the year of acquisition and the subsequent ten years (index = 100 in the year of acquisition)

firms of the R&D cluster are owned by large MNEs competing within sectors dominated by a few global firms (e.g. consumer electronics, communications and software), which view activities in the individual country from a global perspective, and base their strategies less on the specific competences and growth potentials of the individual firm. The MNEs' global perspective often implies that certain activities are transferred from the more nationally oriented sub-sidiaries to regional centres, thus exploiting economies of scale.[13]

CONCLUSION

The above analysis has demonstrated that the manufacturing firms acquired by foreign owners do not constitute a homogeneous group which follows the same development pattern. Three basic types of acquired firm were identified, classified as market, production and R&D clusters, based solely on their different owner-ship motives and MNE roles.

The next phase of the analysis showed that each of the three clusters was characterized by a characteristic level and pattern of competences which – independent of their relation to the MNE – would make them prone to very different patterns of development and growth. Firms of the market cluster generate few of their competences internally, rather these are transferred from the rest of the MNE. They have relatively few competences which can generate lasting competitive advantages independent of the MNE affiliation, and they demonstrate the weakest development in employment of the three clusters. For these firms, acquisition has primarily resulted in a further focus on sales and marketing, mainly in Denmark.

Firms in the production cluster primarily base their development on independently generated valuable and durable competences in the form of specialized production knowledge achieved by combining knowledge about concrete products and production processes with specialized customer insight. Their knowledge, being less codified and formalized, is by nature more difficult to imitate and transfer to other MNEs. To these firms, the effect of the acquisition seems to be a significant strengthening of development activities, further specializing those competences which prior to the acquisition represented the strengths of the firms.

The R&D-oriented firms have both more formalized R&D activities and a development of knowledge which combines many different competences. To these firms, acquisition has led mainly to a strengthening of their research and development assets.

Thus, it is typical of the acquired firms that their strengths are further upgraded, while their weaker aspects are reduced and left to other parts of the MNEs. Foreign acquisitions thus lead rather to furthering the firms' own specialization than to a new orientation of the firms' fundamental competences. The subsidiary's post-acquisition development can be explained as an effect of both its MNE role and of its competences, but in the sense that they reproduce and reinforce one another.

The competence-based theory has emerged as an explanation of the firms' long-term results from market-based competitive relations. Here, the theory has been applied to illuminate how firms develop under multinational ownership; that is, how they are fitted into the MNEs' various sub-strategies, and how they are specialized, and their competences developed, after acquisition. The competence-based analysis has to a limited extent been used in theoretical studies of MNE–subsidiary relations (Kogut and Zander 1992, Helleloid 1992), but as far as we know it has not been used in similar empirical studies on the effects of acquisition.

The present study shows that important aspects of the effects of acquisition on subsidiaries are explicable from a competence-based approach. This explanation also throws new light on related issues, including the question of MNEs' allocation and localization of their R&D capacity. Recent studies have described the MNEs' localization of R&D outside their native country, emphasizing concentration close to the home base, even in those cases where the MNE demonstrates a strongly globalized activity pattern (Patel and Pavitt 1992). Foreign localization of the MNE's R&D has also been explained by referring to different types of efficiency gain pertaining to R&D activity itself (Dunning 1994, Granstad, Håkanson and Sjölander 1993).

Compared to other recent studies, the present analysis seems to indicate that in many cases, localization will be an effect of indivisibility and the synergy asset between R&D competence and other types of competences within the acquired firm. The production cluster in particular demonstrated that R&D capacity must be maintained and developed *within* the given subsidiary, if the advantages of learning-based development capability in this type of firm are to be exploited. Thus, the competence-based view substantiates the argument that the development and growth of acquired firms inevitably must be characterized by a certain autonomy, which also specifies some of the mechanisms behind the emergence of so-called heterarchical relations within MNEs (Hedlund 1986). Furthermore, it has been substantiated why autonomy will be predominant within certain types of firm (particularly the production cluster) and absent within others.

NOTES

1 The authors gratefully acknowledge the helpful comments of Lee Davis, Jens Frøslev Christensen, Nicolai Juul Foss, Christian Knudsen and Peter Maskell.
2 The study is presented in detail in Valentin and Pedersen, 1993.
3 The concept of MNE role focuses on the processual aspects of the acquisition (organizational and strategic aspects), whereas the concept of motive focuses on the immediate economic rationale underlying the acquisition. There is a close coupling between the two concepts since ownership motive is decisive for the firm's MNE role.
4 There is a certain affinity between this analytical model and Forsgren's (1989) 'Political View of the International Firm' which he uses to analyse Swedish acquisitions of foreign firms. Both Forsgren and the present chapter attempt to analyse the effects of foreign acquisitions as an interplay between some MNE strategic factors and the firm's independent potential for development. The primary difference is that while Forsgren links the firm's independent potential for development to the local network relations, we link it to the competence basis of the firms. By emphasizing the importance of the subsidiary's internal dynamics the analysis is much in keeping with the so-called 'heterarchical' perception of MNEs (Hedlund 1986) even though the development of acquired firms has not, to our knowledge, been studied from a competence-based perspective in a form comparable to the present analysis. Because they are both based on the competence-based theory of the firm, the model is in part parallel to Helleloid's model (1992) even though his argument pertains to green-field investments (as opposed to acquisition).
5 'Manufacturing firm' is defined as including software companies.
6 For a further description of the total data base, see Valentin and Pedersen, 1993.
7 Cluster analysis is a statistical procedure by which cases are classified so as to be very similar to others in the cluster with respect to some predetermined selection criterion. Clusters successfully formed by this procedure will have high internal homogeneity and high heterogeneity in their relationship to other clusters.
8 Simultaneously we attempted to conduct the cluster analysis on the basis of as few

and as simple variables as possible, leaving it to the next step in the analysis to examine if further characteristics of the firm were distributed systematically on the identified clusters.

9 Other indicators of the firms' activities have been attempted, such as turnover, return on sales, return on equity; however, it proved impossible to construct long, continous time series for these indicators, among other reasons because some of the firms for competitive reasons did not wish to inform us about their total turnover. Apart from this, these indicators are much more fluctuating than employment.

10 Of the total of 101 acquired firms, 70 were acquired during the period 1975–90. However, for some of these it has not been possible to collect information on employment prior to the acquisition. In connection with the acquisition, one or several companies are often reconstructed, which makes it difficult to collect comparable figures for employment before and after the acquisition. This is, for example, the case if the acquired firm was a division of a larger company and did not publish an independent financial statement. Among the 70 firms acquired during this period it has been possible to collect comparable information on 38 firms.

11 As an alternative to this explanation of differential growth in the clusters we have tested if the growth of the firms was rather conditioned by links to the domestic market. The reason for this explanation is that, given the limited size of the Danish home market, firms which specialize in servicing this market are bound to be subject to a limit for growth. Testing this explanation by correlating the annual growth with the home market's share of the firm's sales the two dimensions prove to be completely independent of one another. In other words, the orientation towards the home market is not in itself impeding growth.

12 Several case studies of Danish firms acquired by MNEs confirm this development pattern. Furthermore, Table 9.3 demonstrated that the Danish subsidiaries within the production cluster exploited the MNE's technical competences less, caring more about managerial competences and financial resources.

13 An example of this is the mobile telephone sector: during the 1970s and the 1980s Philips and Motorola placed important production and development activities in Denmark which during the 1990s have been transferred to other European subsidiaries due to a shift in the dominant technology from the Nordic NMT system to the European GMS system.

REFERENCES

Barney, J. (1991) 'Firm Resources and Sustained Competitive Advantage', *Journal of Management* 35: 99–120.

Dierickx, I. and Cool, K. (1989) 'Asset Stock Accumulation and Sustainability of Competitive Advantage', *Management Science* 35: 1504–11.

Dunning, J. H. (1981) *International Production and the Multinational Enterprise*, London: Allen and Unwin.

Dunning, J. H. (1988) 'The Eclectic Paradigm of International Production: A Restatement and Some Possible Extensions', *Journal of International Business Studies* 19: 1–31.

Dunning, J. H. (1992) *Multinational Enterprises and the Global Economy*, Reading, Mass.: Addison-Wesley.

Dunning, J. H. (1994) 'Multinational Enterprises and the Globalization of Innovatory Capacity', *Research Policy* 22.

Forsgren, M. (1989) *Managing the Internationalization Process – The Swedish Case*, London: Routledge.

Granstad, O., Håkanson, L. and Sjölander, S. (1993) 'Internationalization of R&D –
A Survey of Some Recent Research', *Research Policy* 22.

Grant, R. M. (1991) 'The Resource-based Theory of Competitive Advantage', *California Management Review* 33: 114–35.

Hedlund, G. (1986) 'The Hypermodern MNC – A Heterarchy', *Human Resource Management* 25.

Helleloid, D. (1992) 'A Resource-based Theory of the Multinational Enterprise', paper presented for EIBA Annual Meeting, Reading, December 1992.

Kogut, B. and Zander, U. (1992) 'The Knowledge of the Firm in the Choice of the Mode of Knowledge Transfer', paper presented for EIBA Annual Meeting, Reading, December 1992.

Lippman, S. and Rumelt, R. P. (1982) 'Uncertain Imitability: An Analysis of Interfirm Differences in Efficiency under Competition', *Bell Journal of Economics* 13: 418–38.

Nelson, R. R. and Winter, S. G. (1982) *An Evolutionary Theory of Economic Change*, Cambridge, Mass.: Harvard University Press.

Patel, P. and Pavitt, K. (1992) 'Large Firms in the Production of the World's Technology: An Important Case of Non-Globalization', in O. Granstad, L. Håkanson and S. Sjölander (eds) *Technology Management and International Business*, Chichester: Wiley.

Penrose, E. (1959) *The Theory of the Growth of the Firm*, Oxford: Oxford University Press.

Reed, R. and DeFillippi, R. J. (1990) 'Causal Ambiguity, Barriers to Imitation, and Sustainable Competitive Advantage', *Academy of Management Review* 15: 88–102.

Teece, D. J., Pisano, G. and Shuen, A. (1990) 'Firm Capabilities, Resources and Concept of Strategy', CCC Working Paper. no. 90–8. University of California at Berkeley.

Valentin, F. and Pedersen, T. (1993) *Udenlandsk ejet industri i Danmark – Virksomhedsprofiler og udviklingsmønstre*, Copenhagen: Industri- og Handelsstyrelsen.

WHITHER THE COMPETENCE PERSPECTIVE?

Nicolai J. Foss

INTRODUCTION: ECONOMICS AND THE FUTURE DEVELOPMENT OF THE COMPETENCE PERSPECTIVE

The various chapters in this book have all been concerned with refining and/ or extending the competence perspective. Rather than trying to pull these discussions together, my design in this chapter is to speculate on the future development of the competence perspective. In particular, I shall argue that the process of theoretical development of the competence perspective is to a large extent steered by the kind of economics that competence-based scholars choose primarily to rely on.

The competence perspective shares at least one important characteristic with the Porter-inspired industry analysis framework: they both significantly rely on economics in order to put forward new arguments, clarify terminology, interpret existing insights and criticize other approaches. However, on closer inspection it seems to be *different kinds* of economics that underlie these two approaches to strategy. While the doctrinal antecedents of the Porter industry analysis framework are clear and unambiguous, namely industrial organization (henceforth, 'IO') economics in the Bain/Mason tradition (Porter 1981), things are different with respect to the competence perspective.

The competence perspective has been argued to stem from, rely on, or be compatible with a wide variety of economic approaches, such as evolutionary economics (Foss, Knudsen and Montgomery 1995; Godfrey and Hill 1993), the new industrial organization à la Tirole (1988) and Shapiro (1989) (Ghemawat 1991b), Chicago industrial economics (Barney 1991, Conner 1991), and the Austrian school of economics (Wensley 1982, Jacobson 1992, Godfrey and Hill 1993, Man 1993).[1] Moreover, in this book, Christian Knudsen (chapter 2) explores the prehistory of the competence perspective and traces it back to, among other sources, Marshall's writings – a view that is reinforced by Brian Loasby's chapter (3).

Thus, many and quite different economic approaches are seen as compatible with or as being able to play a foundational role for competence-based research. Some recent commentators (Mahoney and Pandian 1992) see this as a strength

175

rather than as a weakness: it means that the competence perspective is ideally suited to further the conversation within the strategic management field.

However, there are reasons to caution against uncritically endorsing this pluralistic stance. For it can be interpreted to mean that the competence perspective should draw freely on just *any* kind of economics. But, as I shall argue, it is not sensible for the competence perspective as an emerging approach to draw extensively on widely different and even conflicting approaches, such as, for example, the new industrial organization and evolutionary economics.

Thus, choices have to be made; but choice is only important to the extent that the different options over which the choice is made differ in their consequences. Therefore, important questions include the following. Which kind of economics should the competence perspective rely on? And which criteria should we adopt for making this choice? What are the opportunity costs of choosing to found the competence perspective on alternative economic approaches?

The following take some stabs at these issues. Specifically, I discuss the potentialities of *new industrial organization* (henceforth, 'new IO'), *Austrian economics* and *evolutionary economics* with respect to the furtherance of the competence perspective. In my opinion, these three approaches are the most obvious contenders for serving a foundational role for the competence perspective.[2]

In order to isolate which of these three may be the most helpful, I first briefly discuss the competence perspective in context – more precisely, as part of a broader economic turn within strategy thinking – and discuss the central characteristics of the competence perspective. I point out that the competence perspective exists in two versions: a relatively 'formal' version which draws on neoclassical equilibrium methodology (e.g. Lippman and Rumelt 1982, Barney 1986a, Wernerfelt 1995), and a less formal version that is more oriented towards process (Prahalad and Hamel 1990, Hamel and Prahalad 1993, Hamel and Heene 1994). This distinction is related to Knudsen's discussion in chapter 2, since he also introduces an overall distinction between more equilibrium-oriented and more process-oriented versions of the competence perspective.

I next turn to a discussion of the potentialities of three economic approaches with respect to the furtherance of the competence perspective, concluding that evolutionary perspectives are best able to further the competence perspective. This is because more 'dynamic' issues seem to be increasingly relevant and important to competence-based scholars. And evolutionary economics better than, for example, new IO enables us to address and understand processes of asset accumulation, competition in terms of the accumulation of asset stock, technological competition, and so on – all issues that seem to be increasingly pressing to both practitioners and scholars.

Thus, although these issues may seem rather abstract, they should ultimately be of relevance to practitioners, too. There is much evidence that the competence perspective has already had a great impact on managerial practice,[3] and it seems likely that this impact is going to increase in the future. However, the foundations of the competence perspective are unclear and its implications are not fully unfolded. There can be little doubt that a future competence perspective primarily influenced by new IO is bound to produce managerial implications that are different from those produced by a competence perspective that is primarily influenced by evolutionary economics.

THE COMPETENCE PERSPECTIVE IN CONTEXT

Economics and strategy

As I noted in the introductory chapter to this book, it is a prevalent recognition today that economic theory is crucial to the strategy discipline. Economics is thought of as being able to further conversation within the strategy discipline (rather than to block it), among other things, because economics provides a relatively clear and unambiguous language in which strategy issues may be precisely represented and conceptualized. To strategy scholars who subscribe to the view that in general more economics means a more healthy strategy discipline,[4] a related – crucially important, but much too neglected – question must be: which *kind* of economic theory should we draw on?

Although economists undoubtedly are in agreement on the importance of some crucial organizing concepts and insights (such as scarcity, incentives and self-interested behaviour), these may nevertheless be focused in many different ways and lead to widely divergent conclusions. For example, a Marxist may use the assumption of self-interested behaviour to argue that the market is inherently 'anarchic', whereas an Austrian economist may use the same assumption to argue that there is in the market an inherent tendency towards an equilibrium state. Analogously, strategy scholars may use economics in different ways, may draw on different kinds of economics, and may therefore reach different practical implications.

In the mid-1970s, 'economics' meant to strategy scholars such as Richard Caves and Michael Porter the Bain/Mason structuralist approach in IO. To Caves and Porter, basic IO concepts such as entry barriers and the collusion such barriers may foster offered an explanation of, for example, the observed persistence of above-normal profit. However, it was not entirely unproblematic to rely on IO in strategy research. For example, Joe Bain (1959) explicitly excluded from the focus of IO any 'internal approach, more appropriate to the field of management science, such as could inquire how enterprises do and should behave in ordering their internal operations and would attempt to instruct them accordingly' (pp. vii–viii). As this indicates, the would-be importer of IO to the strategy field confronted a basic translation problem, deriving from the explicit dissociation from any 'internal approach, more appropriate to the field of management science' (ibid.).

Furthermore, IO was static, did not seriously consider the diversified firm, saw the firm as a unitary decision-maker, and had an industry, rather than a firm, focus (Scherer 1980, Porter 1981). This was much in contrast to the

177

strategy literature that from its emergence in the beginning of the 1960s saw strategy as involving entrepreneurial action in an uncertain and hard-to-predict environment (Ansoff 1965), did not neglect the large, diversified corporation (Chandler 1962), and was very much about the internal workings of the firm (Bower 1970).

Although Porter was well aware of the problems this raised for an application of IO to the strategy discipline (Porter 1981), many of the unfortunate characteristics of IO did in fact carry over to his industry analysis approach (Porter 1980). An example is the black-box conceptualization of the firm that is characteristic of older IO and which is clearly present in *Competitive Strategy*. Although it is by no means illegitimate *per se*, this conceptualization may direct attention away from aspects of the firm that may be crucially important to strategy research.

The competence perspective and the industry analysis framework

Proponents of the competence perspective (such as Barney 1991) have seen the neglect of the resource and competence side of firms as a major weakness of the Porter industry-analysis approach. Clearly, it may be analytically permissible to 'black box' the firm for some purposes, such as understanding short-run business strategy. This is because such issues do not necessarily involve significant changes in the firm's stock of resources.[5] But this procedure may block understanding in other respects, such as explaining the direction of the firm's diversification activities (Montgomery and Wernerfelt 1988), the inter-firm (imitation) barriers that block the equalization of rents over firms (Rumelt 1984, Wernerfelt 1984), and the growth strategies of firms (Penrose 1959). A satisfactory understanding of such issues would seem to make it necessary to treat the resource side of firms in some detail.

Finally, it has been argued that by concentrating excessive attention on product-market strategies, the Porter framework neglects the costs of implementing strategies (Barney 1986a: 1231; Dierickx and Cool 1989). Resources must be acquired or built in order to implement product-market strategies, and the cost at which this can be done influences returns. This implies that the factor-market distribution of information matters for the distribution of the returns of product-market strategies, since factor-market prices to some extent reflect relevant information. In fact, as argued by Barney (1986a), firms can only obtain competitive advantage if they are lucky or possess superior information. The competitive advantage obtained by luck or superior information is sustainable to the extent that various 'isolating mechanisms' (Rumelt 1984), such as patents or 'causal ambiguity', are present. This implies that an equilibrium may exist with firms characterized by sustained differential efficiencies (Lippman and Rumelt 1982).

Equilibrium and the competence perspective

Although some attention has recently been paid to various economic approaches as precursors of and potential allies to the competence perspective (e.g. Conner 1991, Mahoney and Pandian 1992), the extent to which the competence perspective draws on *modern neoclassical equilibrium methodology* has not been made clear.

However, the influence is clearly there. For example, Barney's (1986a) factor-market logic essentially draws on the rational-expectations methodology of modern macroeconomics (e.g. Lucas and Sargent 1981)[6] and the efficient market theory of modern finance theory (e.g. Fama 1976). According to Barney (1986a), firms can only hope to obtain a competitive advantage if factor markets are not efficient in the sense of the finance concept of 'strong efficiency' (that is, prices reflect all information) and/or expectations are not fully rational. Clearly, these are instances of equilibrium methodology, since the equilibrium concepts of efficient markets and rational expectations are used as a benchmark for inquiring into firms' possibilities of obtaining competitive advantage.

As a further example of the role of equilibrium methodology, consider the concept of 'sustained competitive advantage'. This is defined as the advantage that lasts after all attempts at imitation have ceased (Barney 1991: 102). Again (zero-imitation) equilibrium is utilized as a yardstick to define and understand (sustained) competitive advantage. But there is a problem here. For using an equilibrium notion to define the concept of sustained competitive advantage implies that the concept loses direct contact with reality. For example, sustainability is not a matter of calendar time. It is a matter of the 'logical time' of equilibrium models, and cannot be directly translated into real time.[7]

Furthermore, sustained competitive advantage exists only in (zero-imitation) equilibrium (see Lippman and Rumelt 1982); it simply makes no sense to speak of sustained competitive advantage outside of equilibrium, because equilibrium is *defined* as the absence of imitation. Given that one of the central aims of the competence perspective is to uncover the sources of *sustained* competitive advantage (Barney 1991, Peteraf 1993) in terms of concepts such as rareness, non-imitability, non-substitutability, and so on, of resources and capabilities, it appears that much of the important structure of the competence perspective is solidly founded on equilibrium methodology. Since, from an economic perspective, the pursuit of competitive advantage is usefully seen as involving the exploitation of some disequilibrium somewhere in the economic system, a too heavy reliance on equilibrium methodology would seem seriously to impede understanding these disequilibrium aspects of strategy.

However, it is possible to distinguish between two overall versions of the competence perspective – and one of these does not rely on equilibrium methodology to the same extent as the other. Thus, there is a more 'academic' and equilibrium-oriented version of the competence perspective;[8] it is essentially the one I have discussed above. But there is also a more informal or managerial version that I here take to be exemplified by Prahalad and Hamel's influential article on 'The Core Competence of the Corporation' (1990). In the following, I briefly outline some overall differences between the two versions of the competence perspective.

Varieties of the competence perspective

The more informal strand of the competence perspective differs from the formal strand by drawing less on economics and by being less oriented towards equilibrium methodology. For example, in Prahalad and Hamel's (1990) article, there is no attempt at all to conceptualize and assess the crucial concept of 'core competence' in terms of economics.[9] Relative to the more formal version of the competence perspective, there is much more emphasis in Prahalad and Hamel's work on dynamics, learning, innovation and process issues (see also Hamel and Heene 1994, Prahalad and Hamel 1994). Terms such as 'changing opportunities' (Prahalad and Hamel 1990: 81), 'collective learning' (p. 82), 'unanticipated products' (p. 81), and so on, are centrally placed in the discussion.

In the more formal versions of the competence perspective, such dynamic phenomena enter the picture because they allow theorists to tell a (loose) story about how competitive advantages may arise (see Rumelt 1984). But the greater part of the interest concerns how advantages are made sustainable, not really how these advantages are initially established.[10] This is, however, what interests Prahalad and Hamel.

These differences may be argued to derive simply from the circumstance that Prahalad and Hamel (1990) wrote for managers, that more formal versions of the competence perspective are written for academics, and that their ideas are just popular expressions of more formal competence insights. This, in turn, would imply that there is no real difference between the informal and the formal competence perspective at deeper theoretical levels, and that the more 'informal' work does not really add anything new. I do not think this is completely correct. For example, as already pointed out, the informal version of the competence perspective is explicit about issues such as learning, innovation and change that are not to the same extent present in the more formal versions of the competence perspective.

Evolutionary economists Richard Nelson and Sidney Winter (1982: 46) noted the simultaneous existence in economics of two different styles of theorizing, which they called 'formal' and 'appreciative' theory. As they explain:

> When economists are doing or teaching economic theory *per se* . . . the theoretical work is stark, logical, formalized. In contrast, when economists are undertaking applied work . . . or are explaining to an audience interested in the question *per se*, why certain economic events happened, theoretical ideas tend to be used less formally and more as a means of organizing analysis. These two different styles of theorizing, we shall call *formal* and *appreciative*.

(ibid., emphasis in original)

180

Nelson and Winter's distinction applies to the two versions of the competence perspective. In terms of their distinction, what I have called the 'informal' version of the competence perspective is an instance of Nelson and Winter's 'appreciative' theory, while the other, equilibrium-oriented, version represents 'formal' theory. Why is it that both economics and the strategy discipline (and presumably other disciplines too) are characterized by an appreciative and a formal segment?

In economics the fundamental reason why applied work often has an appreciative character is because it involves applying a timeless equilibrium model to an inherently dynamic reality (O'Driscoll and Rizzo 1985: 24). To use earlier terminology, it is a matter of translating the logical time of formal models to the historical time of reality – an enterprise involving bending and twisting the relevant theory, adding *ad hoc* assumptions and insights, using sometimes awkward proxies, supplementary 'stories', and so on.

For example, application of basic timeless (comparative-static) and equilibrium-oriented price theory to economic reality often necessitates introducing supplementary, but *ad hoc*, assumptions. An economist who uses basic price theory to analyse the economic effects of, say, some change in tastes will often supplement his or her analysis by introducing people imbued with entrepreneurial spirit who are able to discover and act on the new profit opportunity. But price theory does not formally warrant this; it has no place for the entrepreneur (see Kirzner 1973).

By the same token, much of what writers such as Prahalad and Hamel say is not warranted in the same sense by the more formal version of the competence perspective. For example, concepts such as 'stretching' or 'leveraging' resources (Hamel and Prahalad 1993) are difficult to interpret and understand in terms of the formal competence perspective. This does not mean that they are wrong or irrelevant; on the contrary, appreciative work may provide grist for the formal scholar's theoretical mill.

In disciplines where this feedback relation does obtain, progress is, among other things, a matter of practice being allowed to influence theorizing significantly and to indicate new problems to be solved. In disciplines where this feedback relation does not obtain, and some would single out neoclassical economics here (Nelson and Winter 1982: 48), conceptualization of empirical reality is completely dictated by which theoretical tools are currently available. It is hard to deny that because of its inherent orientation towards practice, progress in strategy research cannot be completely theory-driven. An implication is that strategy research can never be only applied microeconomics and/or game theory.

All this matters crucially to the future evolution of the competence perspective for a number of reasons. There is a real possibility that the differences between the formal and appreciative versions of the competence perspective may increase. This may happen if the more formal version of the competence perspective becomes even more stark, formalized, abstract, and unwilling to let practice significantly influence theorizing. Or, it may happen if the more appreciative version of the competence perspective takes on a life of its own and becomes unwilling to draw on more basic, formal competence research.[11]

This is where the issue of which kind of economics competence-based scholars draw on becomes important. For the future direction of the competence approach – including whether the two versions of the approach will converge or diverge – will to a significant extent depend on the kind of economics that competence-based strategy scholars decide to draw on. For example, there is a danger that the competence perspective may come to rely on overly formal economic theories and neglect the appreciative dimension. In the following section, I consider three economic approaches and evaluate their ability to serve a foundational role for the competence perspective.

THREE ECONOMIC APPROACHES AND THE COMPETENCE PERSPECTIVE

Questions asked by the competence perspective

It has become increasingly clear that what, in large part, separates economic approaches is the asking of different questions (Robinson 1977, O'Driscoll and Rizzo 1985: 17). For example, neoclassicists ask questions that differ from those asked by Austrians (Jacobson 1992).

Approaches to strategy ask different questions too. For example, the Porter industry-analysis perspective implies a certain set of questions, while the competence perspective implies another set. Since the competence perspective implies a specific set of questions, the nature of this set may indicate which economic approaches are in the best position to further research within the competence perspective. Strategy scholars may ask questions that are best addressed and understood by drawing on, for example, evolutionary economics, or they may ask questions that are best approached in terms of insights from the new IO. Which questions are asked by competence-based strategy scholars?

As indicated earlier, the overall research objective that informs the work of competence-based scholars is *to account for the creation, maintenance and renewal of competitive advantage in terms of the characteristics and dynamics of the internal resources of firms* (Wernerfelt 1984, Dierickx and Cool 1989, Barney 1991, Peteraf 1993, Williams 1994). This broad definition has a number of specific implications.

Most importantly, it must imply that firms are taken to be different in terms of their endowments of resources; heterogeneity is the basic condition of competitive advantage (Barney 1991). It also means that the mechanisms that sustain competitive advantage must be given great attention. It may be agreed that we know relatively much about these issues; since Lippman and Rumelt (1982) they have been central in what I have called the more 'formal' competence-based research.

182

But the themes of creating and renewing competitive advantage must imply that attention is paid to entrepreneurship broadly conceived (Rumelt 1984, Jacobson 1992) and to processes of resource-accumulation (Dierickx and Cool 1989, Prahalad and Hamel 1990). These issues may not be completely consistent with equilibrium reasoning. For example, processes of resource accumulation, particularly when they concern accumulation of 'invisible' resources of the competence or culture type, involve path-dependence, (collective) learning, and unanticipated consequences, notions which are hard to make consistent with basic equilibrium methodology (see Nelson and Winter 1982, Dosi *et al.* 1988). Accordingly, they have been offered relatively little attention within the more formal competence-based research. However, the more dynamic issues may be ultimately the most interesting, as argued by evolutionary economist Sidney Winter (1995: 151):

> Although the specific [managerial] challenges differ widely across resources, they typically involve both a static and a dynamic aspect. The static aspect consists of employing the resource to operate a flow of quasi-rents in the near term. In the explanation of interfirm profitability, differences at a given point in time, it is this static aspect of differing resource endowments that dominates the picture. The most interesting strategic issues, however, involve the dynamic aspect – the challenge of leveraging the existing resource position into a more favourable future position.

While we know much about 'the static aspect', we are still largely in the dark about the 'most interesting strategic issues', such as the dynamics of asset accumulation, or, more broadly, the creation and renewal of competitive advantage.

In the next three subsections, I discuss the potentialities of alternative economic approaches – new IO, Austrian economics and evolutionary economics – with respect to their ability to further research within the competence perspective and given the above identification of the competence-based research programme. I argue that the new IO is unlikely to help satisfactorily in addressing the above issues, that Austrian economics may provide inspiration, but is too general, and that evolutionary economics is the most likely source of substantial inspiration.

The new industrial organization

The upsurge in work within the new IO took place almost simultaneously with the emergence of both the competence perspective and the formal evolutionary approach (Nelson and Winter 1982), namely in the beginning of the 1980s. Most research has been concerned with game-theoretic studies of behaviour and performance in imperfectly competitive markets (Tirole 1988, Shapiro 1989, Schmalensee and Willig 1989, Saloner 1994). Specifically, a game between competing firms is specified and solved using the concept of Nash equilibrium or one of its refinements (such as 'sub-game perfection').

According to Carl Shapiro (1989), recent work in new IO can be *identified* with 'the theory of business strategy'. Shapiro further asserts that 'At this time, game theory provides the only coherent way of logically analyzing strategic behavior' (1989: 125). This may sound like a provocative dismissal of the work of people who have used other approaches when addressing strategy. However, one should bear in mind that game-theoretic work in IO implies a quite distinct conception of what 'strategic behavior' means: a firm acts strategically when it engages in behaviour that by influencing rivals' expectations of its future behaviour is able to influence the behaviour of those rivals significantly.

Note that a competence-based understanding of strategy as involving the accumulation and protection of rent-yielding resources would on this new IO understanding of strategy not necessarily be about strategy at all.[12] However, the pioneering contribution of Wernerfelt (1984) emphasized that there is not necessarily an antagonism between the competence perspective and IO-inspired strategy perspectives, but rather a duality. As Wernerfelt speculated, 'these two perspectives should ultimately yield the same insights' (1984: 171).

This conciliatory reading may be supported in various ways. To begin with, note that firms in the new IO are not homogeneous; for example, they may differ not only in terms of their cost structures but also in terms of their reputations (Tirole 1988: 256). Another similarity is that the assumptions of factor/resource indivisibility and immobility are central to both approaches. For example, the theory of contestable markets (Baumol, Panzar and Willig 1982) demonstrates that completely mobile factors cannot be sources of sustained competitive advantage. It is only in the presence of exit-barriers, and therefore immobile factors, that firms may realize returns in excess of the competitive level. Although focused somewhat differently, this insight with its emphasis on 'sticky' resources seems consistent with competence-based analysis (Ghemawat 1991b). In spite of such apparent similarities between the competence perspective and IO-inspired strategy thinking, there are also deep-seated differences; and I shall argue that these are so important that they overwhelm the similarities identified above.

For example, it can be argued that the new IO approach to strategy only really works in connection with analysis of situations in which the players are on an almost equal footing in terms of their endowments of resources and competences. If there are disproportionately large cost, quality, etc. differences between firms, the ploys carried out by much less efficient rivals will not fundamentally harm the much more efficient firms. More importantly, one may distrust the basic assumption of IO-inspired strategy thinking that firms are continuously engaged in playing games against each other. Instead, it may be asserted that a larger part of firms' activities concern games against nature. Thus, activities such as trying to get the production process right, trying to find out the preferences of consumers, designing an efficient organization, and so on, do not necessarily – if at all – involve a strategic dimension, as understood in game theory.

However, in my opinion the crucial issues have to do with the concepts I outlined previously as indicative of the kind of questions scholars working with a competence perspective typically ask. In other words, the discussion turns on whether heterogeneity, learning, process, path-dependence, entrepreneurship, endogeneity of competitive advantage, and so on, are included and conceptualized. I here argue that while these concepts are crucial to the competence perspective, they are not placed centre-stage in the new IO.

As asserted above, it clearly *is* the case that firms may be heterogeneous in the new IO. Furthermore, some strands of contractual economics are clearly compatible with the new IO (Grossman and Hart 1986, Tirole 1988: 21–60). In other words, it would be wrong to accuse the new IO of not having a theory of the firm or of conceptualizing the firm as a 'black box'. However, what may be argued is that although firms in the new IO are assumed to be different, the sources of this heterogeneity are seldom made clear. And to the extent that they in fact are made clear, they differ from the sources identified by the competence perspective.

In general, the most important reasons why firms differ are because they:

1 are placed in different environments,
2 come equipped with different initial endowments,
3 learn differently,
4 are subject to different discretionary actions from management.

Point 1 is the conventional economic explanation of firm variety (Nelson 1994: 253), while point 2 represents the new IO approach to accounting for variety. For example, in new IO models of technological competition, firms make different *initial* R&D draws, face different constraints and incentives, and accordingly make different strategies (Tirole 1988: chapter 10). In contrast, points 3 and 4 are not featured in new IO as explanations of firm heterogeneity, whereas they are central in the competence perspective. In new IO, the differences are already *there*, and do not change.[13]

In this view, strategy becomes primarily a matter of deploying given resources to a product market and utilizing them in sophisticated plays and counter-plays (Teece, Pisano and Shuen 1990). Strategy becomes a matter of extracting maximum monopoly rents out of 'fixed factors over the planning horizon' (Caves 1984: 128) by 'playing the game' in an intelligent way. Longer-run strategic issues relating to the development and accumulation of resources do not enter the picture. The critique that Edith Penrose (1959: 1) directed towards the neoclassical theory of the firm of her time seems also appropriate in connection with the new IO: 'there is no notion of an *internal* process of *development* leading to cumulative movements in any one direction'.

Thus, while firms in the new IO are clearly different, the sources of heterogeneity are given and fixed. In contrast to the competence perspective, firms do not themselves create their own opportunity set. Ultimately, this may arguably be reduced to a matter of differences in underlying conceptualizations of agency.

Clearly, the relevant conceptualization in the new IO is one that presumes very large cognitive powers on behalf of agents: in game-theoretic new IO, a strategy involves anticipating any and all actions that other players might take in all future stages of the game, and calculating the optimal response (Caves 1994: 14). Since all players are able to do this, the equilibrium position is essentially given from the beginning. Players cannot be surprised by unexpected events, there is never any difference between the competence of players and the difficulty of decision problems (see Heiner 1983), and although agents may formally learn in Bayesian games, their learning *functions* never change (O'Driscoll and Rizzo 1985: 37).

This means that there cannot be any failed strategies and wrong conjectures, no need for restructuring organizations in the face of, for example, new competition from innovative entrants, no 'emergent' (unintended) strategies (Mintzberg 1994), and no accumulation of resources (except as represented in a trivial way by learning by doing) – in short, there can be no *process*.

In my opinion, the above are major differences from the basic thrust of the competence perspective that should lead us to question seriously the usefulness of the new IO with respect to the furtherance of the competence perspective. However, (formal) competence-oriented scholars may draw on the new IO because of its technical attractions. In fact, Wernerfelt (1995: 134) utilizes the assumption of given initial resources in a way that seems to bring him closer to the new IO than to the competence perspective:

> In its simplest form the resource-based approach to strategy is derived in a static model. Given an exogenously specified set of interfirm resource differences, one can derive equilibrium strategies as functions of these differences and interpret profits as returns to the resources.

In its less 'simple', but more appreciative (and perhaps more representative), versions, the competence perspective does not start out with a given 'exogenously specified set of interfirm resource differences'. Instead, differences arise from differential learning, innovation, path-dependences, and so on (Prahalad and Hamel 1990). Since the new IO has little to say about these issues, I suggest we take a look at economic approaches that may have more to say about them.

Austrian economics

Robert Jacobson (1992) contrasted what he called 'the Austrian theory of strategy' with IO-inspired strategy thinking, essentially identifying this purportedly Austrian theory with the competence perspective. Other scholars have also argued that Austrian economics may be helpful to strategy research (Wensley 1982, Godfrey and Hill 1993, Man 1993). It therefore seems appropriate to consider the role of Austrian economics with respect to the furtherance of the competence perspective.

Austrian economics originated with the marginalist revolution in economics around 1870.[14] Some of the many themes that Austrians have addressed – such as methodology, capital theory, monetary theory and business cycle theory – are not relevant here. Work that is relevant is that on entrepreneurship and the market process, exemplified by Mises (1949), Hayek (1948) and Kirzner (1973).

Key to the seminal contributions of Mises (1949) and Hayek (1948) is to develop a process conceptualization of the market that differs from the standard neoclassical one. Markets should not be approached in terms of numbers of sellers and buyers, concentration or whether sellers can influence price. Such conceptualizations are, because of their static nature, likely to obscure the rivalrous nature of market activity seriously and to lead attention away from the prime mover of the market, the entrepreneur. The entrepreneur has been most carefully discussed in the Austrian literature by Israel M. Kirzner (1973). According to him, entrepreneurs discover hitherto undiscovered opportunities for profitable trade, to wit, exhibit the entrepreneurial quality of 'alertness'. However, as Kirzner (1973: 73) himself makes clear, innovation is not featured in his theory, and he even dissociates himself from the Schumpeterian notion of the innovative entrepreneur.

In the Schumpeterian system entrepreneurship is a matter of introducing new processes of production, new products, forms of organization, and so on (Schumpeter 1934). This is clearly related to the competence perspective. Entrepreneurship is formally portrayed in the competence perspective as a matter of drawing from a distribution of productive efficiencies when entering an industry and paying an irrecoverable 'entry fee' (Lippman and Rumelt 1982). This formal representation is intended to capture the uncertain nature of entrepreneurial ventures. The appreciative competence literature emphasizes even more the forward-looking role of entrepreneurship and its ability to imagine and create the firm's opportunity set. For example, Prahalad and Hamel (1990: 80) take a very Schumpeterian view of management, thinking of its 'critical task' as 'creating products that customers need but have not yet even imagined', that is, to innovate products. This is conceptually distinct from Kirzner's view of the entrepreneur.

It is furthermore important to understand that Kirzner and other Austrians are primarily interested in the entrepreneur because it allows them to construct a dynamic theory of the market process. The Austrian theory of the *market* process is not a theory of the individual actors on the market *per se*.[15] Arguably as a result of this, there is no Austrian theory of the firm, its organization, boundaries or productive competences (Foss 1994b). As Loasby (1989: 157) observes, 'the behaviour of large firms is a neglected area of Austrian economics', and as two Austrian economists noticed, 'there is no . . . Austrian theory of the firm' (O'Driscoll and Rizzo 1985: 123). Since the competence perspective is first and foremost about the firm and firm strategy, it is therefore doubtful how much direct inspiration may be gained from Austrian economics. There are other reasons why scholars are unlikely to benefit directly from Austrian economics.

Strategy scholars have increasingly turned towards economics because, among other things, they believe that economics may increase the problem-solving ability of strategy thinking, make strategy thinking more susceptible to confrontation with empirical reality, make concepts less ambiguous, and increase fruitful dialogue between strategy scholars (Camerer 1985; Montgomery, Wernerfelt and Balakrishnan 1989; Rumelt, Schendel and Teece 1991, 1994). Can strategy scholars get these benefits from Austrian economics? In my opinion the answer is largely in the negative. For example, because of its strongly anti-empirical stance (see, for example, Mises 1949), Austrian economics may halt rather than improve testing and confrontation with empirical reality. It is also doubtful whether Austrian economics would bring more conceptual clarity to the field and thus improve dialogue between scholars. Austrian economics simply has not conceptualized many concepts and phenomena relevant to strategy research and, most importantly, the firm.

Although Austrian economics is unlikely to be of little direct use in strategy research in general, and in the competence perspective in particular, it does provide a germane overall vision of the economic process as a matter of disequilibrium, entrepreneurship, coping with ignorance and learning (O'Driscoll and Rizzo 1985, Jacobson 1992). This vision differs strongly from the new IO emphasis on equilibrium states and unlimited rationality. But we do not necessarily have to go to Austrian economics for this vision; it may also be found in evolutionary economics (Nelson and Winter 1982: chapter 2). And, as I argue in the next subsection, evolutionary economics is likely to be of more direct inspiration for competence-oriented scholars than either the new IO or Austrian economics. For example, modern evolutionary economics pays attention to the dynamic processes that interest appreciative competence-oriented scholars, while it is still able to satisfy the demands of more formal scholars with respect to rigour, formalization, and so on.

Evolutionary economics

Although evolutionary approaches have a long history in economics and although prominent economists such as Alfred Marshall and Joseph Schumpeter endorsed evolutionary modes of thought,[16] they have never been a part of mainstream economics (Hodgson 1993, Andersen 1994). Arguably, some of this has to do with the great diversity that characterizes evolutionary approaches. There are evolutionary theories about the individual decision-maker at one end of the spectrum, and there are evolutionary theories of secular changes in national economies at the other end (see Dosi *et al.* 1988). But it has also been a constant problem that evolutionary economists have not been unanimous about what is meant by a theory being 'evolutionary'. Is it just that the theory is about irreversible change? Or, is it rather that it uses analogies to central concepts from evolutionary biology?

An important characteristic of modern evolutionary economics (Nelson and Winter 1982, Dosi *et al.* 1988, Metcalfe and Gibbons 1989, Andersen 1994) is its orientation towards *population dynamics*, implying an orientation towards the population level and a view of heterogeneity of the (rather inflexible) members of a population as driving the evolutionary process (for the organization-theory equivalent, see Hannan and Freeman 1989). This is focused by providing analogies to three central mechanisms of evolutionary biology, to wit, *variation*, *heredity* and *selection*.

By 'variation' is meant that members of a population differ with respect to at least one trait of selective significance; 'heredity' means there exist copy mechanisms that ensure stability of traits in the species under consideration; and 'selection' means that some species are better adapted to the pressure of the environment, and as a result increase in weight through differential reproduction. In economics, the firm level normally provides the analogies to the first two evolutionary mechanisms. Firms differ in terms of their endowments of resources, strategies, efficiencies, realized performance, and so on. This provides an analogy to the concept of variation. Furthermore, firms' innovative efforts introduce new variation. The analogy to heredity is to be found in the firm's competences which both transmit information over time and make firms relatively inflexible. Finally, market competition and firm growth and decline provide the rather obvious analogy to the mechanism of selection through differential reproduction.

The most important recent contribution within this kind of evolutionary theory is undoubtedly Nelson and Winter's book, *An Evolutionary Theory of Economic Change* (1982). It was with the publication of this book that the contours of a unified and rigorous evolutionary research programme began to take shape (Andersen 1994: 18). Nelson and Winter stand directly in the tradition of the biological analogy that was given its first articulate statement by Armen Alchian (1950). In their formal models, firms are primarily conceptualized as bundles of hierarchically arranged routines, representing 'the skills of the organization'. These are rather inflexible (but may be changed through process innovation), and thus provide a rationale for the relative rigidity of behaviour that is necessary for selection to work.[17]

In Nelson and Winter's early writings (including their 1982 book), there is little interest *per se* in firm strategies, mainly because of the population-dynamic orientation. However, firm behaviour is in no way unimportant in evolutionary economics: it is after all on the firm level that analogies to heredity and variation are found. And crucial evolutionary concepts such as adaptation, learning, search and path-dependence mostly relate to this level. Furthermore, as I explain in the following subsection, evolutionary economists have recently turned their attention increasingly towards the firm level.

Phylogenetic and ontogenetic evolutionary economics

Within biology, it is customary to make a distinction between '*phylogenetic*' and '*ontogenetic*' evolution (Richards 1992). Phylogenetic evolution is a matter of what was earlier called 'population dynamics'. In contrast to the population perspective in phylogenetic evolution, ontogenetic evolution concerns the development of the individual organism. While the greater part of evolutionary economics has been directed towards phylogenetic evolution (that is, evolutionary change at the industry level), there has recently been a number of important attempts to approach firm-level ontogenetic evolution. For example, both Richard Nelson and Sidney Winter have since the publication of their joint 1982 book pursued a more ontogenetic style of analysis (Nelson 1994; Winter 1987, 1988, 1990). Other important examples include the many recent papers on technology strategy from an evolutionary perspective (Burgelman and Rosenbloom 1989, Metcalfe and Gibbons 1989, Kogut and Zander 1992), the recent 'dynamic capabilities approach' (Teece, Pisano and Shuen 1990, Langlois 1992), and the increasing interest that Oliver Williamson's (1985) transaction-cost economics has met with among some evolutionary scholars (such as Dosi, Teece and Winter 1992).

In its firm-oriented, ontogenetic guise, the evolutionary approach draws heavily on Penrose (1959), who presented the first comprehensive ontogenetic theory of the firm, *and* who is one of the strongest influences on the competence perspective. According to Penrose, there is no optimum size ('equilibrium') of the firm, since firms continually generate excess resources that may profitably be deployed to 'neighboring' product markets. There is a continuous evolution of the individual firm, and the emphasis on increasing and related diversification is just a part of this evolutionary story, albeit the one for which she is best known.

Although Penrose's story is ontogenetic, it is not in principle incompatible with a broader phylogenetic story. For firms have different rates of growth, and those kinds of firm that exhibit higher rates of growth will over time dominate in the overall population. In other words, ontogenetic and phylogenetic modes of analysis are not in principle incompatible (see Metcalfe and Gibbons 1989). Most importantly, it is not at all necessary for application of evolutionary arguments to assume that agents are completely unable to adapt to changed circumstances, and are completely ignorant and myopic. However, what *is* important is that complete flexibility and strong rationality assumptions (*à la* the new IO) are ruled out.

By focusing on the 'unfolding process' (Penrose 1959: 1) of the growth of the individual firm, an ontogenetic story of firms better allows us to understand why firms differ, giving us an improved basis for discussing *how* such differences matter (see Nelson 1994). That is, we are more detailed and explicit about a necessary element in the overall evolutionary explanation.

However, this is not necessarily to say that the fundamental evolutionary mechanisms are inapplicable to the organizational level. On the contrary, Herbert Simon (1962) long ago explicitly tied organization-level learning dynamics to evolutionary theory by arguing that processes of search and discovery can be conceptualized in terms of variety and selection. Thus, it is not necessarily sloppy terminology to say of a firm that it is 'evolving' rather than 'developing'.

In the following subsection, I make and try to substantiate two related claims: evolutionary economics may assist the competence perspective to the extent that the competence perspective is about ontogenetic evolution, and it may supply a much needed theory of phylogenetic evolution to the competence perspective.

Evolutionary economics and the competence perspective

The (set of) evolutionary approach(es) and the competence perspective are both characterized by emphasizing fundamental heterogeneity of firms as a *necessary* starting point for theorizing, but have traditionally justified this differently. Evolutionary economists have been interested in heterogeneity, because it is a necessary part of a population-dynamic (phylogenetic) approach (Andersen 1994). Competence-oriented scholars have been interested in heterogeneity because heterogeneity is the basic condition of competitive advantages (Barney 1991). Their attention has been more directed towards the ontogenetic aspect, that is, the development of the individual firm. But, as asserted earlier, phylogenetic and ontogenetic evolution are not incompatible. For example, it is because some firms evolve superior bundles of resources and therefore gain competitive advantage (competence-perspective insight) that they may increase in weight in the overall population of firms (evolutionary insight). In other words, there is a close complementarity between the two approaches here. Some similarities are briefly considered next.

Both the evolutionary approach and the competence perspective are founded on a (Penrosian) notion of the firm as a knowledge-creating entity. In both it is fundamentally the firm's path-dependent, hence, 'sticky', knowledge endowment that makes it differ in important respects from other firms, and allows it to articulate rent-seeking strategies that differ from those of other firms. For example, there is much similarity between the focus on routines/organizational capabilities in formal evolutionary economics (Nelson and Winter 1982: chapter 5) and the concern with 'core competence' in the more appreciative versions of the competence perspective (such as Prahalad and Hamel 1990). Moreover, there is an interesting connection to the evolutionary argument that firms are inert. This argument does not amount to the proposition that firms are completely unable to change. Rather, it is a much more subtle argument that some parts – perhaps the crucial ones – are much less likely than other parts to change rapidly in response to outside changes. It is widely recognized that the resources that matter most for firm success – such as technological competences, culture, reputation, and so on – are best viewed as *stock variables* that can only be gradually changed by appropriately chosen input flows (Dierickx and Cool 1989).

Furthermore, the competence perspective and the evolutionary approach both have fundamentally an efficiency approach to firm performance (Nelson and Winter 1982, Barney 1991) (in contrast to the market-power perspective of the new IO). This indicates that the competence perspective and evolutionary economics may benefit from a closer liaison (see also Teece 1990; Teece, Pisano and Shuen 1990; Nelson 1994). I here indicate some areas where arguments derived from evolutionary economics may further the competence perspective.

Developing competence-perspective arguments

I have argued that the research interests of competence-oriented scholars concern the creation, maintenance and renewal of competitive advantage in terms of the internal resources of firms. However, formal competence research has tended to cast this within an equilibrium mould, whereas appreciative research within the competence perspective has shown too little rigour. The evolutionary approach may help overcome this schism. This is because the evolutionary approach focuses on process, change, disequilibrium, and so on, and thus is compatible on the substantive level with appreciative work within the competence perspective, while at the same time being capable of *formally* addressing these phenomena (see Nelson and Winter 1982; Dosi *et al.* 1988; Silverberg, Dosi and Orsenigo 1988; Metcalfe and Gibbons 1989; Andersen 1994), thus meeting the demand for rigour of formal competence-based scholars. In other words, like the new IO, evolutionary economics is capable of dressing its arguments in a formal garb (although formal models usually have to be simulated rather than analytically solved), but it does this with less affront to realism than the new IO does.

For example, Luigi Marengo (1992) develops a formal simulation model of a firm in which agents do not have any prior knowledge of the environment they are facing, but are able to learn and coordinate their actions through a common knowledge basis. Marengo is particularly interested in the coordination of individual learning processes inside the firm, and how a stock of organizational knowledge emerges from the interaction of these learning processes. In his simulation model, agents do not have any prior knowledge of the environment they are facing and they do not possess a shared partition of the states of the world (that is, there is no common knowledge).

However, such a shared partition is necessary for coordination – for example, understanding the demand of the exogenous market and coordinating this with the different shops inside the firm – to take place. And, in fact, as demonstrated by Marengo's simulations, coordination emerges gradually and spontaneously, as agents interact under given organizational structures and under the impact of given environments. Thus, spontaneous order may arise within the planned order of the firm, as it were (to borrow terminology from Austrian economics).

This is an important evolutionary contribution towards better understanding of the more 'emergent' aspects of the internal organizations of firms, something about which contemporary orthodox theory is almost entirely silent. It captures much of the meaning of what appreciative competence scholars mean by 'core competence' (Prahalad and Hamel 1990). Moreover, it goes a long way in accounting for the ultimate sources of firm heterogeneity: because of the role of random influences and the path-dependent nature of collective learning processes, these are particularly likely to be the key causal forces behind the emergence of essential variation among firms.

An improved understanding of the dynamics of competitive advantage

My conceptualization of the overall research interests of competence-oriented scholars incorporates what may be called 'the dynamics of competitive advantage', that is to say, the creation and renewal of competitive advantage. This, in turn, requires an understanding of entrepreneurship, learning, innovation, and so on (Barney 1986b) as the mechanisms that initiate and renew competitive advantage, in addition to an understanding of the mechanisms that maintain (sustain) competitive advantage. Typically, it is the last issue that has been given most attention within the competence perspective, while the issues that relate to the creation and renewal (for example, through innovation) have been comparatively more neglected, at least within formal research within the competence perspective.

Since evolutionary economics, in contrast to the new IO and Austrian economics, is explicitly concerned with processes of technological change and development (see Dosi *et al.* 1988), it is eminently suited to assist understanding of the dynamics of competitive advantage. For example, evolutionary economists emphasize the many types and dimensions of innovations. By implication, some types of innovation may change the distribution of competitive advantages in a population of firms more than, and in different ways from, other types of innovation. Whether innovations are, for example, 'competence-destroying' or 'competence-enhancing' (Tushman and Anderson 1986) has profound managerial implications. In short, the explicit incorporation of the process of technological change in evolutionary economics better allows understanding the dynamics of competitive advantage.

Evolutionary economics may also assist in understanding the issue of sustainability of competitive advantage in terms of the characteristics of resources. Nelson and Winter (1982: chapters 4 and 5) gave the organization aspects of firms some attention, and there has been much contact between organization theory and evolutionary economics (ibid., Burgelman and Rosenbloom 1989, Marengo 1992). For example, the important concept of *routine* has an underpinning in organization theory (Nelson and Winter 1982). Competence-perspective scholars have not typically been much interested in organization theory, although it has been recognized that insights from organization theory may assist in understanding sustained competitive advantage (Barney 1991: 116). By making clearer the organization-theory aspect of firm heterogeneity, evolutionary economics may assist further understanding of sustained competitive advantage in terms of the characteristics of firms' organizations (such as tacit aspects, complexity, etc.).

The role of the environment

The competence perspective has recently been criticized for being overly 'introspective' (Porter 1994: 445), that is, too much concerned with the internal resources of firms and too little with how firms position in product markets. Clearly, the competence perspective does play down the role of the environment (Barney 1991: 100); it is present – after all, reference is often made to competitive imitation, factor-market competition, and so on – but it is not analysed in much depth (however, see Amit and Schoemaker 1993; Foss and Eriksen 1995).

In contrast, the environment is explicitly factored in and analysed in evolutionary economics. The population-dynamics perspective of much evolutionary economics inherently involves the environment. But another, and perhaps more pertinent, source of evolutionary interest in the environment stems from the technology orientation of evolutionary economics in which innovations are seen to be strongly connected (Teece 1990: 61).

For example, evolutionary economists have suggested that technologies often develop as connecting structures, called 'paradigms', 'regimes', 'dominant designs', or 'design configurations' (Dosi *et al.* 1988, Metcalfe and Gibbons 1989). These are characterized by certain products, by certain (standardized) ways of producing these products that are shared among a population of firms, and by certain learning structures (for example, the new biotechnology defines a technological paradigm). Producing within a technological paradigm requires access to certain resources, and the paradigm, in turn, influences firms' asset-accumulation processes so that firms follow path-dependent 'technological trajectories' (Dosi *et al.* 1988). Technological ferment may render obsolete technological paradigms and destroy the basis of firms' competitive advantages by introducing new resource requirements (Barney 1986b: 796).

These evolutionary ideas have a number of fertile implications for the competence perspective. For example, the notion of technological paradigm (or similar notions) supports identification of, for example, the present and future resource needs of a firm that considers entering the paradigm. By pointing out that technological development is path-dependent, evolutionary economics provides guidance to the direction of firms' processes of resource accumulation. In short, evolutionary economics contributes an understanding of the environment that in contrast to that of the new IO is explicitly dynamic, highlights technological development, and in many ways is directly consistent with insights from the competence perspective.

Paul Robertson's contribution to this book (chapter 5) is an example of an attempt to combine a competence perspective with an evolutionary theory of the environment. Thus, Robertson examines the dynamics of competitive advantages and also of transaction costs in a real-time setting; for example, transaction costs decline in the long run, as norms and technical standards become established. Another example is the work of Dosi, Teece and Winter (1992) on 'corporate coherence', in which normative propositions about the extent of diversification are derived from a framework that incorporates both a competence-based theory of the firm and an evolutionary theory of the environment.

CONCLUSION

In this chapter, I have discussed how the emerging competence perspective relates to three important economic approaches – namely, the new IO, Austrian economics and evolutionary economics. I began by placing the competence perspective in the context of a broader tendency towards an economic orientation within strategy research, and by noting the co-existence of two different kinds of the competence perspective: a formal, equilibrium-oriented, kind and an appreciative, process-oriented, kind.

Moreover, it was argued that the competence perspective is about the creation, maintenance and renewal of competitive advantage in terms of the internal resources of firms, and that this conceptualization placed restrictions on which kinds of economics the competence perspective could fruitfully draw on.

Specifically, the new IO is too equilibrium-oriented and too formal to capture the more processual aspects of the competence perspective, and although Austrian economics provides a germane vision of the economic process, it is not about the firm and is too vague and general. However, evolutionary economics dovetails in important dimensions with the competence perspective (for example, with respect to how firms should be conceptualized), and is clearly able to further the competence perspective. For example, it contributes a much needed analysis of the environments of firms, and brings in the dimensions of technological competition, learning, disequilibrium and path-dependence.

Although I have come out largely in favour of evolutionary economics, I do not say that competence-oriented scholars may only draw important inspiration from evolutionary economics. There is something to learn from, for example, the new IO and particularly from pondering the phenomena theorized by new IO scholars: product-market tactics, commitment strategies, entry-deterrence, and so on, represent real phenomena that should be included in a comprehensive strategic theory. What I have argued is that it is the *research style and assumptions* of the new IO, rather than the phenomena it highlights, that are not fully consistent with the competence perspective. In terms of research style and assumptions, evolutionary economics offers greater attractions. It is more similar to the competence perspective, it is able to address the questions that interest competence-oriented scholars, and it is relatively rigorous.

In other words, evolutionary economics is *better* able to help scholars working within the area of competence-based theories of the firm to address the questions that interest them than are alternative approaches. In particular, to the extent that more dynamic issues relating to learning and asset accumulation take increasing prominence, competence-based scholars are increasingly likely to gain from a cross-fertilization with evolutionary economics.

NOTES

1 Other influences include the mainstream of American strategy thinking (Mahoney and Pandian 1992), transaction-cost economics (Conner 1991, Mahoney and Pandian 1992), and Schumpeterian economics (Rumelt 1984, Barney 1986b, Jacobson 1992). Of course, all competence-based strategy scholars regard the influence from Edith Penrose's classic, *The Theory of the Growth of the Firm* (1959), as beyond dispute (e.g. Barney 1991: 99; Mahoney and Pandian 1992: 363).

2 The remaining approaches are much less obvious in this respect. For example, while transaction-cost arguments are undoubtedly important to the competence perspective (see, e.g. Peteraf 1993), the transaction-cost approach is only concerned with organization and exchange aspects of firms, not with production, accumulation of resources, and so on (Winter 1988, Foss 1993, Robertson, chapter 5). It is therefore not likely to play a foundational role for the competence perspective, although transaction-cost arguments are to some extent compatible with competence arguments (see Conner 1991, Peteraf 1993).

3 For example, it is reported (Hamel and Heene 1994: xxvi) that the most reprinted *Harvard Business Review* article ever is Prahalad and Hamel's 1990 article, 'The Core Competence of the Corporation'.

4 Not all subscribe to this view, however; see, for example, Hirsch, Friedman and Koza (1990).

5 This is analogous to the standard definition of 'the short run' in economics, which is defined as that period of time in which there are no changes in the real capital stocks of firms.

6 In the context of economic models, rational expectations implies that price expectations held by agents coincide with the objective distribution implied by the model. The deterministic version of rational expectations is perfect foresight.

7 Barney (1991: 102) explicitly makes this point. For discussions of the complex issue of time in economic models, see Shackle (1972) and O'Driscoll and Rizzo (1985).

8 Exemplified by Lippman and Rumelt (1982), Wernerfelt (1984, 1995) and Barney (1986a, 1991).

9 However, it should be noted that much of what Prahalad and Hamel say may be given an interpretation in terms of, for example, Dierickx and Cool's (1989) emphasis on processes of asset accumulation. The former pair's point that advantage results from being able to build stocks of core competences 'at lower cost and more speedily than competitors' (1990: 81) is consistent with Dierickx and Cool's (1989) overall perspective, and their investigation of the mechanisms that may in fact allow firms to accomplish this. Wernerfelt (1995) is a recent attempt to model processes of asset accumulation formally. Eriksen and Mikkelsen (chapter 4) also add conceptual meat to the core competence skeleton.

10 For example, in the Lippman and Rumelt (1982) model, establishing competitive advantage is portrayed as a matter of firms drawing from a distribution of production efficiencies.

11 That this may be a real danger is indicated by a comparison between, for example, Hamel and Prahalad (1993) and Wernerfelt (1995). Although both these contributions are about processes of resource accumulation, there is a tremendous distance between them in terms of mode of exposition, level of abstraction, attention paid to dynamics, and so on, and it seems difficult to relate the two.

12 To the extent that processes of resource accumulation capture interest within the new IO, it is primarily in connection with accumulation of excess capacity that may support the credibility of threats (Tirole 1988: 255). Of course, these differences reflect the difference in terms of the dominant product-market perspective of the

new IO and the more factor-market/internal-accumulation-oriented perspective of the competence perspective.

13 In contrast, in evolutionary economics firms are sometimes assumed to be initially identical but to 'grow' heterogeneity as they learn from their own internal experiments and from interaction in the market (see Silverberg, Dosi and Orsenigo 1988).

14 Loasby (1990) is a good overall introduction to Austrian economics.

15 In much the same way, neoclassical price theory is not a theory of producers and consumers *per se*, but a theory about their interaction.

16 Schumpeter may well be taken to be the patron saint of modern evolutionary economics (Andersen 1994). It is not uncommon to consider Schumpeter to be an important representative of the Austrian school (e.g. Jacobson 1992), because of the attention he paid to disequilibrium and the role of the entrepreneur. As prominent Austrians (Hayek 1948: 91; Kirzner 1973: 73) have repeatedly emphasized, this is rather problematical; in many ways (particularly with respect to methodology), Schumpeter differed from the Austrian school.

17 If all firms are able to adapt instantly and flexibly to changed circumstances, there cannot be any selection by the environment.

REFERENCES

Alchian, A. A. (1950) 'Uncertainty, Evolution, and Economic Theory', in A. A. Alchian, *Economic Forces at Work*, Indianapolis: Liberty Press, 1977.

Amit, R. H. and Schoemaker, P. J. H. (1993) 'Strategic Assets and Organizational Rent', *Strategic Management Journal* 14: 36–46.

Andersen, E. S. (1994) *Evolutionary Economics: Post-Schumpeterian Contributions*, London: Pinter Publishers.

Ansoff, H. I. (1965) *Corporate Strategy*, New York: McGraw-Hill.

Bain, J. S. (1959) *Industrial Organization*, New York: Wiley.

Barney, J. B. (1986a) 'Strategic Factor Markets: Expectations, Luck and Business Strategy', *Management Science* 32: 1231–41.

Barney, J. B. (1986b) 'Types of Competition and the Theory of Strategy: Toward an Integrative Framework', *Academy of Management Review* 11: 791–800.

Barney, J. B. (1991) 'Firm Resources and Sustained Competitive Advantage', *Journal of Management* 17: 99–120.

Baumol, W. J., Panzar, J. C. and Willig, R. D. (1982) *Contestable Markets and the Theory of Market Structure*, New York: Harcourt, Brace, Jovanovich.

Bower, J. L. (1970) *Managing the Resource Allocation Process*, Harvard Graduate School of Business Administration.

Burgelman, R. A. and Rosenbloom, R. S. (1989) 'Technology Strategy: An Evolutionary Process Perspective', *Research on Technological Innovation, Management and Policy* 4: 1–23.

Camerer, C. (1985) 'Redirecting Research in Business Policy and Strategy', *Strategic Management Journal* 6: 1–15.

Caves, R. E. (1984) 'Economic Analysis and the Quest for Competitive Advantage', *American Economic Review, Papers and Proceedings* 74: 127–32.

Caves, R. E. (1994) 'Game Theory, Industrial Organization, and Business Strategy', *Journal of the Economics of Business* 1: 11–14.

Chandler, A. D. (1962): *Strategy and Structure: Chapters in the History of the Industrial Enterprise*, Cambridge, Mass.: The MIT Press.

Conner, K. R. (1991) 'A Historical Comparison of Resource-based Theory and Five Schools of Thought within Industrial Organization Economics: Do We Have a New Theory of the Firm?', *Journal of Management* 17: 121–54.

Dierickx, I. and Cool, K. (1989) 'Asset Stock Accumulation and Sustainability of Competitive Advantage', *Management Science* 35: 1504–11.

Dosi, G., Freeman, C., Nelson, R. R., Silverberg, G. and Soete, L. (1988), *Technical Change and Economic Theory*, London: Pinter Publishers.

Dosi, G., Teece, D. J. and Winter, S. G. (1992) 'Towards a Theory of Corporate Coherence,' in G. Dosi, R. Giannetti and and P. A. Toninelli (eds) *Technology and Enterprise in a Historical Perspective*, Oxford: Clarendon Press.

Fama, E. (1976) *Foundations of Finance*, New York: Basic Books.

Foss, N. J. (1993) 'Theories of the Firm: Competence and Contractual Perspectives', *Journal of Evolutionary Economics* 3: 127–44.

Foss, N. J. (1994a) *The Austrian School and Modern Economics: Essays in Reassessment*, Copenhagen: Copenhagen Business School Press.

Foss, N. J. (1994b) 'The Theory of the Firm: The Austrians as Precursors and Critics of Modern Theory', *Review of Austrian Economics* 7: 31–65.

Foss, N. J. and Eriksen, B. (1995) 'Industry Capabilities and Competitive Advantage', in C. A. Montgomery (ed.) *Resource-based and Evolutionary Approaches to the Firm*, Boston: Kluwer.

Foss, N. J., Knudsen, C. and Montgomery, C. A. (1995) 'An Exploration of Common Ground: Integrating Evolutionary and Resource-based Views of the Firm', in C. A. Montgomery (ed.) *Resource-based and Evolutionary Approaches to the Firm*, Boston: Kluwer.

Ghemawat, P. (1991a) *Commitment: The Dynamics of Strategy*, New York: The Free Press.

Ghemawat, P. (1991b) 'Resources and Strategy: An IO Perspective', Mimeo, Harvard Business School.

Godfrey, P. C. and Hill, C. W. L. (1993) 'Grounding Strategic Paradigms: Logical Positivism, Realism, and the Resource-based View of the Firm', Mimeo, Graduate School of Business Administration, University of Washington.

Grossman, S. and Hart, O. (1986) 'The Costs and Benefits of Ownership: A Theory of Lateral and Vertical Integration', *Journal of Political Economy* 94: 691–719.

Hamel, G. and Heene, A. (1994) *Competence-based Competition*, New York: John Wiley.

Hamel, G. and Prahalad, C. K. (1993) 'Strategy as Stretch and Leverage', *Harvard Business Review* 69: 75–84.

Hannan, M. T. and Freeman, J. (1989) *Organizational Ecology*, Cambridge, Mass.: Harvard University Press.

Hayek, F. A. von (1948) *Individualism and Economic Order*, Chicago: University of Chicago Press.

Heiner, R. A. (1983) 'The Origin of Predictable Behavior', *American Economic Review* 73: 560–95.

Hirsch, P. M., Friedman, R. and. Koza, M. P (1990) 'Collaboration and Paradigm Shift', *Organization Science* 1: 87–97.

Hodgson, G. M. (1993) *Bringing Life Back into Economics*, Cambridge: Polity Press.

Jacobson, R. (1992) 'The "Austrian" School of Strategy', *Academy of Management Review* 17: 782–807.

Kirzner, I. M. (1973) *Competition and Entrepreneurship*, Chicago: University of Chicago Press.

Kogut, B. and Zander, U. (1992) 'Knowledge of the Firm, Combinative Capabilities, and the Replication of Technology', *Organization Science* 3: 383–97.

Langlois, R. N. (1992) 'Transaction Cost Economics in Real Time', *Industrial and Corporate Change* 1: 99–127.

Lippman, S. J. and Rumelt, R. P.(1982) 'Uncertain Imitability: An Analysis of Interfirm Differences under Competition', *Bell Journal of Economics* 13: 418–38.

Loasby, B. J. (1989) 'A Subjective Appraisal of Austrian Economics,' in B. J. Loasby *The Minds and Methods of Economists*, Cambridge: Cambridge University Press.

Loasby, B. J. (1990) 'The Austrian School', in D. Mair and A. G. Miller (eds) *A Modern Guide to Economic Thought*, Aldershot: Edward Elgar.

Lucas, R. E. and Sargent, T. (eds) (1981) *Rational Expectations and Econometric Practice*, London: Allen and Unwin.

Mahoney, J. T. and Pandian, J. R. (1992) 'The Resource-based View within the Conversation of Strategic Management', *Strategic Management Journal* 13: 363–80.

Man, A.-P. de (1993) '1980, 1985, 1990: A Porter Exegesis', Management Report Series No. 166, Rotterdam School of Management, Erasmus Universiteit Rotterdam.

Marengo, L. (1992) 'Structure, Competence, and Learning in an Adaptive Model of the Firm', Papers edited by the European Study Group for Evolutionary Economics, #9203.

Metcalfe, J. S. and Gibbons, M. (1989) 'Technology, Variety, and Organization', *Research on Technological Innovation, Management, and Policy* 4: 153–93.

Mintzberg, H. (1994) *The Rise and Fall of Strategic Planning*, New York: Prentice-Hall.

Mises, L. von (1949) *Human Action: A Treatise on Economics*, London: William Hodge.

Montgomery, C. A and Wernerfelt, B. (1988) 'Diversification, Ricardian Rents, and Tobin's q', *RAND Journal of Economics* 19: 623–32.

Montgomery, C. A., Wernerfelt, B. and Balakrishnan, S. (1989) 'Strategy Content and the Research Process', *Strategic Management Journal* 10: 189–97.

Nelson, R. R. (1994) 'Why Do Firms Differ, and How Does It Matter?', in R. P. Rumelt, D. E. Schendel and D. J. Teece, *Fundamental Issues in Strategy: A Research Agenda*, Cambridge, Mass.: Harvard Business School Press.

Nelson, R. R. and Winter, S. G. (1982) *An Evolutionary Theory of Economic Change*, Cambridge, Mass.: Belknap Press.

O'Driscoll, G. P. and Rizzo, M. (1985) *The Economics of Time and Ignorance*, Oxford: Basil Blackwell.

Penrose, E. T. (1959) *The Theory of the Growth of the Firm*, Oxford: Oxford University Press.

Peteraf, M. (1993) 'The Cornerstones of Competitive Advantage: A Resource-based View', *Strategic Management Journal* 14: 179–91.

Porter, M. E. (1980) *Competitive Strategy*, New York: The Free Press.

Porter, M. E (1981) 'The Contributions of Industrial Organization to Strategic Management', *Academy of Management Review* 6: 609–20.

Porter, M. E. (1994) 'Towards a Dynamic Theory of Strategy', in R. P. Rumelt, D. E. Schendel and D. J. Teece, *Fundamental Issues in Strategy: A Research Agenda*, Cambridge, Mass.: Harvard Business School Press.

Prahalad, C. K. and Hamel, G. (1990) 'The Core Competence of the Corporation', *Harvard Business Review* 66: 79–91.

Prahalad, C. K. and Hamel, G. (1994) *Competing for the Future*, Cambridge, Mass.: Harvard Business School Press.

Richards, R. J. (1992) *The Meaning of Evolution*, Chicago: University of Chicago Press.

Robinson, J. (1977) 'What Are the Questions?', *Journal of Economic Literature* 15: 1318–39.

Rumelt, R. P. (1984) 'Towards a Strategic Theory of the Firm', in R. B. Lamb (ed.) *Competitive Strategic Management*, Englewood Cliffs, NJ: Prentice-Hall.

Rumelt, R. P., Schendel, D. E. and Teece, D. J. (1991) 'Strategic Management and Economics', *Strategic Management Journal* 12: 5–29.

Rumelt, R. P., Schendel, D. E. and Teece, D. J. (1994) 'Afterword' in *Fundamental Issues in Strategy: A Research Agenda*, Cambridge, Mass.: Harvard Business School Press.

Saloner, G. (1994) 'Modeling, Game Theory, and Strategic Management', in R. P. Rumelt, D. E. Schendel and D. J. Teece, *Fundamental Issues in Strategy: A Research Agenda*, Cambridge, Mass.: Harvard Business School Press.

Scherer, F. M. (1980) *Industrial Market Structure and Economic Performance*, Chicago: Rand-McNally.

Schmalensee, R. and Willig, R. (eds) (1989) *Handbook of Industrial Organization, Vol.1.*, Amsterdam: North-Holland.

Schumpeter, J. A. (1934) *The Theory of Economic Development*, Cambridge, Mass.: Harvard University Press.

Shackle, G. L. S. (1972) *Economics and Epistemics*, Cambridge: Cambridge University Press.

Shapiro, C. (1989) 'The Theory of Business Strategy', *RAND Journal of Economics* 20: 125–37.

Silverberg, G., Dosi, G. and Orsenigo, L. (1988) 'Innovation, Diversity and Diffusion: A Self-Organisation Model', *Economic Journal* 98: 1032–54.

Simon, H. A. (1962) 'The Architecture of Complexity', *Proceedings of the American Philosophical Society* 106: 467–82.

Teece, D. J. (1990) 'Contributions and Impediments of Economic Analysis to the Study of Strategic Management', in J. W. Fredrickson (ed.) *Perspectives on Strategic Management*, Grand Rapids, Mich.: Harper.

Teece, D. J., Pisano, G. and Shuen, A. (1990) 'Firm Capabilities, Resources and the Concept of Strategy', Mimeo, University of California at Berkeley.

Tirole, J. (1988) *The Theory of Industrial Organization*, Cambridge, Mass.: MIT Press.

Tushman, M. L. and Anderson, P. (1986) 'Technological Discontinuities and Organizational Environments', *Administrative Science Quarterly* 31: 439–65.

Wensley, R. (1982) 'PIMS and BCG: New Horizons or False Dawns?', *Strategic Management Journal* 3: 147–58.

Wernerfelt, B. (1984) 'A Resource-based View of the Firm', *Strategic Management Journal* 5: 171–80.

Wernerfelt, B. (1995) 'Resource-based Strategy in a Stochastic Model,' in C. A. Montgomery (ed.) *Resource-based and Evolutionary Approaches to the Firm*, Boston: Kluwer.

Williams, J. R. (1994) 'Strategy and the Search for Rents: The Evolution of Diversity among Firms', in R. P. Rumelt, D. E. Schendel and D. J. Teece *Fundamental Issues in Strategy: A Research Agenda*, Cambridge, Mass.: Harvard Business School Press.

Williamson, O. E. (1985) *The Economic Institutions of Capitalism*, New York: The Free Press.

Winter, S. G. (1987) 'Knowledge and Competence as Strategic Assets', in D. J. Teece (ed.) *The Competitive Challenge*, Cambridge, Mass.: Ballinger.

Winter, S. G. (1988) 'On Coase, Competence and the Corporation', *Journal of Law, Economics and Organization* 4: 163–80.

Winter, S. G. (1990) 'Survival, Selection, and Inheritance in Evolutionary Theories of Organization', in J. V. Singh (ed.) *Organizational Evolution: New Directions*, London: Sage.

Winter, S. G. (1995) 'Four Rs of Profitability: Rents, Resources, Routines, and Replication', in C. A. Montgomery (ed.) *Resource-based and Evolutionary Approaches to the Firm*, Boston: Kluwer.

INDEX